Children and Sports Training

Children and Sports Training:

How Your Future Champions Should Exercise to be Healthy, Fit, and Happy

by Józef Drabik, Ph.D.

Stadion Publishing Company, Inc.
Island Pond, Vermont

Stadion Publishing Company, Inc.
Post Office Box 447
Island Pond, VT 05846, U.S.A.
http://www.stadion.com

Publisher's Cataloging in Publication
(Prepared by Quality Books Inc.)

Drabik, Józef.
Children and Sports Training: how your future champions should exercise to be healthy, fit, and happy / by Józef Drabik.
p. cm.
Includes bibliographical references and index.
Preassigned LCCN: 92-85419
ISBN 0-940149-02-8 (hard)
ISBN 0-940149-03-6 (soft)

1. Physical education for children—Study and teaching. 2. Physical education and training—Study and teaching. I. Title

GV361.D73 1995 613.7'1
QBI95-20151

Translated by Thomas Kurz
Edited by R. Scott Perry
Cover Design by Lightbourne Images © 1996
Drawings by Mikolaj Zagorski
Printed in the United States of America

Synowi Piotrowi

Warning—Disclaimer

The author and Stadion Publishing Company are not liable or responsible to any person or entity for any damage caused or alleged to be caused directly or indirectly by the information contained in this book.

Consult your physician before starting any exercise program.

Contents

Foreword

This book is different from other books on sports training and fitness for children. It gives the reader much more than the usual information on the importance of early development of aerobic endurance and the standard precautions against certain exercises. Its most important contribution is in the explanation of "sensitive ages" for development of movement abilities (endurance, coordination, speed, strength, flexibility) and what exercises to use for developing these abilities at any given age. The existence of sensitive ages is related to sex differences and the need to develop separate programs of exercises for girls and boys from the onset of puberty. It is perhaps "politically correct" to have girls and boys exercise together, but it is certainly harmful to them. The exercises that fully develop the potential of a 12-year-old girl will harm a 12-year-old boy. Exercises that are good for the boy are less challenging for the girl and thus hold her back. The consequence of not doing just the right kind of exercises at just the right age is reduced fitness and athletic potential lost forever. In the case of girls it is easier to inflict lasting damage because their sensitive ages are shorter than boys'.

Another unique feature in this work is a set of physical education lessons and workout examples that show how to teach skills while maintaining a high level of activity and effort intensity. Dr. Drabik and I were startled to learn that many American p.e. teachers do not know how to teach skills without interrupting the flow of activity. To some that we have talked to, it was inconceivable that children can be taught a volleyball technique, for example, while they constantly move so their heart rate stays above 150 beats per minute. They assumed it was necessary to teach by making children stand and listen to lengthy descriptions accompanying the teacher's demonstration.

The lesson plans in this book show how to teach on the move.

THOMAS KURZ❑

Preface

In the U.S.A. more and more children are participating in organized sports outside of a school setting. Unhappily, both the number and the gravity of sports injuries have also risen dramatically so that children are now suffering injuries once limited to professional athletes. And in a curious paradox, even though more children are participating in sports training, there are also signs—obesity, inability to perform basic fitness exercises— that more U.S. children are unfit than ever before.

Training and attitudes are the issues.

Training and attitudes are also the issues for countries of the former Soviet Bloc, but from a different perspective. Until the recent past, results were what counted in sports for those countries, never mind at what cost these results were achieved. If human dignity or health were compromised, so be it. The attitude was the individual for sports, not sports for the individual.

With respect to children, this attitude showed itself in an insistence on early sports specialization. Fitness preparation narrowed to include only sport-specific exercises. Unsuitable training loads that violated ethics and the basic principles of methodology and instruction for children were the rule. "The [short-term] end justifies the means" seemed to be the unofficial slogan of a sports establishment that could and did suppress the opinions of those who had the best interests of children in mind.

Short-term, results-oriented thinking does not very often lead to long-term sports success. Worse, such thinking can lead to grave consequences for all children: injuries as a result of improper training that overloads young bodies and a cavalier acceptance of doping, to mention only two. Finally, children may develop—and indeed many have developed—a negative attitude toward sports and fitness in general, which can cause a lowering of overall fitness and health for whole populations.

Sound methods of sports training for children exist. In the United States there is an increasing receptivity to the knowledge springing from the research of former Soviet Bloc countries. Now that the socialist party and the socialist state have lost their grip on education, there is a climate open to reconsidering the primitive application of natural selection principles such as "The weak will drop out, the strong will survive." The weak of today may be the strong of tomorrow, of course, and weeding them out leads to the loss of future talent.

With such shortsighted attitudes gone for good, it is time to give a hearing to the best of training techniques. Sports training that benefits children rather than exploiting them, leaving them susceptible to injury, or turning them off to sports is what this work is about.

Acknowledgments

I would like to thank Professor Dr. Joachim Raczek of Poland for permission to use his research throughout this book and Thomas Kurz for translation, valuable tips on making my advice easier to apply in practice, and for adding research data from sources in the United States.

I am also grateful to all authors and researchers, Polish and foreign, to whose works I refer so often in this book.

INTRODUCTION
WHY CHILDREN SHOULD EXERCISE

Exercise affects the whole body, including one's brain. Aerobic exercises (simple and repetitive) cause an increase in the number of capillaries supplying the cerebellum. Learning new skills increases the number of synaptic connections between brain cells (Black 1990). A fit cardiorespiratory system, the result of systematic aerobic activity, is more resistant to coronary heart disease, hypertension, stroke, and varicose veins. Regular activity reduces stress level.

There are more benefits, but you get the idea. Exercise is essential to health, fitness, and happiness. But to get these benefits one has to do it, and childhood is the time to get into the exercise habit.

During the preschool years there are several movement skills a youngster should master—including running, jumping, hopping, throwing, catching, kicking, balancing, and climbing. Lack of these generic skills—learned by age 4 or 5—makes it difficult for the child to catch up with peers and may cause him or her to quit physical activities. Practice time, the example of correct role models, and well-informed parents or teachers who know when, how, and what skills to teach will remedy this.

In this book you will learn methods of developing all of a child's movement abilities, but that does not mean a teacher, coach, or parent should strive to develop all of them to the maximum in a child.

Not everybody can develop every motor ability equally easily or to an equally great degree. Some people's genes predispose them to the easy acquisition of great strength,others great endurance, others speed, yet others coordination. Coaches who spend a lot of time on developing an athlete's endurance, for example, when the individual is predisposed for great strength, are not going to improve competitive results and can weaken the great strength potential (Novikov and Chuiko 1984). To give you a practical example, a young wrestler who has tremendous strength will dominate his opponent before endurance comes into play. Making this wrestler stress endurance in his workouts will put him at a disadvantage against someone who is genetically predisposed to develop endurance. He will lose his strength advantage but never match the endurance of someone naturally predisposed to it.

The general principle follows: In training and exercise, work to accentuate the positive. Then, if time and energy permit, work on lagging qualities. In this way you will maintain the motivation of the young athlete to work out and make him or her receptive to the idea of doing other exercises. Exercises and training that emphasize abilities in which a young athlete is genetically predisposed to excel will make him or her happy. And a happy youngster is more willing to engage in other forms of training that promote his or her general health and fitness.

PART 1
BASIC CONCEPTS

1

THE CONCEPT OF PHYSICAL FITNESS

Everyone has different fitness. It changes with time, place, type of work, and situation. It is a result of everyday activity and genetically encoded individual potential. Physical fitness on the one hand is motor achievements (speed, strength, and endurance, for example), and on the other hand it is physiological achievements (a person's response to effort, for example). Physical fitness finds its expression in two aspects: dynamic, or motor achievements, and static, or "medical" fitness (Hebbelinck 1984).

Physical fitness is the foundation of sports performance.

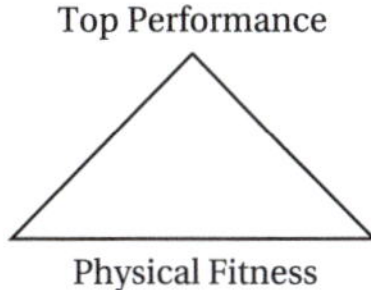

Figure 1. Physical fitness—the foundation of sports performance

With a concept of such basic importance, you would think it likely to be very well understood and defined. It is not. The concept of physical fitness is one of the fuzzier concepts in physical education and sports sciences. It is still a subject of research and theoretical inquiries. Here are some definitions of physical fitness that have been put forward.

Physical fitness is:

1. The ability to perform everyday tasks willingly, without excessive fatigue, and with enough energy left to enjoy physical activities in free time as well as for meeting unexpected events demanding physical efforts (Clarke 1959).

2. The state of the organism determining the organism's level of ability for activity (Larson 1966).

3. The ability to perform motor activity demanding significant involvement of strength, speed, dexterity, agility, endurance, and other motor abilities, or the level of development of motor abilities evaluated by tests that do not require proficiency at sports technique (Denisiuk and Milicerowa 1969).

4. A manifestation of the good shape of organs and the high level of an organism's function, expressed by effectively solving versatile motor tasks and determined by the degree of development of motor abilities (Sozanski 1975).

5. The ratio of effectiveness to predisposition (Wolanski and Parizkowa 1976).

6. A manifestation of a life-style, of a system of values; it is an ability to manage motor tasks in sports, in work, and in everyday life (Przeweda 1985).

7. An indicator of the biological value of a human (Drozdowski 1986).

8. The entirety of a person's abilities and skills that makes it possible to efficiently perform all movement activities (Szopa 1993).

As the above list of definitions shows, fitness is variously defined and some definitions are wider than others. In any case fitness means the ability to move adequately and effectively in life. This ability is not given to you once and for all, nor to all in equal measure. Fitness has to be striven for and developed so it can serve you as long as possible.

Structure of physical fitness

The different models people have developed to describe physical fitness reflect the diversity of definitions that exist.

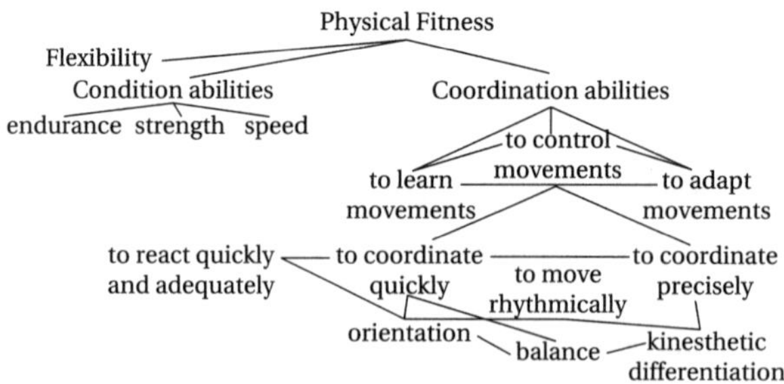

Figure 2. Structure of physical fitness according to Gundlach (1970), as expanded by Raczek (1986)

Gundlach and Raczek emphasize (figure 2) the difference between conditioning abilities, which are easy to improve and are determined mainly by energy sources, and the coordination abilities, more difficult to improve and determined by the nervous system. They also believe that flexibility is mainly an anatomical quality, one that is not dependent on other abilities.

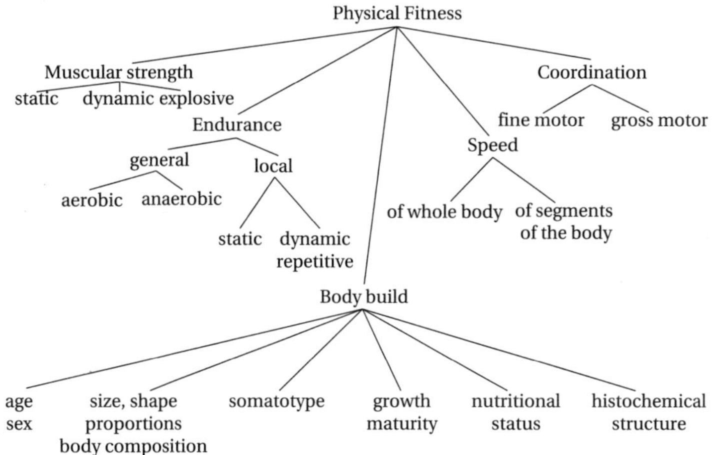

Figure 3. The factors and components of physical fitness according to Hebbelinck (1984)

Hebbelinck, on the other hand, shows (figure 3) that physical fitness is related to factors of body build, which is reasonable considering the close relation between the structure and function of the body.

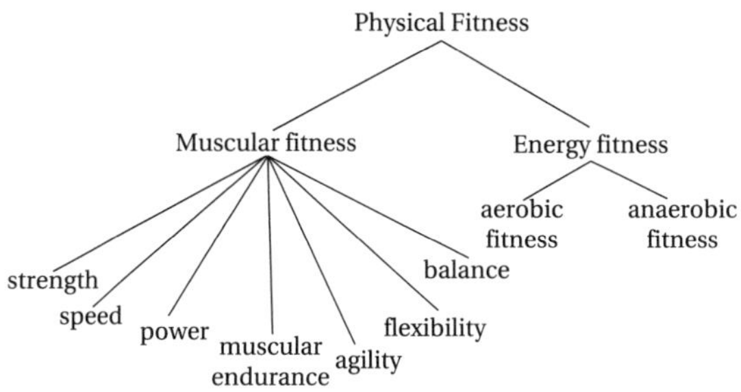

Figure 4. Structure of physical fitness according to Sharkey (1986)

Sharkey's concept (figure 4) is more practical for a coach because it emphasizes two types of fitness, muscular fitness and energy fitness, which differ in the ways they are developed.

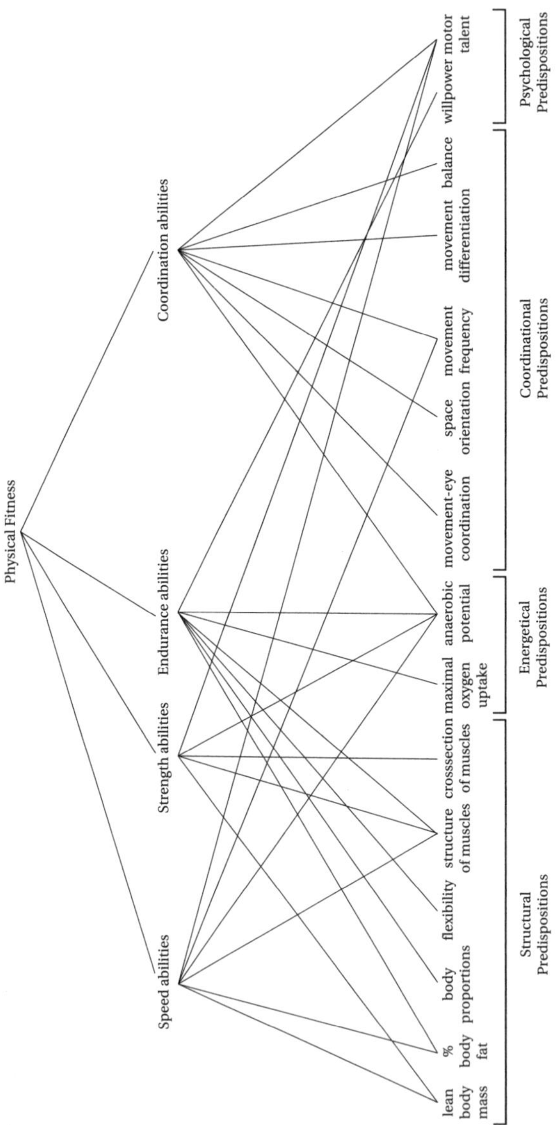

Figure 5. Structure of connections among predispositions and abilities according to Szopa (1989a)

Szopa relates (figure 5) four motor abilities (speed, strength, endurance, coordination) to four groups of predispositions that those abilities are based on. These interrelations of motor abilities and predispositions have to be taken into account in selection for sports.

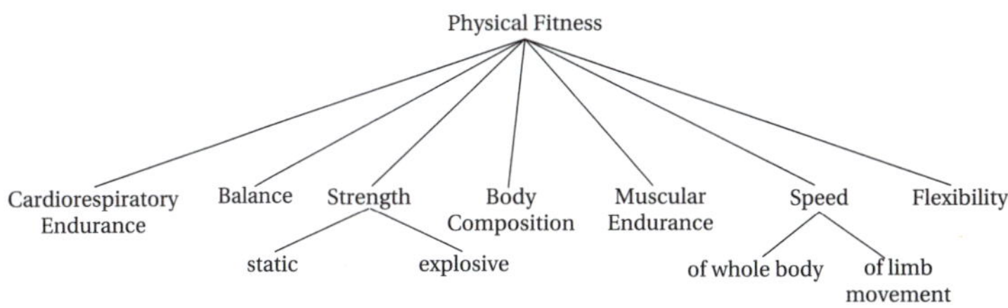

Figure 6. Components of fitness according to EUROFIT (1988)

The authors of EUROFIT (a European test of physical fitness) show a concept in figure 6 that is similar to Sharkey's in its lack of emphasis on coordination abilities.

All these concepts of physical fitness help give a fuller idea of its essence. Fitness applies to an individual as a whole and is a product of both the structure and the function of his or her body. Such an understanding of fitness helps you realize its complexity.

Goals of children's physical fitness training

Independent of the various formulations of the concept of fitness and the various concepts of its components, training for physical fitness has the following goals.

- To develop a person's function versatilely
- To raise the level of motor abilities
- To prevent the negative results of one-sided, specialized training loads

These goals attest to the significance of an athlete's physical fitness preparation. This significance is reflected (table 1) in the percentage share of workouts dedicated to physical fitness in consecutive years of athletic training (Filin 1987).

Table 1. Share of workouts dedicated to general physical fitness in long-term athletic training

year	1	2	3	4	5	6	7	8
%	70-80	70	60	60	50	50	40	40

Considerations for choosing methods of physical fitness training

1. Age. The volume and intensity of exercises developing physical fitness and the methods to apply these means depend mostly on the child's age, and more precisely, on the stage of the child's biological development. A general scheme taking age into account, accepting Sharkey's conception of fitness structure, is shown in table 2. Note the greater volume—usually three times greater or more—of exercises developing energy fitness as compared to muscular fitness.

Table 2. Age as the basis for choosing method (author's interpretation of Sharkey's [1986] concept)

	Muscular fitness		Energy fitness	
age	methods	time	methods	time
6-10	Resistance of own body weight; flexibility exercises	15 min. 3 times per week	Simplified team games; emphasis on play; avoid formal training methods	up to 4 hours per week
11-14	Resistance allowing more than 10 repetitions per set to develop strength-endurance; flexibility exercises	30 min. 3 times per week	Team games; introduction of long, easy intervals	4-6 hours per week
15-19	Resistance that limits number of repetitions to less than 10 per set to improve strength and develop power; flexibility exercises	45 min. 3 times per week	Moderate length and short intervals; regular training at the anaerobic threshold	6-8 hours per week

Table 3 provides the details that show you the way to stress training of particular motor abilities, or components of physical fitness.

Table 3. Possibilities for beginning and intensifying training of particular components of fitness in various age groups (Grosser, Starlschka, and Zimmerman 1983)

Elements of fitness	Age groups (in years) F=females M=males intensity: + low, ++ moderate, +++ high							
	5-8	8-10	10-12	12-14	14-16	16-18	18-20	20 and over
maximal strength				+F	++F +M	+++F ++M	+++F +++M	+++F +++M
explosive strength			+F	++F +M	+++F ++M	+++F +++M	+++F +++M	+++F +++M
strength-endurance				+F	++F +M	+++F ++M	+++F +++M	+++F +++M
aerobic endurance		+F +M	+F +M	++F ++M	++F ++M	+++F +++M	+++F +++M	+++F +++M
anaerobic endurance				+F	++F +M	+++F ++M	+++F +++M	+++F +++M
speed of reaction		+F +M	+F +M	++F ++M	++F ++M	+++F +++M	+++F +++M	+++F +++M
maximal speed (acyclic and cyclic)			+F	++F +M	++F ++M	+++F +++M	+++F +++M	+++F +++M
coordination	++F ++M	++F ++M	++F ++M	+++F +++M	+++F +++M	+++F +++M	+++F +++M	+++F +++M

2. **Sensitive periods.** The pace of development of particular motor abilities during an individual's biological development is not the same for boys and girls. You began to make this connection in your examination of table 3, where training for particular abilities often started earlier for girls than boys. The effect of intensive training of a particular motor ability is greater if this training takes place during the so-called sensitive period in development of this ability (Raczek 1989).

Table 4. Sensitive periods in development of motor abilities for girls (F) and boys (M) (Guzalowski 1977):
***H** - period of high pace of development; **M** - period of moderate pace of development; **L** - period of low pace of development (empty fields indicate a very low pace of development, its stagnation or regress)*

Age	7-8		8-9		9–10		10-11		11-12		12-13		13-14		14-15		15-16		16-17	
F-female M-male	F	M	F	M	F	M	F	M	F	M	F	M	F	M	F	M	F	M	F	M
absolute static strength	L		L	L			H	L	M					M		L	H	L		H
speed	H	H	H	H	M	L	H						H				L	L		
speed-strength (standing broad jump)	L				H		H	L	H				L	M		M				
static strength-endurance	M				H		M		H					M	M	H				H
dynamic strength-endurance			M		H		H		H	H								M		
anaerobic endurance (500 meter run)			L	H	M		M	H	H			H				M			L	
flexibility (sit and reach)	L				L	H			M				M	H	H			H	H	
Age	7-8		8-9		9-10		10-11		11-12		12-13		13-14		14-15		15-16		16-17	

From comparing data compiled by various authors on sensitive periods you can see they are not always the same. It is because the data was collected from different populations (table 3—German, table 4—Russian) developing at a different pace, and the tests evaluating the same motor abilities were often different. Treat the sensitive periods shown in this chapter as tentative guidelines. You need to verify them with the population of children that you work with.

These sensitive periods are the periods in human life when the organs and systems that determine a given ability (balance, endurance, speed, or any other ability) are undergoing intensive development. It is then that they are most receptive to a training stimulus developing that ability. The most effective course of action in developing any ability is to help that naturally occurring development and act according to its rhythm and direction. The training has to target those abilities that are not fully matured and, by well thought-through methods, facilitate their development beyond what an individual could do on his or her own. The period of greatest development of motor abilities, unaided by training, is shorter for girls than for boys. Training is most effective when it stimulates maturing abilities rather than those already matured.

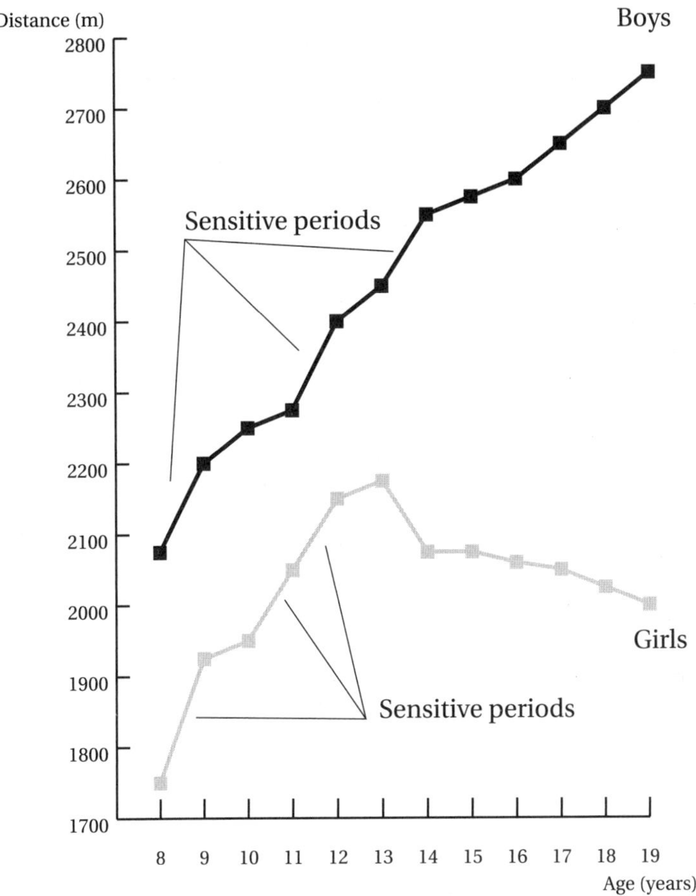

Figure 7. Average results of a 12-minute run (Cooper test) of Polish boys and girls (n=12250) and sensitive periods in development of their endurance (Drabik 1989)

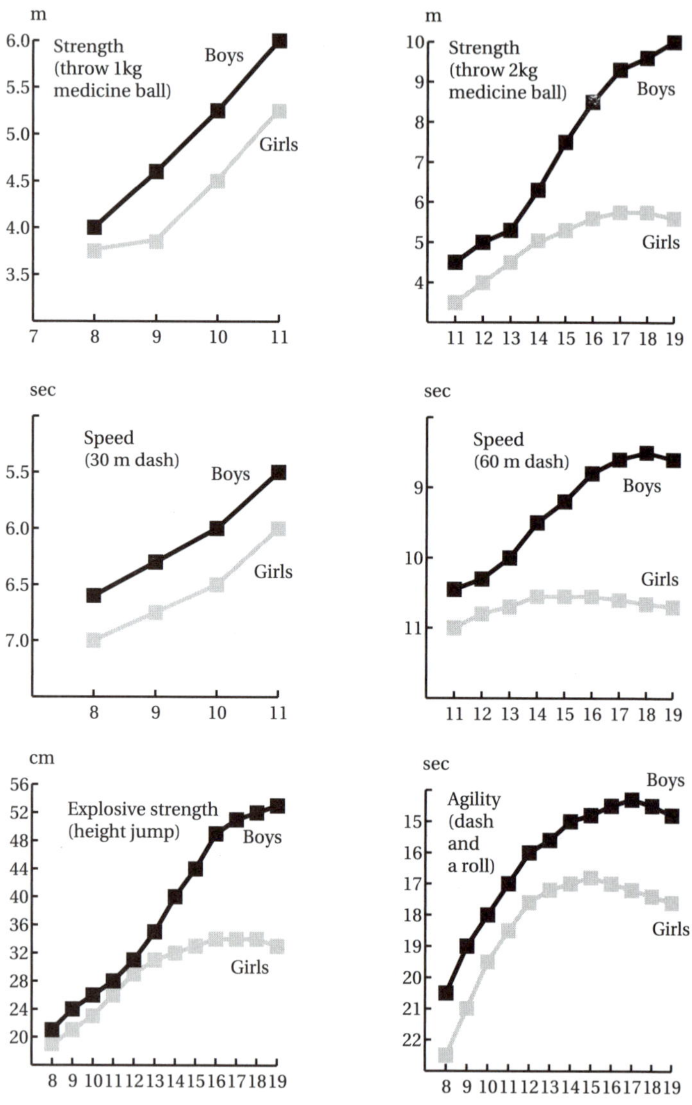

Figures 8-13. Development of selected motor abilities (Denisiuk and Milicerowa 1969)

3. Demands of a sports discipline. Another consideration for physical fitness training is the particular demands of the sports discipline the young athlete is readying him- or herself for. The range of fitness training, its main stress, and the choice of training methods all depend on the sports discipline.

In kayaking, for example, the ultimate goal of fitness training will be developing strength and strength-endurance. (For short distances pure strength will be more important; the longer the distance the greater will be the importance of endurance.) Analyses of a kayaker's effort show that 60% of the energy comes from aerobic processes and 40% from anaerobic.

Table 5. Importance of aerobic and anaerobic power (speed of biochemical reactions) and of aerobic and anaerobic capacity (volume of substrates in biochemical processes) in kayaking (Bellotti et al. 1978)

	Type of Process					
	Aerobic		Anaerobic (lactacid)		Anaerobic (alactacid)	
Distance	capacity	power	capacity	power	capacity	power
500 m	+	+	+++	+++	+++	+
1000 m	+	+++	+++	+++	+++	+
10000 m	+++	+++	+	+	+	

To develop the muscular aspects of a kayaker's fitness, a trainer ought to stress:

- explosive and dynamic strength, using repetitive isotonic and isokinetic exercises; and
- strength-endurance, using repetitive efforts of medium and long duration.

To develop energy fitness, a trainer would:

- improve aerobic potential by continuous, repetitive, and interval methods—long and short distances at 50-80% of maximum heart rate; and
- enhance anaerobic fitness by choosing interval methods—medium and short distances at over 80% of maximum heart rate. (Anaerobic intervals are only applied after children turn 14 or 15.)

The preceding example taken from kayaking shows how general fitness training is incorporated into sports training. Apply the same way of thinking to all sports.

4. Optimalization of the level of physical fitness. You only want to devote the time and effort necessary to develop aspects of physical fitness to the point where they will help, not hurt, the requirements of your particular sports discipline. Optimalization of physical fitness is necessary because there is no world championship in general physical fitness. The need to pursue levels of physical fitness just enough and no more is substantiated more seriously by other aspects of athletic training. The great training loads athletes are subjected to and, related to these loads, the exploitation of an athlete's body both demand a search for those training regimens that have an immediate effect on sports results. Obviously excessive muscle mass resulting from too much or the wrong strength training will interfere with performance in endurance sports or in sports that require utmost precision and speed of movements. On the other hand, not having enough strength will interfere with technique and endurance. So, the optimalization of the development of strength, or of any other ability, is necessary. That will leave you more time to develop other abilities and skills and save you from overtraining (Sharkey 1986).

Determining the optimal level of development for components of fitness is not always easy, and it is not equally important for every component. It is relatively easy in the case of strength. For example, in cyclic sports such as kayaking strength is at an optimal level if the maximal strength of an athlete is 2.5 times greater than the strength required for a single repetition of a typical movement (Sharkey 1986). In the remaining components of fitness, determining optimal level is more difficult. Some facts are known, however. Excessive flexibility of the spine is detrimental to performance in the high jump, for example, and several years of developing aerobic endurance by running results in lowering the explosive strength needed by a volleyball player.

Models of masters—top performers in their discipline—help with determining optimal fitness development.

Example 1. Boxing (Wazny 1989): Physical fitness 50%, of which 45% is speed and strength, 35% agility, 20% endurance

Example 2. Bicycling, track (Wazny 1989): Physical fitness 50%, of which 40% is speed-endurance, 20% speed, 20% endurance, 10% strength, 10% coordination

5. **Structure of a workout.** In the main part of the workout special exercises should precede general exercises, speed exercises should precede strength exercises, and strength exercises should precede endurance exercises. In technical workouts technical exercises should precede fitness exercises.

6. **Sex.** Boys and girls develop at a different pace. It is assumed that girls are two years ahead of boys in biological development. This difference shows in the sensitive periods. A different pace of development must affect your choice of training loads in the development of physical fitness.

You will learn considerably more about the implications of these differences in development in chapters 2 and 3.

Your understanding of physical fitness and its implications for sports training of children is the beginning of wisdom. Now you need to supplement that knowledge with an exploration of the implications of biological development for children's health, fitness, and happiness.

2

BIOLOGICAL DEVELOPMENT AND SPORTS TRAINING

Body build

Physical characteristics develop in stages, with each stage having its own dynamics. In the ages 5-7 the average increase of height is 5-7 cm (2-3 in) and of weight approximately 2-3 kg (4-7 lb) per year. In the fifth year of life height is usually twice that of the height at birth and the weight is five times the weight at birth (Bogdanowicz 1968).

Intermediate school age (7-11) is characterized by a slowdown of the pace of growth in favor of changes in the structure of the body and its general strengthening. Increases in weight become greater than increases in height. This creates better opportunities for increasing a child's physical activity.

The pace of physical development reaches its maximum around 11 or 12 years for girls and 13 or 14 for boys. It is associated with the so-called pubertal growth spurt. At this stage increases in height are again proportionately greater than the increases in weight. Yearly increase of height reaches 8-10 cm (3 to 4 in). At the next stage, after age 13 for girls and 15 for boys, the height increases become smaller but weight increases more intensively.

This changing relationship of height to weight is expressed in weight-height indexes such as the body mass index (BMI), expressed as weight/height^{2}x100.

Body build (height, mass, proportions) is one of the basic considerations in choosing a sports discipline and achieving success in one's sport. BMI is one of the indicators of body build and at the same time it is considered a simple indicator of body fat content. Body fat content has significantly greater influence on results in endurance runs than body mass. You need to keep in mind the differences in BMI between boys and girls as well as the differences among different age groups of the same sex so that you can choose wisely among methods of endurance training. For example, the fact that 83.2% of 8-year-old children share common values of BMI means that the majority of boys and girls of that age can use the same endurance exercises.

At the ages of 13-15 the average values of the BMI for girls are slightly higher than for boys. For girls of that age endurance efforts are more difficult than for boys—this applies particularly to girls 14-15 years old. From an endurance training point of view this is a more difficult period for girls than for boys because of the girls' body build.

Physique and body build dynamics change dramatically with the onset of puberty. The stage of puberty is characterized by great variability in physical, psychological, and motor development within the same age groups. Individuals of equal age differ significantly because some mature faster than others. This has great significance for sports because most often the individuals maturing faster are seen as more fit at the time. Their fitness advantage may derive from their greater biological maturity, however, which is why prognoses of future sports performance are often wrong. For long-term training the best prospects are individuals who are fit but maturing later.

Research does not provide definite proof of increasing height as a result of training. The influence of exercise on body mass and body circumferences is documented, however. Correctly applied and well-controlled physical loads benefit somatic development. Excessive loads disturb growth processes, especially before puberty.

Movement apparatus

Physical activity stimulates the development of bones and ligaments, increasing their ability to withstand effort. The greater elasticity of a child's bones (as compared to an adult's) facilitates the development of flexibility and protects from sudden trauma. A child's pliable bones are susceptible to deformation by excessive repetitive mechanical stress. Mechanical overload may damage growth plates. This happens most often in 10- to 14-year-olds. The growth plates are most susceptible to crushing or pulling apart. Weakness of joints and ligaments is a decisive factor that limits the magnitude of training loads for children and youth.

The work capability of children's muscles differs from that of adults. Because of children's high metabolic rate their muscles fatigue quickly. Recovery is also quick, however, thanks to this same high metabolism and an ability surpassing adults' to supply oxygen to these muscles. Muscle excitability between the ages of 5 and 10 reaches levels typical for adults.

Muscle innervation in children—the growth of motor nerve endings into muscle fibers' interior and the entwining of a muscle fiber's nuclei and blood vessels—is completed around the age of 6 years. It has great importance in neuromuscular coordination and thus, in learning movement skills. Innervation occurs earlier in great muscles than in small ones. This is why a child can master swimming, bicycling, or skating sooner and more easily than precise hand movements such as catching a ball.

Nervous system

In the child's cortex the processes of stimulation dominate processes of inhibition. Processes of inhibition, as well as the reactivity of the whole nervous system, develop gradually with age. As reactivity increases, the number of mistakes go down, particularly between 5 and 10 years old (Wolanski 1979).

The process of developing conditioned reflexes is of great importance. At the age of 6 years these reflexes are changeable and impermanent. Children typically exhibit weak inhibition, poor concentration, high excitability, and generalization in their reaction to stimuli. All these factors often cause improper reaction to external stimuli, especially in situations demanding quick adaptation or sudden changes of direction and of character of movement. Conditioned reflexes become more permanent and are quickly automatized in the ages of 10 to 12, while during puberty these reflexes are more difficult to develop (Wolanski 1979).

There is feedback between the nervous system and physical training—the nervous system plays an important role in a person's adaptation to the loads, and in turn the training loads create new coordinations. These changes will form a basis for developing movement habits and perfect the cooperation among various body systems, including a person's metabolic mechanisms (Raczek 1987b).

Cardiorespiratory system

A child's more frequent and shallower breaths consume less energy than the less frequent and deeper ones of an adult. A child's heartbeats are also more frequent, so the blood circulation in the lungs is faster and the oxygen is more quickly distributed all over the body. The vital capacity of the lungs grows gradually with age, with its increases for older children and youth more correlated with body height than with age (Bogdanowicz 1968).

Mass and volume of the heart grows with age although in relation to body mass these values are similar for both children and adults. Stroke volume and volume per minute is smaller for children than for adults but increases with age. Systolic blood pressure is lower for children than for adults while diastolic is similar. A child's heart works economically because the lower the stroke volume is while the heart's cavities are well-filled the better the economy of the heart's work.

During one's growth and development, the resting heart rate has a tendency to slow down, systolic pressure to go up, heart volume per minute to go up, and the elasticity of arteries to decrease.

Aerobic and anaerobic fitness

Changes within the body influence its ability to perform physical efforts. Adaptability to physical loads is related to development of a person's aerobic and anaerobic potential.

Aerobic fitness relates to a body's intake and efficient use of oxygen. Maximal oxygen intake (VO_2max) increases as a child develops, an expression of the changes of several functions related to his or her body's oxygen use. Thus the VO_2max is an indirect indicator of several cooperating biological functions of the child. Aerobic fitness as it develops in trained and untrained boys and girls ages 8-17 is the subject of figure 14.

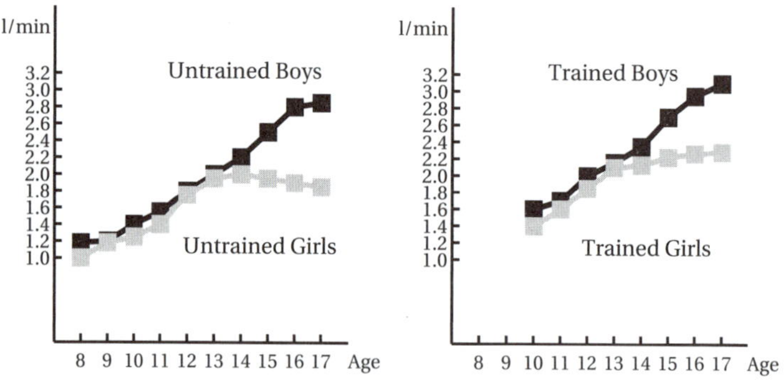

Figure 14. Maximal oxygen intake (VO_2max l/min) of untrained and trained girls and boys (Raczek 1978)

Until the age of 13 there are no significant differences in aerobic fitness between the sexes. In boys the greatest increases of aerobic fitness occur between ages 14-16, and maximal values are reached at the age of 18 or 19; in girls respectively at 11-13 and 14-15. Overlaying the natural speeding up of the development of aerobic fitness with physical fitness greatly improves VO_2max. (See figure 15.)

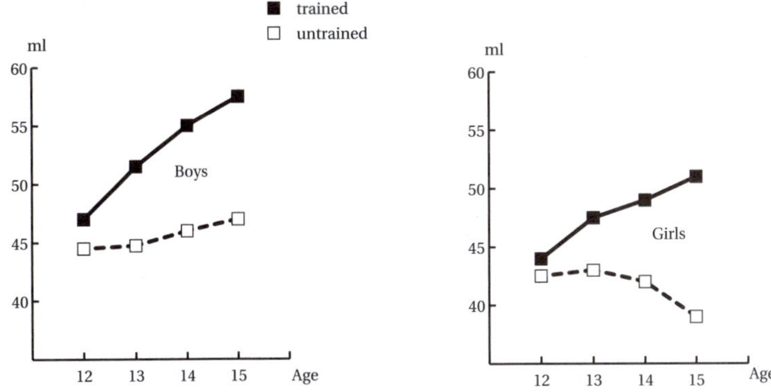

Figure 15. Maximal oxygen intake (VO2max ml/kg · min) of trained and untrained boys and girls (Raczek 1987b)

Anaerobic fitness relates to the ability to continue work when the intensity of work is greater than the supply of oxygen permits. Children have limited ability to perform anaerobic work.

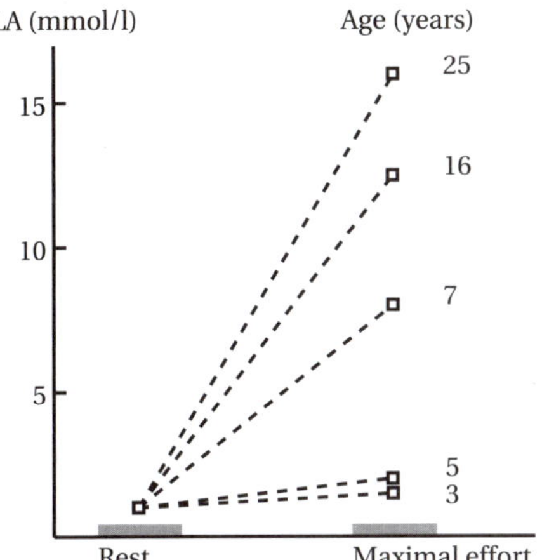

Figure 16. Maximal values of concentration of lactic acid depending on the age (Hollmann et al. 1978)

As you perhaps recall from table 3 (p. 11), anaerobic endurance training for girls would begin at ages 12-14; for boys, at ages 14-16. The measurements of lactic acid (a product of anaerobic work), given by age in figure 16, support these age recommendations.

What you have learned about physical fitness and biological development readies you to consider aspects of recruiting and selecting individuals for sports training. If you are not a coach or trainer, the next chapter will still give you food for thought as you consider your own or your child's talents and abilities.

3

RECRUITMENT AND SELECTION FOR SPORTS

In every sports discipline there is a search going on for individuals with the potential for achieving excellent results in the future. Talented individuals are rare, however, and the probability of discovering them during initial evaluation is small.

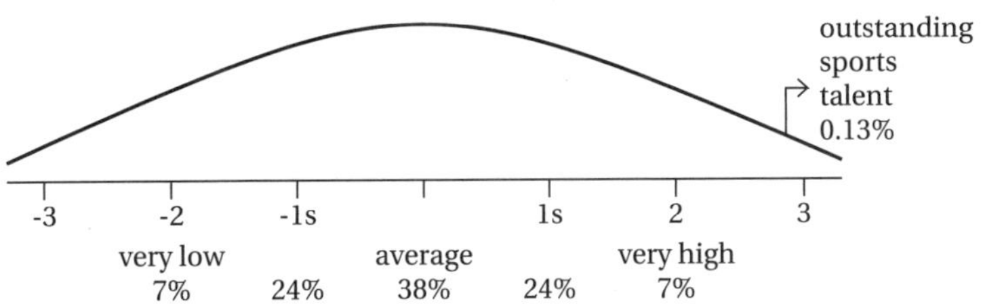

Figure 17. Probability of occurrence of individuals with a particular level of physical fitness (Kovar 1980)

Recruitment

The first step in finding these future champions is recruitment, and the second step is selection. Both these steps are well-intended and needed. They protect lesser talents from future disenchantment and the frustration likely if they fail to satisfy their awakened hopes and ambitions.

Recruitment means pursuing various organized actions that permit the assembly of suitable groups of people ready to undertake sports training. Such actions include arranging:

- announcements in schools;
- letters to parents explaining a new offering;

- meetings with top athletes;
- viewing of instructional movies of a given sports discipline;
- trips to see high-level competitions;
- open workouts; and
- promotional emphasis on given sports disciplines in a school, e.g., photographs from the highest level of competitions, lists of records, and profiles of top athletes.

Informal methods of recruitment include recommendations by p.e. teachers, or coaches, welcoming walk-ins, and buttonholing individuals you deem suitable on the basis of your knowledge and experience if you are a coach or a trainer.

Preferably you will conduct your recruitment activities at the time of the year that makes it possible for candidates to do directed or even specialized exercises. For example, you would recruit for kayaking in the spring, skiing in winter.

Selection

A group assembled as a result of such recruitment has to be subjected to first, initial selection. This selection is aimed at finding the individuals most suitable for a given sports discipline.

Selection is a process consisting of three stages: initial selection, assessment or determination of predispositions, and evaluation. Evaluation then is a continuous process throughout a young athlete's training and development. (See table 6.)

Table 6. System of selection in sports (Filipowicz and Turowski 1977)

Stage of selection	Basic tasks	Basic methods	Scope of interest
First	Initial selection of children for sports training	1. Pedagogical observation 2. Tests 3. Contests—reviews in sports disciplines 4. Sociological examination 5. Medical examination	Children up to 14 years old

Continued on next page

Table 6—continued

Stage of selection	Basic tasks	Basic methods	Scope of interest
Second	Determination of talents and predispositions for a given sports discipline or a group of events	1. Pedagogical observation 2. Tests 3. Control/Test competitions 4. Psychological examination 5. Biomedical examination	Children up to 14 years old
Third	Evaluation of predispositions for meeting specific demands of a given sports discipline or an event	1. Pedagogical observation 2. Tests 3. Control/Test competitions 4. Psychological examination 5. Biomedical examination	Children up to 14 years old and juniors (15-17)

Here is an example showing how the whole process would look for one young athlete whose high potential is realized.

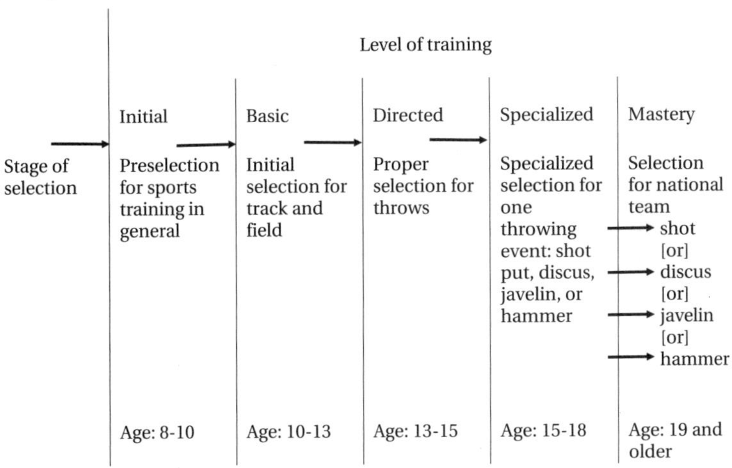

Figure 18. Process of selection for track and field throws (Raczek 1989)

Selection, assessment, and evaluation cycle through the process continually, each time resulting in a further refinement of direction and level of training for the young athlete.

You can get a visual feel for what the process is like overall by studying figure 19.

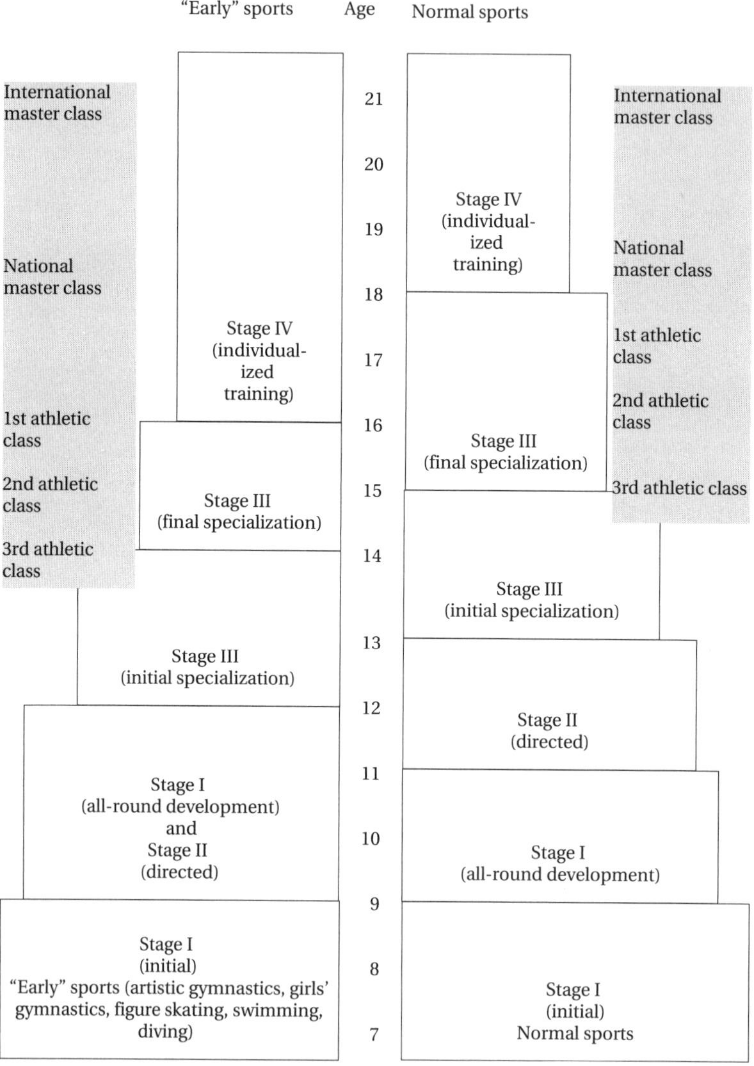

Figure 19. Stages of sports training of children and youth in Poland

Figure 19 will repay your study. The phrases *directed training* and *specialized training* will appear again and again in this work. You need a firm idea of what ages are appropriate for what stages, and this figure supplies that data.

Stage I—Initial selection

The criteria of initial selection are related to a person's:

- health and functional state;
- biological age;
- body type;
- psychological dispositions; and
- movement fitness.

Each criterion has its own considerations to take into account.

Health and functional state. It should go without saying that any child to be involved in sports should have a complete medical examination first. Not so obvious, perhaps, is that the child's functional state should also be assessed.

Functional state is a phrase that stands for the "biochemical efficiency" of an individual's body. A high level functional state is one of the fundamental preconditions of outstanding sports performances. In a laboratory setting you can evaluate functional state by measuring maximal oxygen intake (VO_2max—see table 7), anaerobic threshold, anaerobic capacity, and anaerobic power.

Table 7. Approximate values of maximal oxygen intake (VO_2max in ml/kg/min) in 10- to 18-year-old athletes

Boys

Age	Average	Above Average	High	Very High
10	44.8-51.4	51.5-56.2	56.3-59.8	>59.8
11	46.5-52.3	52.4-57.7	57.8-62.4	>62.4
12	46.6-52.8	52.9-58.6	58.7-63.8	>63.8
13	47.8-54.0	54.1-59.3	59.4-64.5	>64.5
14	48.8-55.4	55.5-59.7	59.8-67.4	>67.4
15	48.0-55.8	55.9-60.1	60.2-67.9	>67.9
16	48.2-56.6	56.7-60.5	60.6-68.2	>68.2
17	48.5-56.5	56.6-62.1	62.2-68.5	>68.5
18	49.8-56.8	56.9-62.5	62.6-70.5	>70.5

Continued on next page

Table 7—continued

Girls

Age	Average	Above Average	High	Very High
10	42.6-47.0	47.1-52.7	52.8-58.3	>58.3
11	42.2-46.4	46.5-53.4	53.5-59.2	>59.2
12	43.2-47.0	47.1-52.9	53.0-58.7	>58.7
13	44.5-48.1	48.2-53.9	54.0-58.9	>58.9
14	42.2-46.0	46.1-52.8	52.9-57.9	>57.9
15	42.1-45.7	45.8-51.7	51.8-57.2	>57.2
16	42.7-46.6	46.7-51.9	52.0-58.0	>58.0
17	42.3-46.5	46.6-52.6	52.7-59.0	>59.0
18	43.3-47.0	47.1-53.9	54.0-60.8	>60.8

Such measurements are expensive, time-consuming, and difficult to conduct with large groups, however. You can substitute simple field tests for them with reasonable accuracy. The following functional indicators are relatively stable (with a strong genetic component), and so they have great prognostic value already at the age of 11-12.

Use a 1.5-mile run or a 12-minute (Cooper test) run to evaluate aerobic fitness. When a child's motivation is high, the correlation coefficient is 0.80-0.90 between the results in these runs and aerobic fitness as measured by laboratory tests of maximal oxygen intake. In the course of selection by these tests you can use the results in these runs or, on the basis of these results, estimate the maximal oxygen intake using the data in figure 20 for the 1.5-mile run.

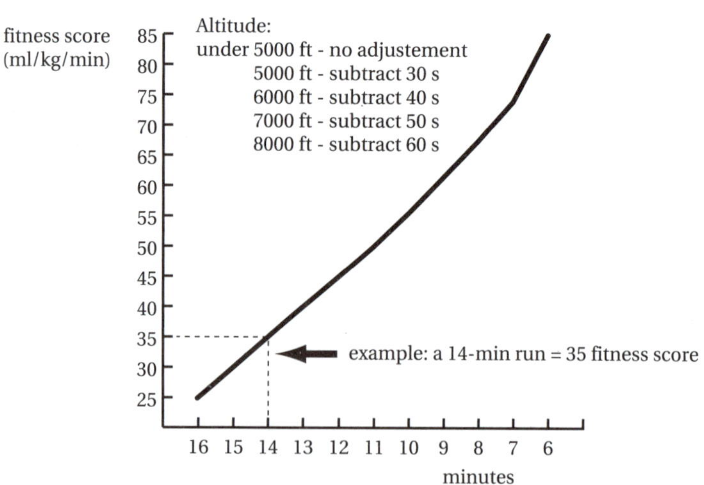

Figure 20. Maximal oxygen intake estimated from the time of running 1.5 mile (Sharkey 1986)

If you elect to use the 12-minute run, use the following equation by K. H. Cooper (Jeannotat 1980):

$VO_2max = 33 + 0.17(x - 133)$

where *x* is the distance (in meters) covered during one minute.

Example: A child covered a distance of 2200 meters during 12 minutes, which means that on the average, in one minute this child covered 183.3 meters. According to the equation his or her VO_2max is 41.5 ml/kg/min.

In case you lack suitable facilities for runs (preferably a 400-meter running track), use the step-test as modified by Montoye.

Equipment: Step 30 cm high, metronome, stopwatch.

Test: After resting 10 minutes in a sitting position, step up and down on the step at the pace of 30 step-ups per minute during 5 minutes. Sit down and rest for 1 minute. Count the heartbeats during the first 30 seconds of the second minute after the effort and multiply their number by 2.

Index of aerobic fitness = t x 100/5.5 x h

where *t* is the time of effort in seconds and *h*-heartbeats in the second minute after the effort

Example: 300 x 100/5.5 x (2 x 60) = 30000/660 = 45.5

Use table 8 to assess the child's initial fitness.

Table 8. Index of aerobic fitness and evaluation of children's fitness (Mazur et al. 1975)

Fitness index	Evaluation
over 60.0	very good
50.1 - 60.0	good
40.1 - 50.0	average
30.1 - 40.0	low
below 30.0	insufficient

To evaluate anaerobic power, use a sprint at 30-60 meter distance or a height jump. To evaluate anaerobic capacity, use a 200-meter sprint; to evaluate tolerance for lactic acid, use an 800-meter run. In all these tests you will have to adopt your own scale of evaluation, probably based on performance relative to others. These indicators of physiological fitness are relatively stable already at age 11-12 and thus of great prognostic value.

Biological age. Among the listed criteria of selection, determining the stage of biological development is particularly important. Biological age is a more accurate indicator of an individual's physical potential than his or her calendar age. This criterion is mostly genetically determined.

Unevenness of the developmental processes in children and youth of the same calendar age is often the source of many pedagogical problems, including difficulties in sports training. There are three methods to determine biological age: an examination of the development of teeth; an examination of wrist X-rays; and determining the stage of sexual maturity. The least expensive and simplest is the third method, which can be determined quite easily at the time of the child's medical exam. (See figure 21.)

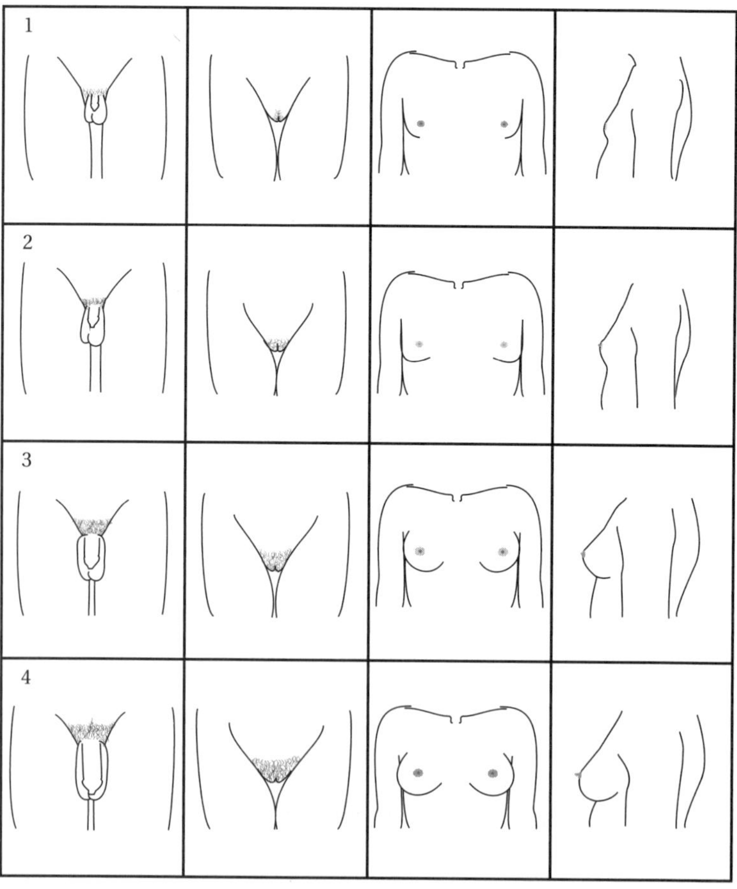

Figure 21. Stages of sexual maturity (Caine and Broekhoff 1987)

Table 9. Five-stage scale of sexual development (Starosta and Handelsman 1990)

Characteristics of sexual maturity	Stages of development				
	I	II	III	IV	V
Breasts	lack of signs of maturing, child's breast	breast gland and nipple slightly raised, diameter of the circle surrounding the nipple slightly increased	further development of the breast (midway between stage 2 and 4)	nipple and the circle surrounding it protrude from the breast (mamma aerolata)	full maturity of the breast—nipple protrudes but not the circle around it;
Density of pubic hair	lack of hair or the same hair as all over the body	single long hairs	more dense and thicker hair	more dense	very dense
Shape of hairs		soft, straight or slightly curling	more curled	curled	very curled
Color of hair		similar to the color of other body hair	darker than other body hair	dark	dark
Shape/reach of hair growth	some fluff on pubic area	in boys at the root of penis, in girls along labia	some over symphysis pubis (center of pubic area)	only around genitals, not on the thighs	hair crosses over to inner thighs
Penis	shape and size the same as in childhood	slight enlargement	visible increase of length	increased size, mainly the thickness	full maturity, the same as adult
Scrotum	shape and size the same as in childhood	enlargement, skin is red and thicker	enlargement	skin is darker	full maturity, the same as adult

Body type. Body type is determined genetically and so it is easy to assess and predict. It is a very important criterion in selection for particular sports. For example, kayakers have strong skeletons, are tall, are massive, have long upper limbs, strong muscles of the rib cage and arms, are mesomorphs. German data (Wozniak 1974) shows that best results among male kayakers are achieved by individuals 180-190 cm (5'11"-6'2") tall, so at age 12 prospective kayakers should have the following minimum dimensions—body height 157-158 cm (5'2"), sitting height 82 cm (32"), reach 157-158 cm (5'2"). At 14 these dimensions are respectively 165-170 cm (5'4"-5'7"), 86-89 cm (34"-35"), and 165-170 cm (5'4"-5'7").

In sports the athlete's height is very important. You should predict the ultimate body height during the initial selection. For this purpose first of all it is necessary to know the stage of sexual maturity as previously described (figure 20 and table 9). For example, assume that a 14-year-old boy, 160 cm (5'3") tall, is in the second stage of sexual maturity. Data from table 10 indicate that he is delayed in sexual maturity.

Table 10. Age and stages of sexual maturity in Polish children (Milicerowa 1973)

	Stage of sexual maturity	Early (before age)	Normal (from - to)	Late (after age)
Boys	2	11.5	11.5-13.5	13.5
	3	12.6	12.6-14.6	14.6
	4	13.2	13.2-15.4	15.4
	5	14.2	14.2-16.6	16.6
Girls	2	10.5	10.5-13.0	13.0
	3	11.4	11.4-13.4	13.4
	4	12.2	12.2-14.4	14.4
	5	12.8	12.8-15.2	15.2

Table 11. Average percentage of ultimate height reached at ages 10 to 17 in early, normal, and late maturing groups of boys and girls (Milicerowa 1973)

Boys Early	Boys Normal	Boys Late	**Age**	Girls Early	Girls Normal	Girls Late
80.7	78.8	76.5	**10.0**	87.2	83.7	79.7
82.0	80.4	78.5	**10.5**	89.2	85.5	82.2
83.5	81.5	79.6	**11.0**	91.0	87.5	84.3
85.4	83.9	81.1	**11.5**	93.2	89.3	85.1
87.5	84.6	82.4	**12.0**	95.1	91.5	87.0
89.9	86.5	83.7	**12.5**	96.6	93.6	89.2
92.2	88.3	85.1	**13.0**	97.7	95.4	92.0
94.2	91.0	87.1	**13.5**	98.5	96.9	93.9
95.8	93.4	88.8	**14.0**	99.1	98.0	95.5
97.2	95.5	90.8	**14.5**	99.4	98.7	96.8

Continued on next page

Table 11—continued

Boys Early	Boys Normal	Boys Late	**Age**	Girls Early	Girls Normal	Girls Late
98.2	97.0	92.8	**15.0**	99.5	99.4	98.1
99.0	98.2	94.6	**15.5**	99.6	99.8*	98.8
99.5	99.0	96.2	**16.0**	99.7	99.9*	99.4
99.9	99.5	97.8	**16.5**		99.9	99.7
	99.9	98.8	**17.0**			

* Diminishing size of the sample population makes these numbers slightly anomalous. The difference is insignificant since the girls are within a fraction of a percent of their ultimate height.

Having determined from table 10 if the child is maturing early, normally, or late, you can take data from table 11 to figure out the ultimate body height in the following equation:

ultimate body height = current height/percentage of ultimate height x 100

In the example of a 14-year-old late-bloomer, his ultimate height would be 180.1 cm (160 cm/88.8 x 100), or about 5'11".

Information on the body types and sizes in the child's family tree is also valuable in estimating suitability for different sports.

Psychological dispositions. You always ought to consider psychological fitness together with pedagogical aspects. Take into account opinions that indicate such psychological features and personality traits as:

- diligence, ambition, systematicness, activity, involvement;
- cooperativeness and responsibility in teamwork;
- attitude toward difficulties;
- interests, motivation for undertaking training; and
- simple reaction time.

As a rule negative opinions or observations would exclude any likelihood of a child's adaptation to training and any chance for desirable progress. Within the scope of the psychological criteria the child's grade average is worth taking into account. Good grades are evidence of talent, intelligence, and the previously mentioned psychological features necessary for a future sports career.

Reaction time, and the coordination related to it, are important psychomotor features in all sports. You can measure it by special instruments or roughly estimate it by means of a striped (one stripe=1 cm or 0.5 inch) stick that has to be caught as soon as a partner releases it. (See illustration page 127.)

Physical fitness. As far as physical fitness is concerned, three elements are important to evaluate:

- levels of development of basic motor (movement) abilities and magnitude of their yearly increases;
- level of mastering basic techniques of various sports; and
- sports results in one's sports discipline and their progression.

During the initial selection it is sufficient to evaluate only the first of these elements. This is not difficult. You can use various tests of physical fitness, as for example AAHPERD test, MOPER test, or the EUROFIT test. Table 12 can help you determine movement potential. At the assessment and evaluation stages of selection you must examine all three elements.

Table 12. Determining the potential of beginning athletes at the initial selection stage (Raczek 1989)

Initial level	Points	Pace of the increase	Points	Total points	Potential
high	3	high	3	6	very high
high	3	average	2	5	high
average	2	high	3	5	high
high	3	low	1	4	average
low	1	high	3	4	average
average	2	average	2	4	average

Raczek (1989) proposes the following movement fitness tests at all stages of selection for track and field.

Stage 1 (initial selection—for track and field in general)

- 60-meter sprint from flying start (result in seconds)
- 12-minute continuous run (result in meters)

- Triple jump on one leg, without pre-run, starting standing on both legs with one leg forward (result in centimeters)

- Overhead throw of a shot backward (result in centimeters)

Convert results to points according to table 13.

Table 13. Evaluation in points of fitness tests results during initial selection, ages 10-11 (Raczek 1989)

Points	12-minute run m	60-meter run s	triple jump on one leg cm	throw of a shot (boys—4 kg, girls—3 kg) cm
20	3000	9.4	580	560
19	2900	9.5	570	550
18	2800	9.6	560	540
17	2700	9.7	550	530
16	2600	9.8	540	520
15	2500	9.9	530	510
14	2400	10.0	520	500
13	2300	10.1	510	490
12	2200	10.2	500	480
11	2100	10.3	490	470
10	2000	10.4	480	460
9	1900	10.5	470	450
8	1800	10.6	460	440
7	1700	10.7	450	430
6	1600	10.8	440	420
5	1500	10.9	430	410
4	1400	11.0	420	400
3	1300	11.1	410	390
2	1200	11.2	400	380
1	1100	11.3	390	370
Additional points over 20	1 point = 100 m	1 point = 0.1 s	1 point = 10 cm	1 point = 10 cm

Stage 2—Assessment of Predispositions

These assessments are to determine predispositions to a group of events.

- 60-meter sprint from low start

- 30-meter sprint from standing and from flying start

- 800-meter run

- Throw shot (girls 3 kg/6.6 lb, boys 4 kg/8.8 lb) either overhead backward or from below waist forward

- Triple jump on one leg, without pre-run, starting standing on both legs with one leg forward

Children who fulfill minimum requirements (see table 14) of these tests can qualify for the next stage of training.

Table 14. Minimum requirements during assessment of predispositions (ages 12-13) in track and field

Tests for sprinters	Results Boys	Results Girls	Tests for jumpers	Results Boys	Results Girls
30 m (flying start)	3.7 s	3.8 s	triple jump	660 cm	640 cm
30 m (low start)	4.7 s	4.8 s	30 m (flying start)	3.9 s	4.0 s
triple jump	640 cm	620 cm			
Tests for runners	**Results Boys**	**Results Girls**	**Tests for throwers**	**Results Boys**	**Results Girls**
800 m	2:25 min.	2:35 min.	throw of a shot	820 cm	720 cm
30 m (flying start)	4.0 s	4.1 s	triple jump	620 cm	600 cm

Stage 3—Evaluation

Moving on to the next level of training—from basic to directed, for example—requires first and second stage tests plus tests of the specific fitness required in a chosen event of track and field. In making selections, observe these cautions.

1. Conduct tests at least twice a year. Effects of training (meaning improved test results) are your first reliable information that a given individual has the required potential—psychologically, physiologically, and physically—for achieving future sports successes.

2. In selecting children for future training, mistakes are inevitable because of the difficulty of predicting further physical, movement, and mental development, as well as the development of a particular child's interests.

3. Don't be discouraged by first or subsequent failures of a young athlete in his or her sports career. An athlete's sports career does not have to be forever tied to one sports discipline. A wise coach will see and point out the potential of his or her charge in another discipline. Knowledge of the common and differentiating dominant features of various sports will help with matching athlete's potential to sports discipline. (See diagram 1.)

standard movements dominant features			nonstandard movements dominant features		
differentiating	common	differentiating	differentiating	common	differentiating
speed	strength	endurance for continuous effort	agility	1. complex reaction 2. endurance for variable efforts 3. strength	1. sense of time and space 2. peripheral vision 3. dexterity at manipulating equipment
track and field multi events middle distance runs swimming bicycling track road weightlifting rowing throws kayaking jumps speed skating hurdles cross-country ski sprints long distance runs			sailing downhill ski ski jumps equestrian sports luges gymnastics sport artistic fencing ice hockey boxing rugby judo soccer wrestling basketball acrobatics volleyball		

Diagram 1. Sports and their dominant features (Szewczyk 1984)

4. From a pedagogical point of view selection ought to be most often affirmative, rarely negative. Every healthy and somewhat movement-talented child who is willing to work ought to be able to find a place in a suitable sport. This does not have to happen immediately, perhaps not even in a few years. There should be no rush in sports training. Even in swimming, considered an "early" sport, children who are successful early do not always grow up to be Olympic champions. Those swimmers who succeeded at age 17 often were not among the best at early stages of their training, as a few examples will make clear.

Dick Shoulberg, swimming coach of Philadelphia Germantown Academy, who coached Olympic swimmers on the 1980 and 1984 U.S. teams and has placed swimmers in the top 10 of national championship swim meets each of the last 12 years, said, "I can't think of a single instance in which a swimmer in the 10- or 12-year age group was among the best swimmers in his class and also went on to compete in the Olympics." He could name, though, many swimmers who were not among the best at age 10, but were among the best at age 17 (Adams 1991).

Breaststroke swimmer Dmitry Volkov, a two-time bronze medalist of the 1986 World Championship, three-time gold medalist of the Goodwill

Games, 1987 European Champion, bronze medalist from the 1988 Olympics in Seoul despite suffering a severe hand injury just two months before the start, as a child was asked to stop coming to the swimming pool because he was "completely hopeless" (Mikulik 1990).

Tennis players Steffi Graf and Boris Becker in their childhood were considered unpromising. They were not put on the children's national tennis team (Mikulik 1990).

Soccer player Igor Byelanov, winner of the Golden Ball, was rejected twice from Odessa soccer school because of "lack of any talent and promise." When he applied for the third time, coach Maslovski admitted him to his group but had no idea what talent Igor had (Mikulik 1990).

"Sport selection satisfies a unique, twofold need: to identify accurately in a small population the very best talent that existed for one or more carefully chosen sports, and to ensure that the expensive coaching, training, and sport-science resources that would have to be put into development of that talent would not be wasted" (Arnot and Gaines 1984).

In appendix B you will find many more tables related to specific sports and their demands for body type and fitness.

4

TRAINING LOADS AND CHILDREN

Loads in sports are the physical and mental efforts of the athlete. They are the most essential element of the sports training process, and if well-matched to the person's potential, they increase his or her efficiency and resilience.

Loads are divided into training loads and competitive loads. Both kinds of loads consist of the same components:

- physical (tonnage, mileage, time);
- physiological-biochemical (heart rate, lactic acid concentration); and
- psychological/mental.

In training, the psychological component is made up of aspects related to difficulty, danger, and boredom; in competition, to aspects of concentration, nervous tension, and the desire to win.

Managing training loads with children and youth is difficult because they are busy growing and maturing. As their bodies grow and change, so do their needs. With children and youth the first priority is to secure sufficient energy for this maturational process, and so keeping the proper ratio of load (work) to rest is the basis of conducting sports training. The duration of recovery should determine dosage of the loads. Recovery too short leads to accumulating fatigue, overexertion, and eventually to overtraining. The magnitude of the load, its volume and intensity, is of secondary importance so long as the magnitude does not drop below the threshold of effectiveness. The threshold of effectiveness of training loads is lower for children and beginners of any age. In both cases training loads are already effective at 50% of their maximal potential, whereas for advanced athletes with many years of training the loads must exceed 80-90% of their potential.

Table 15 provides several clues for quick evaluation of fatigue during a workout.

Table 15. Symptoms permitting an approximate evaluation of the degree of fatigue and the training load during workout (Harre 1985)

Indicator	Fatigue: moderate Load: moderate	Fatigue: high Load: optimal	Fatigue: very high Load: ultimate
Perspiration	light or moderate—depending on temperature	heavy, above waist	very heavy, below the waistline
Breathing	accelerated but even	very fast	very fast, short, and irregular
Precision of movement	normal	flaws begin to appear, lowered precision	big flaws, impaired coordination, lack of precision, uncertainty
Concentration	normal, full attention during explanations	inattention during explanations, lowered ability to apply advice, lowered differentiation (ability to notice differences in the amount of strength applied in the movement)	clearly lowered, nervousness, elongated reaction time
Disposition	good, no complaints	feeling of muscular weakness, lowered efficiency, increased overall weakness	great weakness, pains in muscles and joints
Readiness for effort	good	lowered activity, tendency to prolong rest breaks, but ready to continue the effort	none, longing for total rest
Mood	happy, lively	a bit subdued but happy if the results of the workout are as expected	fear of renewed effort, doubts about the purpose of a workout

Although children adapt to training loads faster than adults and regenerate faster after the work, they develop best with moderate loads.

The main elements of training loads are:

- volume (duration of effort, or mileage, or tonnage, or number of repetitions);
- intensity (frequency of movements, volume of exercises per time); and

• rest periods.

The volume of loads determines an athlete's general development and contributes to his or her long-term maintenance of the achieved level of conditioning. Intensity determines how high a level of conditioning an athlete will reach.

Volume of training and children

The volume of loads is the main developmental stimulus in the first 2-3 years of training. Load volume should be increased as the training process progresses. Here is the correct sequence for increasing volume of loads.

1. Increase the frequency of workouts in a week.

2. Increase the duration of workouts by increasing exercise volume (number of repetitions, mileage, or tonnage).

3. Increase the number of exercises, mileage, or tonnage in a workout without increasing its duration.

There should be no rush to increase the volume of loads. You would, for example, only increase the duration of one workout after 2-3 years of training. Table 16 gives you a sense of the percent of an athlete's capacity you would call on at three different stages of training.

Table 16. Dynamics of training loads volume (Nabatnikowa 1982)

Stage of training	% of target load volume
Directed preparation stage	45-50%
Special preparation stage	70-80%
Stage of maximum results	100%

In the directed preparation stage, exercises have structure and dynamics close to but not the same as the competitive event. For shot-putters, for example, directed preparation training would include various throws of a medicine ball and of other equipment.

In the special preparation stage, exercises developing technique, as well as sport specific motor and mental abilities, have structure and dynamics the same as the competitive event. Starts in competitions are also considered as such exercises. Look at table 17 for some examples in selected sports of these training loads realized.

Table 17. Permissible training loads for young athletes (Nabatnikowa 1982)

		Magnitude of training per year	
Sports discipline	Stage of training	Boys	Girls
Kayaking	directed specialized	2500-2800 km 4000-4500 km	2200-2500 km 3500-4000 km
Rowing	directed specialized	1750-2000 km 2800-3200 km	1350-1500 km 2100-2400 km
Speed skating	directed specialized	1800-2100 km 2400-3000 km	1300-1600 km 1800-2200 km
Swimming	directed specialized	1000-1200 km 1700-2000 km	1000-1200 km 1700-2000 km
Running (middle distances)	directed specialized	1800-2000 km 2800-3300 km	1600-1900 km 2600-3000 km
Running 400 m	directed specialized	220-245 km 340-390 km	210-235 km 330-375 km
Throws	directed specialized	2600-3000 4100-4700 of various throws	2300-2550 3500-4100 of various throws
Cross-country skiing	directed specialized	3000-3400 km 5300-5800 km	2700-3000 km 4500-4800 km

For the volume of training loads to be effective it must exceed a certain threshold value. This value is set individually for every athlete and determining it precisely is difficult. Numerous studies were conducted to find out how to determine this value and certain ranges of effectiveness of training loads have been established (Raczek 1989).

In developing children's endurance in younger school ages (7-11), the minimal effective dose of exercises is approximately 30 minutes per week. With older children (ages 12-15), 60 minutes per week is more effective. Table 18 lists load volumes *per workout* so that you can see how this ideal is realized in practice.

Table 18. Gradation of volume of endurance training loads per workout depending on age (Raczek 1989)

Volume	Age			
	10-12	13-15	16-18	19
high	15-20 min.	20-30 min.	30-40 min.	40-60 min.
medium	10-15 min.	15-20 min.	20-30 min.	30-40 min.
low	5-10 min.	10-15 min.	15-20 min.	20-30 min.

Intensity of training and children

The volume of loads is intertwined with their intensity—the intensity of the exercises you select must be adequate. The evaluation of intensity is much more difficult and less precise than the evaluation of load volume, however.

In practice intensity of an exercise is determined in relation to an individual's best personal result or maximal potential in a given exercise—you describe intensity as a percentage of its maximal value. Example: if the best result in a 100-meter sprint is 12 seconds, running it in 14 seconds computes to an intensity of 86% ($^{12}/_{14}$ x 100 = 85.71 rounded off to 86%); or, if the maximal number of pushups per 30 seconds is 40, then doing 20 in the same time comes out to an intensity of 50%.

A better means of evaluating intensity is through the heart rate. This method indicates changes that are caused by efforts in various intensity zones. It is important to remember that when taking pulse by touch, the heart rate is lower than actual by 15-30 beats per minute in children and by 10-20 beats per minute in youth. Because of this it is best to use an electronic heart rate monitor.

Table 19. Zones of intensity of training loads in strength and in endurance training according to Carl and Martin, after Raczek (1989)

Strength training % of maximum resistance	Intensity zone	Endurance training % of maximal heart rate
50-70%	moderate	50-60%
70-80%	high	60-75%
80-90%	very high	80-90%

Continued on next page

Table 19—continued

Strength training % of maximum resistance	Intensity zone	Endurance training % of maximal heart rate
90-100%	maximal	85-100%

Just as with the volume of loads, intensity also has its threshold of effectiveness. The range of this threshold for children and for beginners is greater than for athletes with a few years of training. Heart rate (see table 20) is an accurate indicator of intensity in cyclic (i.e., repetitive) and in aerobic efforts, but in acyclic and in anaerobic efforts—for example, gymnastics—the heart rate permits a very general and only approximate evaluation of intensity.

Table 20. Approximate values of heart rate and intensity zones (Raczek 1989)

Intensity zone	Age	HR per min. Boys	HR per min. Girls
low	12-15	up to 132	up to 138
	16-19	up to 126	up to 132
moderate	12-15	132-144	138-150
	16-19	126-138	132-144
high	12-15	150-174	156-180
	16-19	144-168	150-174
very high	12-15	180-198	186-204
	16-19	174-192	180-198
maximal	12-15	204 and up	210 and up
	16-19	198 and up	204 and up

In such cases it is better to use parameters of cellular metabolism such as pH or lactic acid concentration, while heart rate after the effort remains a good indicator of recovery—slower decline of the heart rate shows that recovery is difficult because exercises were too intensive.

Table 21. Normal behavior of heart rate after effort (Schilch, Löffler, and Hendel 1975)

HR immediately after effort	HR after 1 min.	HR after 2 min.	HR after 3 min.	HR after 4 min.
180	140	130	120	up to 120

The threshold of effective intensity is fluid, depending mainly on the age and level of fitness. For children and youth a heart rate of 150-180 is considered to be an effective intensity. At such values of the heart rate, a steady state beneficial to the child's development can occur. Of course, with improved athletic shape, the amount of work (load) the child can perform in that steady state increases. For older children, as their ability to perform anaerobic efforts develops, it is necessary to improve it. This requires efforts that result in a heart rate of 170-180 beats per minute to develop both aerobic and anaerobic fitness because they occur at the anaerobic threshold. In table 22 you see this information elaborated further.

Table 22. Values of functional indicators at aerobic (2 mmol/l LA) and anaerobic (4 mmol/l LA) thresholds (Raczek 1989)

	Aerobic threshold			Anaerobic threshold		
			Boys			
Age	HR	%VO_2max	speed (m/s)	HR	%VO_2max	speed (m/s)
9-10	179.5	63.1	2.9	201.3	81.2	3.4
14-15	161.8	66.8	3.5	184.1	85.2	4.3
17-18	154.7	67.5	3.7	182.3	84.1	4.5
			Girls			
9-10	182.2	60.8	2.5	204.0	77.4	3.1
14-15	164.1	62.0	3.0	186.5	80.3	3.7
17-18	160.2	65.8	3.3	184.9	82.7	4.0

Structure of training loads

Loads should be adequate for each training stage. They will differ at the stage of general and of directed preparation, for example. There will always be an inverse relation between their volume and intensity—increasing volume usually requires decreasing the intensity and vice versa.

In managing training loads first you increase the volume. Then, as the child's fatigue resiliency improves, you can gradually increase intensity. Do not rush to increase the intensity of training loads!

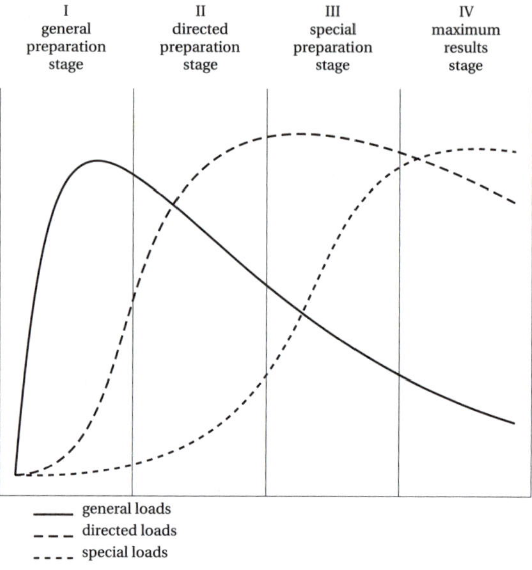

Figure 22. Change of share of particular types of training loads in subsequent stages of training (Raczek 1989)

- General loads—exercises of versatile fitness preparation, of different form and dynamics than competitive actions, that do not teach techniques and tactics of the sport

- Directed loads—exercises that involve the same muscle groups, use the same energy source, and have dynamic characteristics similar to special loads but their form of movement is different. For example, various jumps, different than the actual competitive jump, are directed exercises for jumpers

- Special loads—exercises that have the same form and dynamics as the competitive actions, including exercises developing techniques and tactics of the sport

A close-up look at the data in figure 22 is the subject of table 23. You can see how the emphasis changes over time in the kinds of training and their intensity.

Table 23. Suggested rates of general and special training loads in a yearly training cycle (Nabatnikowa 1982)

Sports	Stage of training	% General loads	% Special loads
Cyclic	Directed	70-80%	20-30%
	Special	30-40%	60-70%
Speed-strength	Directed	70-75%	25-30%
	Special	45-60%	40-55%
Team games	Directed	65-75%	25-35%
	Special	30-40%	60-70%
Individual contact	Directed	60-75%	25-40%
	Special	40-45%	55-60%
Technical	Directed	30-40%	60-70%
	Special	20-30%	70-80%

Table 24. Suggested rates of general and special training loads in speed skating (Nabatnikowa 1982)

Age	10 to 11	12 to 13	14 to 15	16 to 17	17 to 18
% Loads					
General	68-70	64-66	60-65	48-52	40-45
Special	30-32	34-36	35-40	48-52	55-60

Nabatnikowa in table 23 simplified division of the loads to general and special only because these differ most from each other. In reality some of the loads could be classified as directed loads. As figure 22 and table 23 show, therefore, all three kinds of loads are used at any stage of training. No type of load (general, directed, or special) is omitted at any stage of training, only the proportion of these loads changes. And so even during the first year of swimming, at a stage of general preparation, children practice competitive strokes and participate in races, which are exercises of special loads.

In a yearly training cycle (macrocycle) loads should be characterized by variability, and by wavelike increases and decreases of the volume and intensity, as you can see in figures 23 and 24.

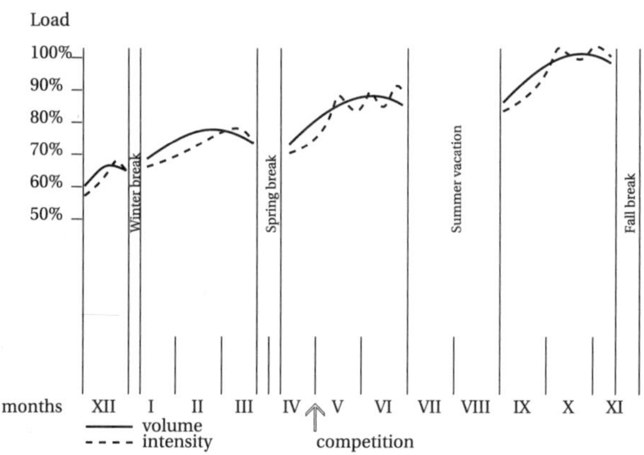

Figure 23. Dynamics of loads in a yearly training cycle for youth (Tschiene 1977)

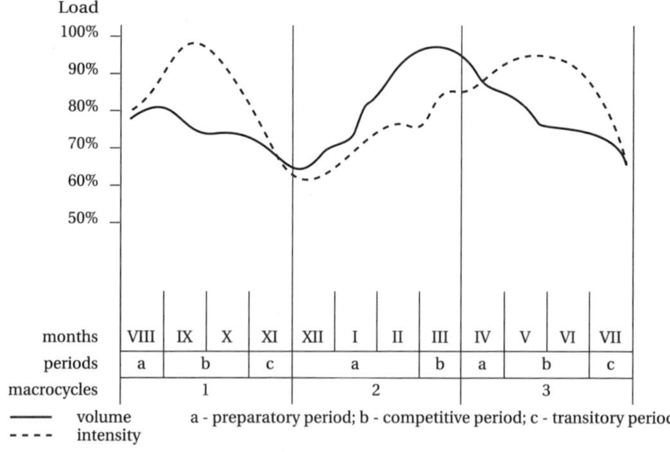

Figure 24. Dynamics of loads for runners at the directed stage of training (Raczek 1989)

It is easiest to regulate loads in a weekly training cycle (microcycle). Here the relationship between the training load and the amount of rest is most important. In a microcycle the principle of varying the loads—high load, then lower or rest—is most visible. With children, you will train at near maximal intensity (determined by heart rate) only once per week.

Table 25. Structure of training loads in a microcycle during the stage of general preparation (Raczek 1989)

Year	day 1	day 2	day 3	day 4	day 5	day 6	day 7
1	low loads		moderate loads		low loads		
2	low loads		moderate loads		low loads		moderate loads
3	low loads	moderate loads		moderate loads	low loads		high loads

The volume and intensity of loads both rise in the stage of directed preparation. (See table 26.)

Table 26. Structure of training loads in a microcycle during the stage of directed preparation (Raczek 1989)

Year	day 1	day 2	day 3	day 4	day 5	day 6	day 7
1	low loads		moderate loads		low loads		maximal loads
2	low loads	moderate loads		moderate loads	low loads		maximal loads
3	low loads	moderate loads	low loads	high loads	low loads		maximal loads

There is another principle for you to observe, too: First apply the loads stressing the neuromuscular system (technical, speed, agility, or strength training) and later the loads that stress the vegetative system (endurance training). During the directed stage of training you can distinguish three types of training loads depending on their energy source. (See table 27).

Table 27. Proportions of training loads of different energy character during the directed preparation stage (Nabatnikowa 1982)

Sport	Load type	Load %	Load volume in km Boys	Load volume in km Girls
Middle distance running	1. aerobic	85-87	1500-1700	1400-1650
	2. mixed	8-11	190-225	145-180
	3. anaerobic	4-5	60-75	55-70
Speed skating	1. aerobic	81-84	1500-2000	1100-1300
	2. mixed	12-15.5	235-260	175-225
	3. anaerobic	3.5-4	65-80	45-60
Rowing	1. aerobic	72-77	1300-1500	1000-1200
	2. mixed	18-22	350-400	265-315
	3. anaerobic	5-6	95-100	75-85
Kayaking	1. aerobic	75-77	1950-2200	1700-1950
	2. mixed	15-18	375-400	345-375
	3. anaerobic	7-8	175-200	155-175
Swimming	1. aerobic	76-78	800-950	800-950
	2. mixed	18.5-21	180-220	180-220
	3. anaerobic	3-3.5	30-35	30-35
Cross country skiing	1. aerobic 2. mixed	(Aerobic & mixed 1 & 2) 84-86.5	(Aerobic & mixed 1 & 2) 2600-2950	(Aerobic & mixed 1 & 2) 2350-2600
	3. anaerobic	13.5-16	400-450	350-400

You can see how all this fits together in table 28.

Table 28. Structure of training loads (in km) during three years of the directed preparation stage (Raczek 1989)

Intensity zone	Boys			Girls		
	year 1	year 2	year 3	year 1	year 2	year 3
RE1 (HR 130-150)	600	850	1325	440	720	1260
RE2 (HR 150-180)	150	274	445	120	220	358
RE3 (HR 170-190)	0	0	105	0	0	70
Speed & rhythm	40	60	100	32	48	94
Competitions	10	16	25	8	12	18
Total	800	1200	2000	600	1000	1800

RE 1 refers to running endurance in the aerobic range. RE 2 means running endurance in the mixed range. And RE 3 is running endurance in the anaerobic range.

Competitive loads and children

Frequency of starts in competitions depends on the level of training experience: the less advanced the child athlete, the less frequent the starts.

Table 29. Number of starts in competitions during the directed preparation stage (Raczek 1989)

Type of event	year 1	year 2	year 3
Cross-country run	4	5	5
Middle distance run	6	8	10
Other track and field events	6	7	8
Total	16	20	23

For young athletes in the specialized stage of training, the number of competitive starts goes up. The competition itself constitutes a fair proportion of their training.

Table 30. Recommended number of starts per year (Nabatnikowa 1982)

Sport	Boys and Girls Ages 15-16	Boys and Girls Ages 17-18
Middle distance running	10-12	12-15
Kayaking	6-8	6-8
Throws	13-16	22-25
Cross-country skiing	17-23	24-30
Volleyball	35-40	45-50

Designing a training program that is appropriate in both load volume and load intensity is the essence of good coaching. Studies have made the process more of a science, but it still has the quality of an art about it as well. Taking into account the young athlete's stage of preparation, biological age, and the needs of the particular sport and tailoring all this to the unique individual before you—these are the factors that make the difference between a good coach and a great one.

5

STAGES OF CHILDREN'S SPORTS TRAINING

You are delving more and more deeply into the kind of thinking and planning a trainer must engage in. You have so far considered the biological development of children and several means of recruiting individuals for sport. You have explored on a large scale the dimensions of the stages of training, and you have begun to examine appropriate training loads for children.

Now you are ready to put one of these stages—the initial, or general development stage—under the microscope. To begin, here in figure 25 is a repeat (at "lesser magnification") of the information you first encountered in figure 19.

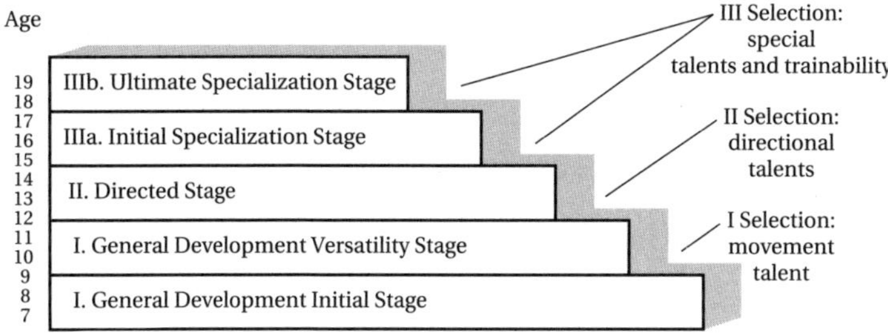

Figure 25. System of youth sports training in Poland and its division into stages

Dividing a young athlete's training into stages and periods within those stages is essential. What makes it so are the many goals and tasks, the need to apply the appropriate loads at the appropriate times, and the necessities of planning training. At the initial stage of training, however, there is still dispute among authorities. Some advise against the periodization of training in the initial stage because of their apprehensions, often justified, of the risk of copying adult athletes' training, the hazards of early specialization and the potential losses from focusing on short-term gains at the expense of proper goals for children's training.

There are three factors that tilt the decision toward some degree of sports-specific training in the initial stage.

1. A diversity of tasks already exists in the early stages of training, in the means, methods, and forms of training.

2. The child will benefit by becoming accustomed early to the wavelike patterns of applying training loads.

3. The coach's work will be simplified considerably insofar as planning and noting increased abilities is concerned.

Taken together these three make a strong argument for plugging in sport-specific training in the initial stage. It is not so much a matter of a strict regimen as it is making sure that the goals and tasks planned for a child are appropriate and will promote the child's all-round development.

In a yearly cycle of training there are three periods: preparatory, main, and transitory. The content of those periods and their structure vary at different stages of the long-term training process.

Kayaking is the example you will study. Kayaking happens to be a sport in which the author has considerable first-hand experience and expertise, which is one good reason to select that sport. Another equally good reason is that kayaking is far enough removed from the casual run of interests that you will be unlikely to be distracted by any preconceptions. And if in fact kayaking is exactly where your interests lie, so much the better! Then you have the bonus of having an initial stage training schema all laid out for you.

In table 31 you can see the content of the periods during the first two or three years of training using the example of kayaking.

Table 31. Main tasks in a yearly cycle of a kayaker's training during the initial stage of preparation (Drabik 1991)

Preparatory period	Main period	Transitory period
1. Developing general fitness—conditioning abilities (strength, speed, endurance) and coordination abilities (agility, dexterity, balance, flexibility)	1. Continuation of work on general fitness	1. Recreational rowing
2. Learning rowing on various types of boats, in the gym on rowing machines, in the kayaking pool, and on open waters	2. Rowing in various types of kayaks and canoes—learning technique and basics of tactics	2. Kayaking excursions and rallies (no competition)
3. Perfecting swimming and learning diving	3. Perfecting swimming and diving	3. Increasing movement potential through other sports (middle- and long-distance running, ball games, bicycling, cross-country skiing), while taking into account functional demands of kayaking
4. Developing adequate attitude (commitment, desire, courage) for workouts on open waters	4. Fun regattas including multiple events and various types of boats	
	5. Watching competitions of juniors or seniors to learn rules and safety	

General fitness preparation during the initial stage of training

Kayaking is one of the strength-endurance sports, which has great bearing on the planning of physical preparation, the choice of the general fitness exercises, and their type. The character of movements in kayaking means, for example, that you would stress strength exercises that developed explosive strength (needed at the start) and endurance (needed while covering the distance). During more advanced stages of training, exercises of general fitness preparation should increasingly rely on directed, and later on special exercises.

Sometimes specialization of general preparation may take place at the initial stage of training. With the youngest kayakers, for example, you could do a strength exercise such as "sawing wood."

You ought to choose general fitness preparation tasks that have a distribution of loads similar to that of competition. For kayakers, this would entail circuit training and a big running play: start with a warm-up of continuous movement across terrain and use its features (ditches, stones, trees). Continue the big running play with running rhythm exercises, accelerations, and running pace exercises at distances of 800-1000 meters repeated 4 to 6 times. Complete the big running play with a cool-down consisting of jogging and calming down exercises. Use continuous and variable methods, e.g., a continuous run at a constant pace during the workout, and the variable method involving continuous work while changing the pace, but not allowing the heart rate to drop below 150.

Fatigue increases fast in long-lasting efforts with a static component (such as sitting, in the case of children rowing). Because of that every once in a while children should come ashore and do some exercises using features of the terrain—leg raises holding a tree, running around trees, climbing trees, slaloming among trees are examples.

In kayaking most of the effort is anaerobic. Until the age of fourteen, a child's potential for anaerobic work is limited. This complicates general fitness preparation for young kayakers. The character of loads in kayaking, however, requires developing both anaerobic and aerobic sources of energy, first aerobic and then mixed—anaerobic and aerobic.

Versatility in strength development is essential. Insufficient strength of the trunk, arms, or legs, as well as any asymmetry of strength among muscle groups will adversely affect technique and the efficiency of rowing. Early fatigue is the consequence, because of short or uneven pulls, or both, on the paddle or oar.

During breaks between sets of general fitness exercises, the child should do flexibility and relaxing exercises.

In kayaking, the goal is to develop the kayaker's fundamental physical characteristics (endurance, strength, speed, speed of muscle contraction, elasticity of muscles). It will also be important to have some features similar to directed and special exercises, as well as exercises that teach the child how to relax muscles while rowing, and any fun activity such as ball games or other totally different activity.

The volume of general fitness preparation should amount to approximately 70-80% of the volume of all workouts. Accent particular movement abilities in accordance with the principles of biological development, among them taking advantage of sensitive periods when the development of a given movement ability accelerates.

General fitness preparation is part of a general outline of training at its initial stage (table 32). Directed and special preparation, which must take place even at the initial stage of training in spite of the great universality of general exercises, is also included in this table.

Table 32. General outline of first years of training using the example of kayaking (Drabik 1991)

Tasks	Means	Methods	Loads
1. All-round development of child's functions	1. Means of all-round fitness preparation (running games, circuits, movement games, ball games, endurance sports)	1. Continuous with moderate intensity and variable with gentle and smooth changes of pace of running, swimming, rowing, bicycling, skiing, or skating	1. Yearly volume of rowing: boys approximately 1000 km, girls approximately 800 km
2. Increasing movement potential	2. Continuous (same pace) and variable (changing pace) rowing for long periods of time, stressing technique	2. Repetitive—mainly for developing skills and habits	2. Intensity approximately 60%
3. Versatile stimulation of development of movement abilities	3. Controlled starts in multi-event competitions (kayaking, canoeing)		3. Frequency of workouts: 3-4 per week
4. Developing aerobic fitness	4. Competitions in other sports		4. Ratio of general loads to directed and special loads: 70-80% to 20-30%
5. Mastering basic technique of rowing in a kayak and in a canoe	5. Means of directed and special preparation		
6. Identifying of talents and interests related to kayaking			
7. Creating work atmosphere guaranteeing mental balance			

There are various ways of choosing and arranging the means of training at the initial stage of children's sports training. Recent studies, however, show that parallel with developing various movement habits by play and games, it is necessary to use special exercises that develop movement potential directly related to a given sports discipline. There is no doubt that at the initial stage of training enlarging the functional potential of the child is a priority. Doing exercises for special preparation is a form of supplementing this task. With the specific demands of kayaking in mind, the following proposal of volumes of means of training seems reasonable. (See figure 26.) This model is certainly subject to debate, because of unavoidable simplifications if for no other reason. But it provides a starting point.

First 12-18 months of initial stage

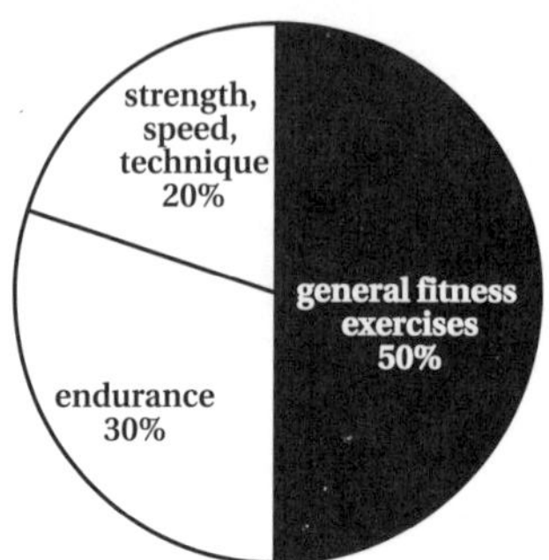

From 12th -18th to 36th month of initial stage

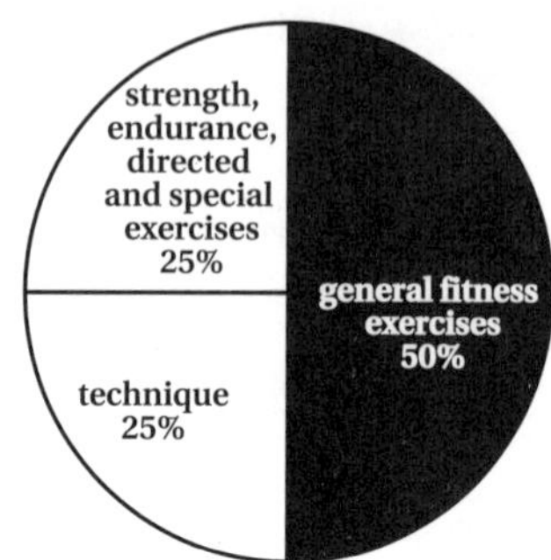

Figure 26. Proposal of ratios of training means in the first 2-3 years, the initial stage, of kayakers' training (Drabik 1991)

These suggestions do not contradict the earlier recommendations regarding the volume of general fitness preparation. Workouts with a strong accent on endurance, or speed, or any other ability, are assumed in the volume of general fitness preparation.

Taking into account the specifics of a child's body on one hand and the necessity of varying the character of training loads on the other hand, here in table 33 are recommendations for volumes (in % of total) of exercises that stress various energy sources in the training of beginning kayakers.

Table 33. Program of general fitness preparation during the initial stage of training, using the example of kayaking (Drabik 1991)

Periods and volume of general fitness exercises in %	Motor abilities, accent, methods	Means/Exercises
Preparatory period Volume of general fitness exercises: 70-80%	**Coordination** Accent on: a. speed and accuracy b. speed, accuracy, and adequacy to a changing situation Methods: repetitive	Coordination will be developed by a majority of the earlier mentioned exercises as well as by the following: 1. Turns and rolls at own and at imposed pace 2. Mirror movements at own pace 3. Movements in atypical positions 4. Additional movements added to exercises (arm exercises while running, for example) 5. Balancing exercises on solid land 6. Balancing exercises in a kayak 7. Learning technique of rowing on various boats

Continued on next page

Table 33—continued

Periods and volume of general fitness exercises in %	Motor abilities, accent, methods	Means/Exercises
Preparatory period Volume of general fitness exercises: 70-80%	**Endurance** Accent on: a. aerobic sources—80-85% b. anaerobic -lactacid sources—approx. 15% c. anaerobic-alactacid sources—approx. 5% Methods: continuous, variable, repetitive	1. Speed-strength play and games 2. Minor ball games (dodgeball, five passes) 3. Simplified ball games 4. Ball games (no outs) 5. Jogging 6. Continuous running along animal shapes drawn on the field 7. Minute runs—who will run for 1 min., 2 min., 3 min., etc. 8. Pyramid runs—1 min. run, 1 min. jog, 2 min. run, 1 min. jog, up to for example 5 min. and then reduce time of the run the same way as it was increased 9. Continuous run in a labyrinth drawn on the ground (diverts attention from fatigue) 10. Run around a triangle with a continuously moving tip (coach or another child) 11. Runs in hilly terrain 12. Runs with change of pace 13. Small running play 14. Run with partner riding a bicycle; change rider every 1000-2000 meters (1 bicycle per 3-5 runners) 15. Interval runs (moderate intensity and not often) 16. Squats until fatigued 17. Easy run with 5 sec. accelerations 18. Triathlons (swimming, bicycling, running; speed skating, cross-country skiing) 19. Continuous rowing in a pool 20. Rowing at variable pace 21. Rowing in touring, slalom, and race kayaks 22. Rowing in a heavy kayak 23. Rowing in a fishing boat 24. Continuous rowing on a selected type of kayak

Continued on next page

Table 33—continued

Periods and volume of general fitness exercises in %	Motor abilities, accent, methods	Means/Exercises
Preparatory period Volume of general fitness exercises: 70-80%	**Speed** Accent on: a. time of single movement b. frequency of movements c. reaction time Methods: repetitive	1. Games and plays involving running 2. Minor ball games 3. Ball games 4. Throwing ball at a moving target 5. Multiple starts on sound signals 6. Short runs at submaximal and maximal speed 7. Runs on an incline 8. Starts from various positions 9. Run with quick turns while maintaining direction 10. Changes of direction of running at signs and sounds 11. Run with change of speed every 5 meters 12. Tag in pairs 13. Running up on a slanted tree 14. Chasing a partner who starts (standing or jogging) 2 meters ahead on a sound signal 15. Races in pairs for a 10-meter distance 16. Track and field throws 17. Accelerations while rowing in a pool 18. Multiple starts in a kayak
Preparatory period Volume of general fitness exercises: 70-80%	**Strength** Accent on: a. explosive strength b. speed-strength Methods: repetitive	1. Jumps over obstacles 2. Runs uphill and downhill (straight up and across the slope) 3. Runs holding hands with slightly resisting partner 4. Runs while pushing partner 5. Jumps from one gymnastic pad to another 6. Jump up while partner presses shoulders down 7. Throwing a ball (basketball, medicine ball) against a wall with both hands and catching it 8. In pairs, pass medicine ball from greatest distance 9. Track and field throws 10. Push-ups 11. Pull-ups 12. Rope climbing 13. Exercises with dumbbells 14. Exercises with an empty bar while sitting or lying 15. Swimming (all strokes) 16. Kayak races using hands instead of paddles 17. Short (200-500 meters) races in various boats
Main period Volume of general fitness exercises: 60-70%	**All movement abilities**	Lower the number of workouts dedicated exclusively to general fitness. Independent of such workouts, include general fitness exercises in technical workouts and in warm-ups on land. Tie general fitness exercises with directed and special exercises. Stress relaxing and playful character of general fitness exercises. Make them into contests.

Periods and volume of general fitness exercises in %	Motor abilities, accent, methods	Means/Exercises
Transitory period Volume of general fitness exercises: 70-80%	**All movement abilities**	1. Kayaking excursions and rallies 2. Outdoor athletics (cross-country runs, jumping exercises, sprints up and down hills, throwing stones) 3. March interspersed with running 4. Hikes on foot and on bicycles 5. Ball games 6. Gymnastics 7. Swimming 8. Winter sports

PART 2
MOVEMENT TRAINING

6

COORDINATION

In many exercises that either are used to develop physical fitness or are a test of it, movement coordination plays a great role. Without good coordination the full motor potential of a person cannot be realized. Mastery of sports technique is impossible without good movement coordination.

Movement coordination is the most complex and the least researched among motor abilities. Even a definition proves elusive. One way to define it is as the ability to accomplish movement tasks that demand cooperation of several parts of the body without mental tensions or mistakes, and with a minimum of effort. Another definition focuses on the various capabilities that accompany coordination: Movement coordination is an ability to perform complex movements, quickly learn new movements, and quickly switch from one set of movements to another. (This last ability is an important component of agility.)

Defining coordination may be difficult, but recognizing its absence is easy. A lack of this ability is evident, for example, if the movement task is to move one's arms in a sagittal plane while jumping up and down and moving the legs in a frontal plane (as in jumping jacks), and instead one ends up moving arms and legs both in the same plane.

The physiological basis of coordination lies in a synchronization of neurological processes in such a way that an excitation of one motor center, directing movements of one part of the body, does not spill over to other motor centers directing other parts of the body.

Practically, most people identify coordination with agility and dexterity. Agility is the ability to perform well-*coordinated*, fluid changes of movements of the whole body quickly, and dexterity is the ability to learn and precisely *coordinate* complicated movements. These descriptions use the term itself to identify what it is, so the cause of understanding is not much advanced, at least as far as coordination's component abilities.

Several authors (Blume, Hirtz, Raczek, Simone) consider the following abilities to be elements of coordination.

- Balance
- Sense of rhythm
- Spatial orientation
- Kinesthetic differentiation
- Reactivity to acoustical and visual signals

According to W. S. Farfiel (1960) there are three levels of difficulty in movement coordination.

First level—performing movements requiring spatial precision; the speed of performing the movements does not matter
Sports application: compulsory program in figure skating

Second level—performing movements requiring spatial precision within time constraints
Sports application: sprinters' low start

Third level—performing movements requiring spatial precision and speed while adjusting to constantly changing conditions
Sports application: contact sports, ball games

Training to enhance the abilities of coordination depends on the development and the degree of maturity of an individual's physiological and neuromuscular functions. Developing coordination is most effective between the ages of 7 and 14, with the most sensitive period being between the ages of 10 and 13. As you have already read (chapters 3 and 4), to be most effective, training should stimulate maturing and not completely matured abilities. Those times when the child's organs and systems related to a particular ability are undergoing intensive development are the times when it is particularly effective to stress training that develops that ability. The most effective course of action in developing any coordination ability is to help this natural development by targeting these abilities that are not fully matured and facilitate their development beyond what the child could do on his or her own.

Sensitive periods

The sensitive periods in the development of elements of coordination are as follows.

- Balance—ages 10 to 11 for boys, 9 to 10 for girls. According to Protasova (1984) balance reaches its fully matured level between 12 and 14.
- Movement adequacy (the choice of movements adequate for the task)—ages 8 to 13, greatest pace of development 9 to 12 for boys and girls
- Kinesthetic differentiation (the ability to correctly estimate differences in form, distance, timing, and the amount of strength required to perform movements)—ages 6 to 7 and then again at 10 to 11 both for boys and girls
- Reaction to acoustical and visual signals—ages 8 to 10 for both boys and girls
- Rhythmic motion—ages 9 to 10 for boys, 7 to 9 for girls
- Spatial orientation—ages 12 to 14 for both boys and girls
- Synchronization of movements in time—ages 6 to 8 for both boys and girls

Coordination (or all the abilities making it up) is formed at a younger school age. Boys have the greatest increases of coordination abilities between the ages of 8 and 9 and then between 11 and 12. Coordination development ends between the ages of 16-18.

Influencing factors

Coordination is affected by the following factors:

1. Intelligence of the athlete. The outstanding athlete is not only well-endowed with movement abilities but also is able to solve complex, unexpected motor tasks.

2. Systematic training. Systematic training improves an athlete's kinesthetic sense and thus improves coordination, precision, and speed of movements.

3. Motor "erudition" (the store of acquired movement skills). Speed of learning and the ability to perfect movements depend on the size of one's stored experiences of movements. Yes, these who have more will get more, easier.

4. Level of development of other motor abilities. The athlete's level of speed, strength, endurance, and flexibility affects coordination. A low level of any motor ability will either directly limit the performance of skills calling for good coordination or make it impossible for the athlete to move fast enough, strong enough, long enough, or with an adequate range of movements to properly perform coordination exercises. On the other hand, good coordination improves strength by engaging the muscles most adequate to a given task in the most efficient order, inhibiting their antagonists, and regulating the frequency of nerve impulses. Coordination affects the speed of movement by regulating the nervous system's capacity to mobilize or change from one movement pattern to another, besides—well-coordinated movements are economical and thus can be faster than the less coordinated.

Coordination can be divided into general and specific. Good general coordination permits quick learning and efficient performance of various, often complicated, movement patterns, no matter what one's sport specialization is. Most (but not all) exercises developing general coordination consist of movements performed for their own sake. The goal is to learn the spatial and temporal form of movements.

General coordination forms the foundation for specific coordination. Every athlete striving for versatile development ought to work on general coordination. Sports specialization must be based on versatility, and thus the athlete must develop general coordination early to provide a basis for special coordination.

Specific coordination allows the athlete to perform techniques in various circumstances smoothly, precisely, and with ease. It is the ability to perform complex actions of one's sports discipline efficiently, and quickly. Specific coordination results from practicing a technique long after mastering its correct external (spatial and temporal) form. The athlete seeks the fine regulation of applied strength and a perfection of timing.

Specific coordination is developed by practicing actions of one's sport (techniques, special exercises) from unusual initial positions; with the weaker limb (right-hander throwing with left hand, boxing with right guard); with changed speed (slower or faster execution of gymnastic combinations, faster prerun in jumps); with added movements (more turns in discus throw); with different equipment, apparatus, partners, or opponents; or in a smaller area (in a smaller ring, court, on narrower support, on a track more densely packed with obstacles).

Coordination training

Coordination training is based on diversity, versatility, and a large number of movements. Children at preschool and specially at early school age should master many of the simple movement skills, especially stressing balance and dexterity for girls because they have a predisposition for excelling in these elements of coordination.

The onset of adolescence is not conducive to developing coordination. During this period strength and speed increase rapidly, which, in combination with significant and sudden body height increases, makes it necessary to adjust all coordination anew. Limit teaching new, complicated movements, instead perfecting and stabilizing the known ones. In the third stage of sexual maturity there are no limits on developing coordination.

The potential development of coordination is determined to a great degree by heredity. Athletes who do not have good coordination, and who learn new coordination skills slowly, are not likely to greatly improve it.

Principles of coordination training

There are five principles fundamental to the task of developing elements of coordination.

1. Increase a child's movement potential from earliest age. Coordination improves thanks to learning new movements, and a high level of coordination permits learning increasingly difficult motor tasks, which is directly applicable in mastering sports techniques. The difficulty of techniques is increasing, so the earlier the athlete starts to learn, the more movement skills he or she has and the better will be his or her coordination and thus the ability to master new sports techniques.

2. Challenge the child by exercises that are difficult yet appropriate for his or her level of biological development, intellectual capabilities, and motor skills. Exercises that are easy are boring and do not develop coordination. Exercises that are too difficult discourage the child from trying. Those exercises should have priority that develop elements of coordination appropriate to which sensitive period the child is in. If the child is in a sensitive period for developing balance but has not developed a good sense of rhythm (which has its sensitive period before balance), put the most stress on exercises developing balance and not on rhythmic exercises. Otherwise the child will end up with a poor or an average sense of both rhythm and balance.

3. Constantly renew and vary the exercises. The preceding two principles make the reasons for this principle clear: The more exercises the athlete knows, the better, and coordination exercises that are already familiar are not fulfilling their purpose.

4. Take the three levels of difficulty into consideration in learning coordination skills. First teach the spatial form of a movement, then teach performing this movement at an assigned speed or at an assigned rhythm, and finally teach how to adjust this movement in changing conditions.

5. Perform already mastered exercises in changing conditions that force changes in the spatial form, timing, and dynamics of this mastered exercise. These changes can be accomplished in the following ways.

- Changes in the direction of movement
- Changes in the starting position
- Changes in the finishing position
- Increasing the range of movements
- Changes in the pace of movement
- Limiting the allotted time
- Adding extra movements
- Adding extra tasks during the exercise
- Changes of the load (changing height of obstacles, weight of equipment, length of a prerun)
- Change of environment (size of exercise area, size, surface and height of support area, type of surface, type of equipment, partner)
- Interfering with sensory control (blindfolding, throwing off balance)
- Changing type of signals in exercises that require reaction to signals
- Performing coordination exercise after some other exercise that interferes with the coordination exercise (balancing after tumbling, precise movements at the end of a workout when children are fatigued)

Methods of coordination training

Hirtz (1976) suggests that the goal of coordination training is to fully develop all neuromotor systems. At the end of high school students have to display a high level of function of all movement control processes. This provides the basis for quick and adequate adjustments to fast-changing situations, for learning and stabilizing new skills, and using them at will. To achieve all these goals requires the young athlete to:

- use various forms of basic movements (marching, running, jumping, balancing, climbing, throwing, catching) in the course of planned and systematic building up of motor "erudition";
- perfect the basic coordination abilities (kinesthetic differentiation, spatial orientation, balance, sense of rhythm, reactivity to signals);
- follow a well thought-through method of learning and solidifying sports skills combining the development of coordination abilities with learning sports skills; and
- combine development optimally of "conditioning abilities" (strength, speed, endurance) with coordination.

In developing coordination you will mainly use the repetitive method of arranging coordination exercises. Typical exercises developing coordination are:

- balancing;
- quick turns and rolls;
- mirroring someone's movements;
- known exercises from new positions;
- known exercises with additional movements; and
- known exercises in new conditions (running in water).

Development of coordination from first grade to tenth grade (from age 6 to 16) is divided into following stages (Marciniak 1990):

1. Grades 1-3 (ages 6-9)

- Secure a wide coordination foundation (learning many basic movements)
- Perfect basic coordination abilities
- Perfect basic movements
- Build a store of running skills

2. Grades 4-6 (ages 10-12)

- Increase the level of basic coordination abilities
- Develop coordination applicable in learning sports skills
- Encourage pupils to perform coordination exercises in spare time

3. Grades 7-10 (ages 13-16)

- Further perfect (partially directed toward needs of a sport) basic coordination abilities
- Combine learned and stable sports techniques with general coordination exercises

These are the means of developing coordination (both general and special) of young wrestlers, for example.

a. Practicing standard wrestling techniques

b. Performing all exercises on the opposite side (right-handers on the left, left-handers on the right)

c. Changes of speed and pace in familiar movements

d. Changing elements of known techniques

e. Adding new movements to a known technique

f. Increasing resistance of the partner as well as practicing against different partners (lighter, heavier, shorter, taller)

g. Learning skills of other sports (acrobatics, gymnastics, ball games, skiing, swimming, or rowing, for example)

As soon as the child learns the rough form movement in a given coordination exercise, add new elements or show a new exercise. You don't want the child prematurely settling on stereotyped techniques.

Coordination exercises demand the highest concentration and optimal stimulation. They mainly stress the nervous system and fatigue it quickly. The best time to perform coordination exercises is at the beginning of the main part of any workout, or even at the end of a warm-up. Do the exercises according to some repetitive method that ensures full recovery between sets of repetitions or attempts. There should not be a workout dedicated exclusively to coordination exercises. It is better to work on coordination in small portions but often rather than in long sessions but rarely. They should rather be done in short blocks within workouts dedicated to some other tasks.

The sequence in learning a new coordination exercise resembles Farfiel's (1960) three levels of difficulty of movement coordination:

1. Learn movements without regard to speed.

2. Increase speed while maintaining precision.

3. Change some movements or perform them in changing conditions.

According to Sledziewski (1989), for children of younger school age (ages 7-12) the most suitable means of developing coordination, or any other ability, are plays, games, and simplified ball games. Workouts or p.e. lessons employing such means suit the child's psyche. Children in the middle school age (ages 12-14) find attractive more difficult exercises such as obstacle courses, mirroring someone else's movement, and acrobatics.

During pubescence, performing coordination (and technical) exercises depends on the dynamics of the "puberty growth spurt" and on the level of previously acquired skills. The less exaggerated is the puberty growth spurt (for example, smaller height increases in a time unit) and the greater a growing child's store of skills, the more it is possible to smoothly increase the volume and difficulty of coordination training. If the puberty growth spurt is great, a coach may choose to limit the amount of difficult coordination exercises in a workout.

Every year a coach or trainer ought to replace 10-20% of the coordination exercises with new ones. This rule is particularly important in sports stressing technique, because the ability to constantly improve technique depends on having a large store of learned movements. Breaking this rule leads to premature freezing (at a level below the future potential of the athlete) of technique, and that limits his or her future development.

Exercises developing balance

Static balance refers to the ability to maintain a vertical position on a narrow area of support, such as standing on a balance beam.

Dynamic balance refers to the ability to maintain balance in motion, without constant contact with any support, as in gymnastic tumbling, for example, or running with a ball while evading opponents in football or soccer.

According to Sledziewski (1989) and Szczepanik (1987), the difficulty of balance exercises has to be gradually increased by reducing the support surface, raising the height of support, and increasing the speed of movements. An athlete's consciousness of risk raises the difficulty of balance exercises.

Here are some examples of exercises to develop balance.

1. Make circles with one leg and both arms (each arm in a different direction) while standing on the other leg.

2. Squat while simultaneously raising both arms; lower the arms when standing up. To increase difficulty, raise and lower the arms twice for each squat.

3. Kneeling on your left knee and supporting yourself on your right hand, make simultaneous circles with your outstretched right leg and left arm.

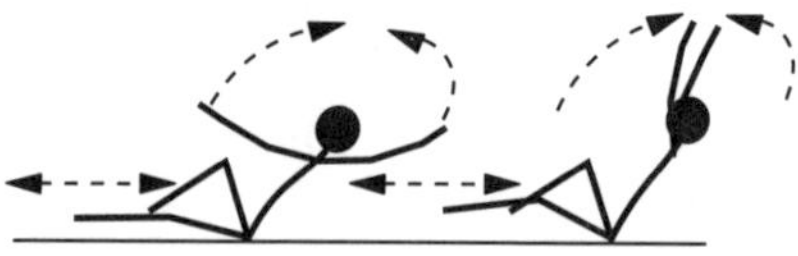

4. Sitting with your legs and feet suspended above the floor, "pedal" with both legs while raising and lowering your arms in the frontal plane.

5. Jump in place, gradually turning around your vertical axis in the air, and make vertical circles in opposing directions with your arms.

6. Jump backward and raise your knees to your chest in flight.

7. Jump in place in a squat, making half-turns around your vertical axis in the air.

8. Exercises on a gymnastic bench or low beam:

a. marching, running sideways first using sliding step and later the more difficult cross step, normal running, jumping;

b. marching backward, marching in a half squat, marching on all fours, marching with turns;

c. passing another athlete in the middle of a bench or beam while marching or jogging; and

d. marching while throwing and catching a ball, marching and evading a thrown ball, marching and dribbling the ball on the floor close to the bench or beam.

9. After several rolls, turns, or flips, perform simple balancing acts—stand on one leg, for example, or walk on the thin straight line.

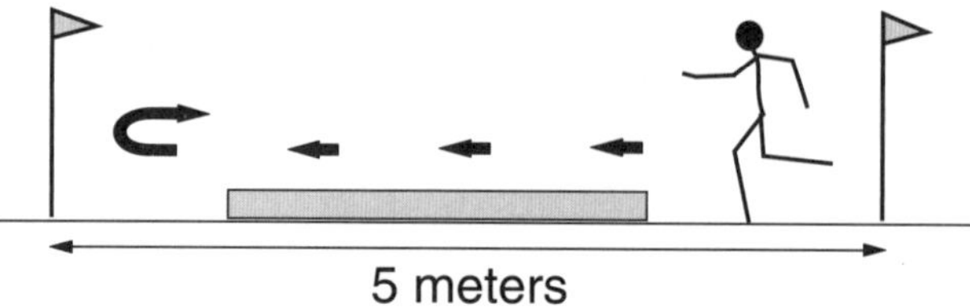

10. Run a short distance—5 meters (5 yards)—at top speed, with part of this distance run on a gymnastic bench or low beam or jumping up and turning, and return.

11. Conduct contests in pairs to knock each other out of balance in jogging, running, or while jumping in the air.

12. Conduct a "cock fight" or a "joust."

13. Juggle a soccer ball with feet and thighs while performing additional movements such as squats, turns, or rolls.

14. Bounce a soccer ball with your head while standing on one leg.

15. Dribble the soccer ball on the ground with the sole of one foot.

16. Stand on the soccer ball with one or with both feet.

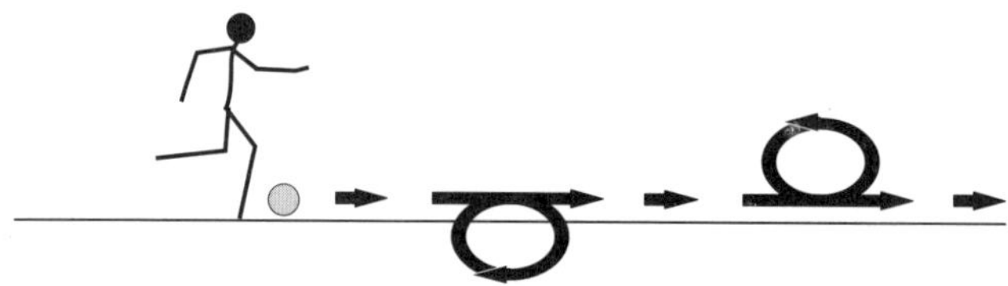

17. Make small fast turns while leading a soccer ball. When turning to the left one's right leg leads the ball, when turning to the right the left leg leads the ball.

Exercises developing a sense of rhythm

Sense of rhythm refers to the ability to determine the extent or range of movements in time appropriate to a given exercise, as well as to the ability to match movements to the rhythm one hears, sees, or feels (Sledziewski 1989). Being able to pick up an opponent's or action's rhythm helps the athlete to anticipate the next moves and to change the rhythm of his or her actions. In boxing, for example, one could adjust his rhythm to confuse his opponent.

Here are some examples of exercises to develop a sense of rhythm.

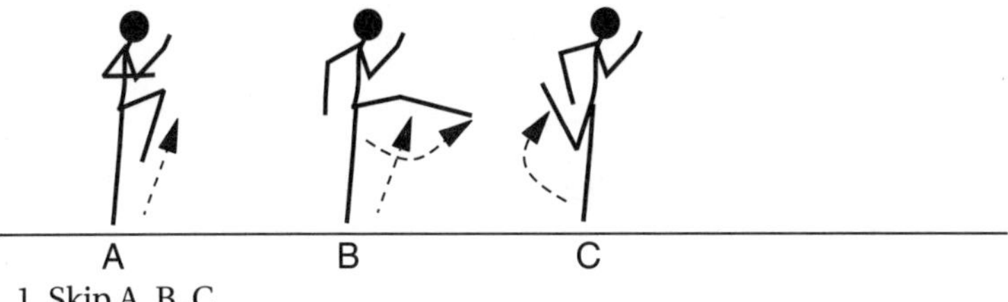

1. Skip A, B, C.

2. Run over 4-8 obstacles (benches, low hurdles) set at uniform distances. Cover the distance between the obstacles in the same number of steps.

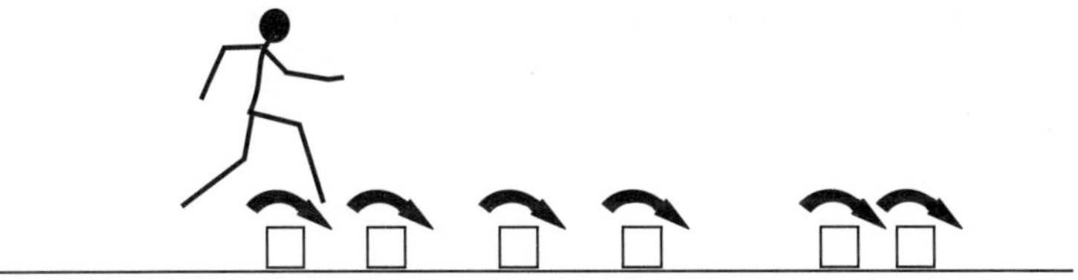

3. Run over 4-8 obstacles set at varying distances. Cover the distance between obstacles in a varying number of steps.

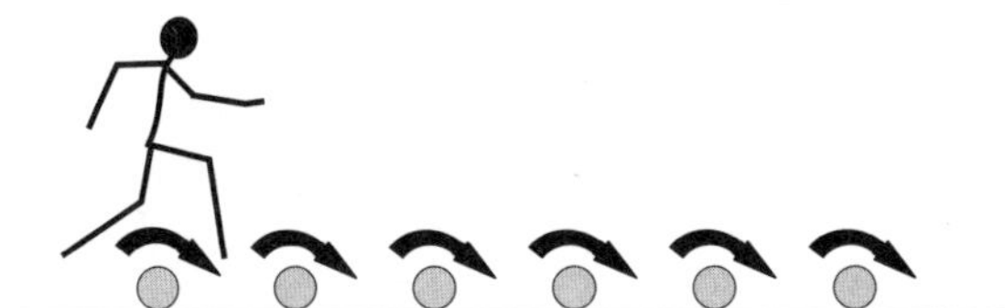

4. Run over several uniformly spaced balls, as for example 10 balls set 1 meter (1 yard) from each other.

5. Run and lead a soccer ball: a. between feet; b. rolling the ball forward or backward with the sole of the foot; or c. rolling the ball with the inside part of the foot while running sideways.

6. Lead the soccer ball through a slalom of posts uniformly spaced 1.5 meters (5 feet) apart.

7. Lead the soccer ball through a slalom and make a feint before each of several posts uniformly spaced 2 meters (7 feet) apart.

8. Kick a soccer ball against a wall 2-3 meters (7-10 feet) away, and when it bounces back kicking it again without stopping it.

9. Any gymnastic or acrobatic exercises performed to music.

Exercises developing spatial orientation

Spatial orientation refers to the ability to sense the position of your body (or of its parts) in space (Sledziewski 1989, Szczepanik 1987).

Here are some examples of exercises to develop spatial orientation.

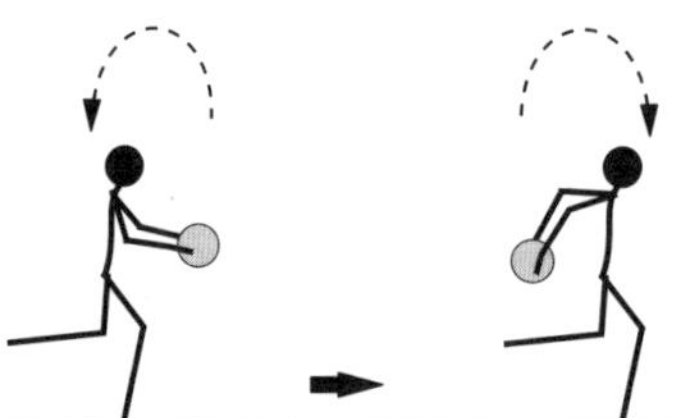

1. Throw a ball overhead in front of yourself and then catch it behind your back, or throw it from behind and catch in front while standing, jogging, or running.

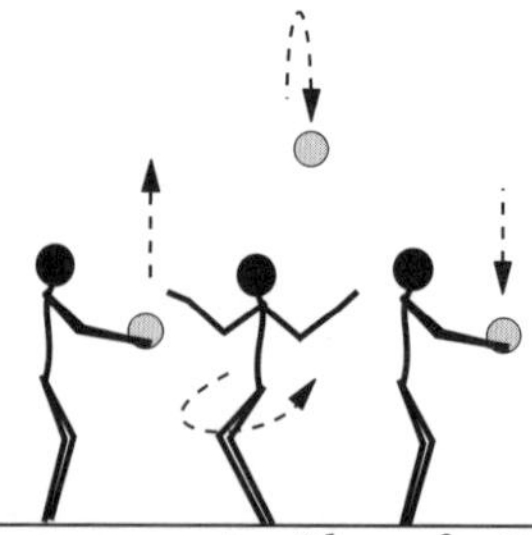

2. Throw a ball about one meter (three feet) above your head but in front of yourself, turn 360 degrees and catch it.

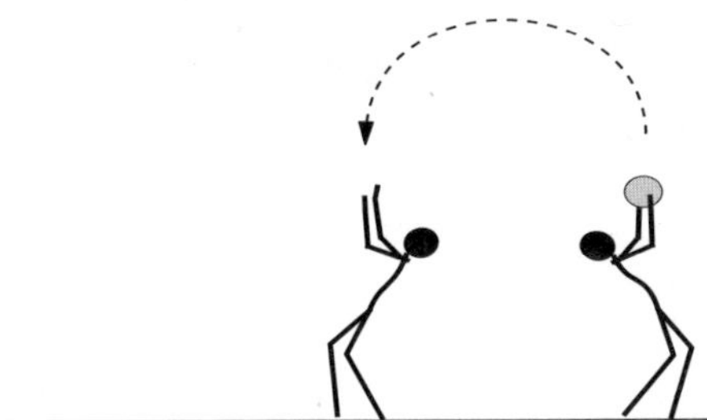

3. You and your partner stand with your backs toward each other and, leaning backward, throw a ball to each other.

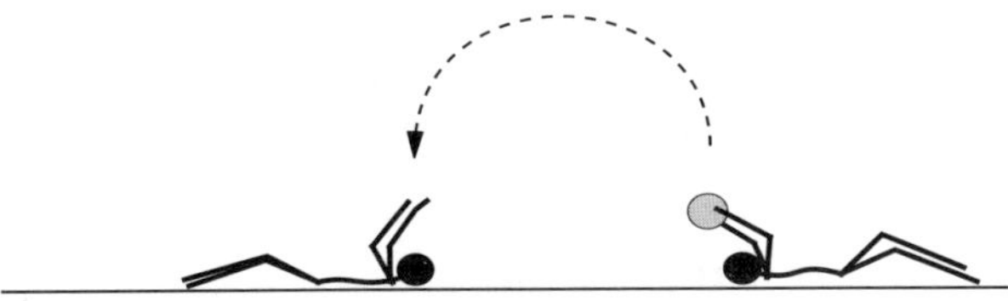

4. You and your partner throw a ball to each other while lying on the floor with your heads toward each other.

5. March on bent legs and roll two balls on the floor with your hands, never losing contact with any ball. Do the same exercise with one hand dribbling one ball while you roll the second ball or throw it up and catch it with the other hand.

6. Throw two tennis balls up (one ball with each hand), make a 360-degree turn, and catch both tennis balls.

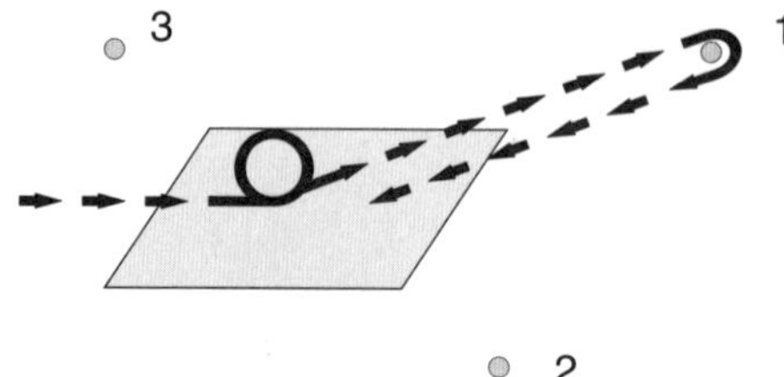

7. Run approximately 5 meters (5 yards) to a gymnastic pad, roll forward, run toward ball #1 and touch it with your left hand, run toward the pad and roll backward, run backward to ball #3 (without turning your head to see the position of ball #3) and touch it with your left hand, run toward the pad, roll forward and continue toward ball #2, touch ball #2 with your right hand, run toward the pad, roll backward, run backward to ball #4 and touch it with your right hand.

8. Bounce off and land on your feet, knees, shoulders, and back on a trampoline.

9. Dive from a platform or from a springboard.

10. Pass the ball to a partner or kick it to a goal after 2-4 rolls or turns.

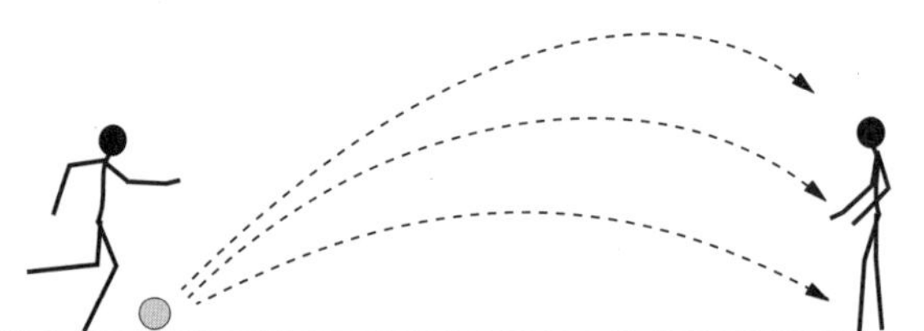

11. Pass the ball to a partner at a distance of 20-25 meters (65-80 feet) aiming at the head, chest, thigh, or feet. The partner with the ball chooses the type of pass, receiving partner has to react.

12. Player standing in front of a goal, facing away from the goal, receives ball from another player (who can pass the ball any way he or she chooses), and immediately turns around and kicks the ball at the goal.

13. Two teams play a ball game on a smaller field, or with several balls in play at the same time;

14. Play a ball game in difficult conditions (on the snow, in tall grass, or on an uneven surface).

Exercises developing speed of reaction

Speed of reaction refers to the ability to quickly respond by movement to a particular stimulus, such as sight, sound, or touch (Sledziewski 1989).

Here are some examples of exercises to develop reaction speed.

1. Catch a ball released by partner. The ball is held in partner's outstretched arms and released by him or her without any warning. The ball is to be caught before it touches the ground.

2. One athlete stands 3-5 meters (10-16 feet) from a wall, facing it. A second athlete stands behind the first and throws tennis balls at the wall. The task of the first athlete is to catch the ball bouncing off the wall. The difficulty of this exercise may be increased by using two balls of different colors (yellow and white, for example) and catching only one of them (for example, yellow).

3. Athletes stand relaxed, legs at a shoulder width, and quickly change positions (squat, sit, lay down) at the instructor's command.

4. Make starts from various positions (sitting, kneeling, laying down, standing) and short sprints of 5-10 meters (or 5-10 yards). The instructor uses various signals, some of which may be false.

5. Athletes exercise in pairs. One performs any movements and the other quickly reproduces them.

6. One athlete runs behind the other and kicks a soccer ball. The athlete in front chases the ball as soon as he or she spies it coming from behind, stops it, and passes it to the athlete who kicked it.

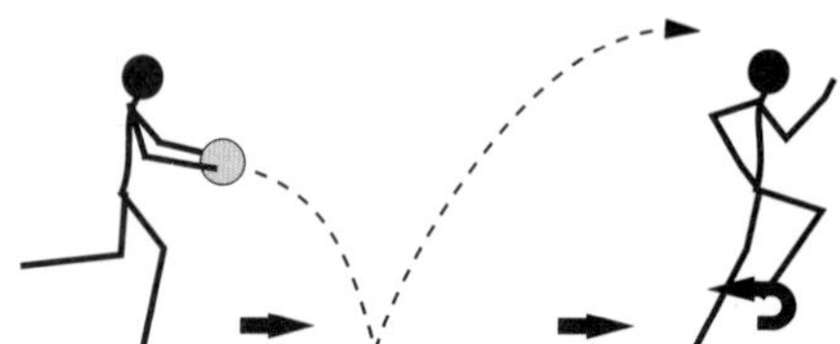

7. One athlete is standing facing forward, or running in front of the other. The athlete behind bounces a ball off the ground behind the first athlete so it overtakes him or her. The task of the first athlete is to play the ball back to the second athlete, preferably before it touches the ground.

Exercises developing synchronization of movements in time

Synchronization of movements in time is perfected by exercises that consist of unrelated movements of two or more limbs or body parts such as your neck, trunk, or hips (Szczepanik 1987). The degree of difficulty is raised by adding more movements of other limbs as well as increasing the difficulty of each movement.

Here are some examples of exercises that develop synchronization of movements in time.

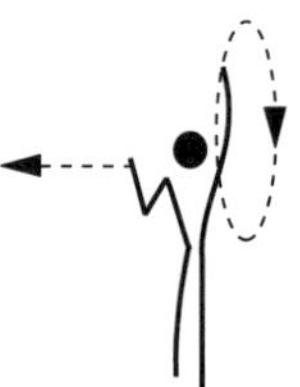

1. Make large circles with one arm and punch to the front or side with the other while standing, jogging, or running.

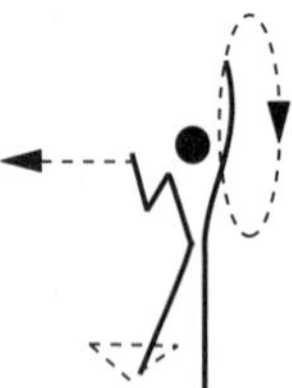

2. Make large circles with one arm and punch to the front or side with the other while standing on one leg and tracing triangles with the other leg.

3. Jump from side to side while raising and lowering arms (one goes up when the other goes down) in a sagittal plane.

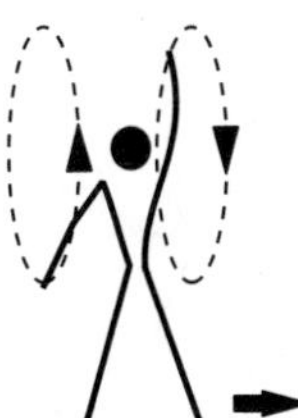

4. Walk sideways making large circles with arms, rotating each arm in a different direction.

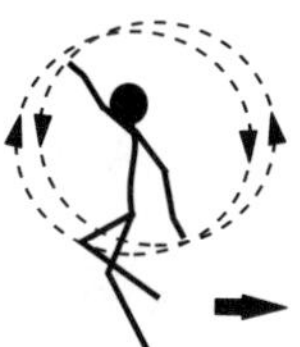

5. Skip backward while making large circles with arms, rotating each in a different direction.

6. Rotate your hips and wrists (arms outstretched on either side), rotating each wrist in a different direction.

7. Rotate your hips and neck in opposite directions.

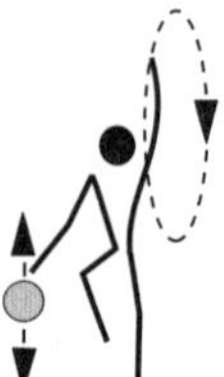

8. Jogging or skipping in place, dribble a ball with one hand and make large circles with your other arm.

9. Jumping up and down, dribble a ball with one hand and make large circles with your other arm.

10. Jump up and down while “boxing” with your arms.

Exercises developing kinesthetic differentiation

Kinesthetic differentiation refers to the ability to discern and finely adjust the muscular tension in movement to achieve a desired result (Szczepanik 1987). In other words, it is an ability to use just the right amount of strength in a movement.

Here are some examples of exercises that will help develop kinesthetic differentiation.

1. Throw balls of various weights and sizes (tennis ball, baseball, volleyball, medicine ball) at a target placed 5-8 meters (5-9 yards) away.

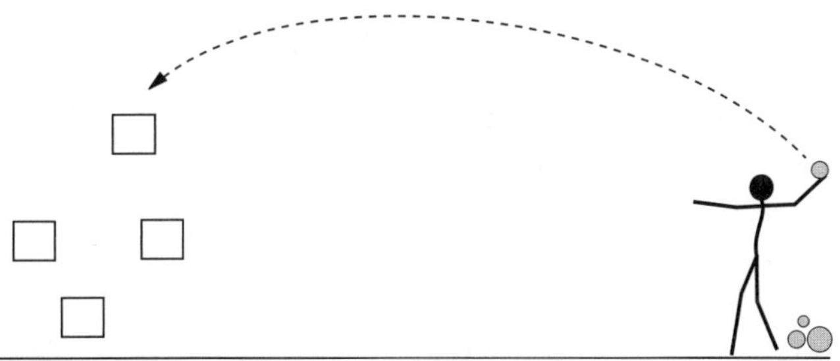

2. Throw balls of various sizes and weights at targets placed at various distances.

3. Make long jumps at an assigned distance that is less than maximal distance for a given athlete.

4. Throw a shot or medicine ball an assigned distance shorter than your maximum.

5. Jump (from a squat) over 5-6 obstacles of various height and depth.

6. Juggle (alone and in pairs) balls of various weight and sizes.

7. Throw or kick a ball against a wall with such force as to make this ball bounce an assigned distance away from the wall.

8. Bounce a ball against a wall with your head while standing, or while jumping.

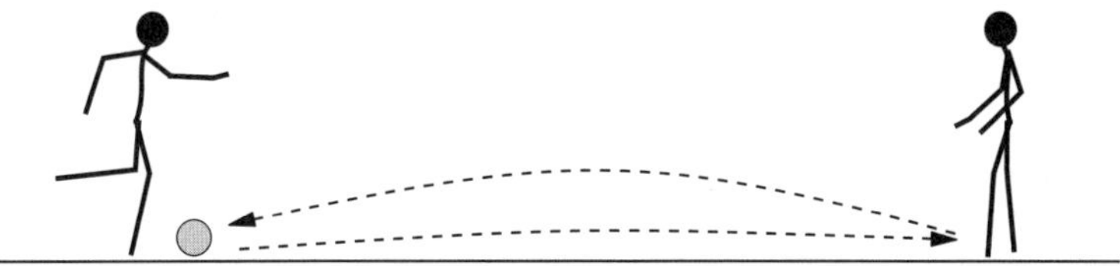

9. Pass a soccer ball between two players 5-10 meters (or 5-10 yards) away from each other, without stopping the ball. Vary the pace of passes, using first the left, then the right leg.

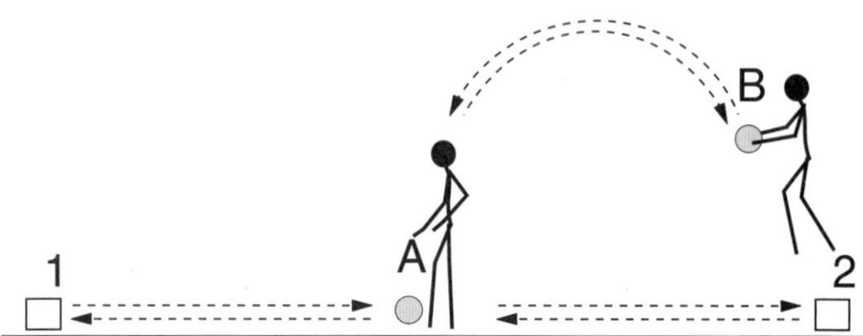

10. Stand between two gymnastic benches or beams. With your left leg, kick ball A toward the first bench, then with your head bounce back ball B thrown by your partner, who stands 5 meters (16-17 feet) away. Then use your right leg to kick ball A toward the other bench, use your head to bounce ball B back to your partner, and repeat.

Exercises developing movement adequacy

Movement adequacy refers to the ability to move in such a way as to accomplish a task with a minimum of effort.

Here are some examples of exercises to develop movement adequacy.

1. Make your way through an obstacle course within an assigned time and with a minimum of effort. (Instructor: Group athletes by weight and compare the expenditure of energy by measuring their pulse rate or breath frequency before and after running the course.)

2. Cover a set distance (on foot, in a kayak, swimming) within an assigned time but with a minimum of movements. (Instructor: Compare athletes within the same weight, height, and strength group.)

3. Receive a ball (in volleyball, team handball, soccer) in such a way that you can pass it to those players who are in a position to execute a successful attack.

4. Cover a set distance over varied terrain (hills) on cross-country skis within an assigned time and with a minimum of effort—which requires proper choice of techniques.

Evaluating movement coordination

The following five-item test was developed and used in the former German Democratic Republic (GDR), or East Germany (Hirtz 1976).

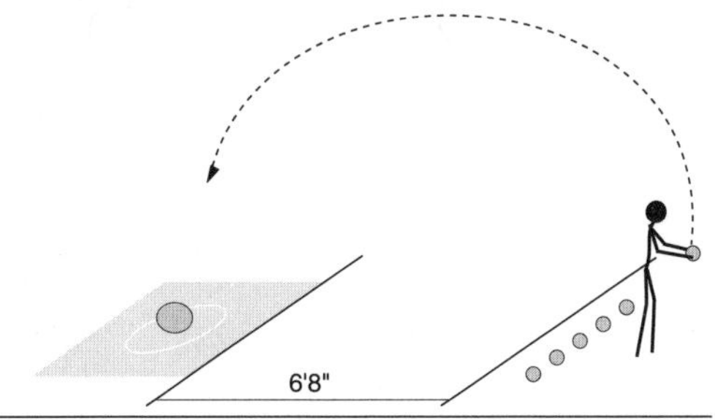

1. Throw backward for accuracy (test of kinesthetic differentiation)

Equipment: measuring tape, 6 baseball or tennis balls, gymnastic hoop, medicine ball 1-kg (2.2 lb), gymnastic pad, chalk

Place hoop on the center of the pad and the medicine ball in the middle of the hoop. Draw a throw line 2 meters (6 feet 8 inches) away from the pad. Place six balls close to this line. The athlete stands with his or her back to the pad, with heels touching the line. The task is to throw a small ball over your head or shoulder and hit the medicine ball without looking back. The athlete makes one trial attempt and then five graded throws. For hitting the medicine ball, 4 points; the pad inside the hoop, 3 points; the hoop, 2 points; pad outside the hoop, 1 point.

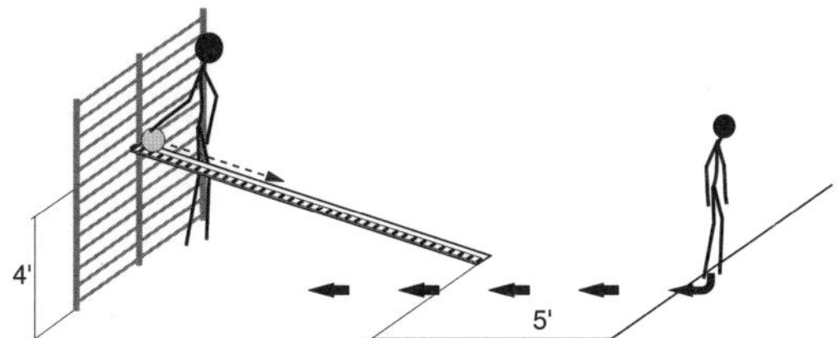

2. Catching a rolling ball (test of complex reaction time)

Equipment: soccer ball, gymnastic bench or beam 4 meters (13 feet 4 inches) long, measuring tape

One end of the bench is attached to gymnastic stalls at the height of 120 centimeters (4 feet). The other end rests on the floor. Measuring tape is attached alongside the surface of the bench. The athlete stands 1.5 meters (5 feet) in front of the floor end of the bench, his or her back to the bench. The coach, standing at the high end of the bench, releases the ball allowing it to roll down the bench and simultaneously gives an acoustic signal. At the signal, the athlete turns around and rushes to stop the rolling ball. The smaller the distance traveled by the ball, as shown by the measuring tape, the better is the reaction time.

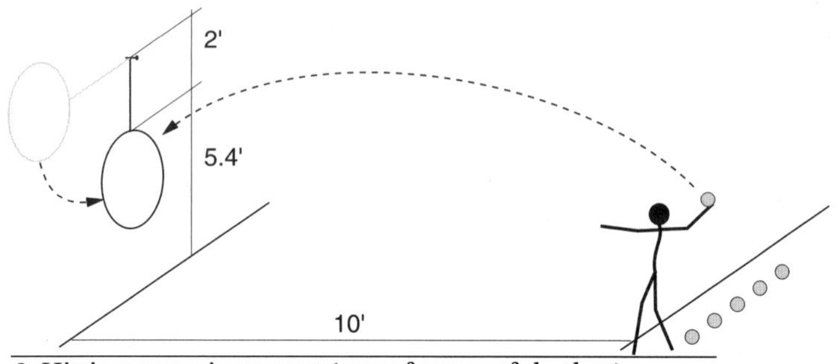

3. Hitting a moving target (test of sense of rhythm).

Equipment: Hula hoop or gymnastic hoop, diameter 80 cm (2 feet 8 inches), 60 cm (2 feet) of twine or a jumping rope, 6 small balls (tennis or baseball), chalk

Suspend the hoop from 60 cm (2 feet) of the rope or twine attached to a wall at 220 cm (7 feet 4 inches) above the floor. The throw line is drawn 3 meters (10 feet) from the wall. Place 6 balls in front of this line. The athlete stands behind the line and takes one ball. The coach lifts the hoop until the rope is nearly parallel to the floor and releases it. The athlete has to hit the wall inside of the hoop during its first swing. Hitting the wall inside the hoop gives 2 points, hitting the hoop itself gives 1 point. Six throws are made, and the worst one does not count. Maximal number of points is 10.

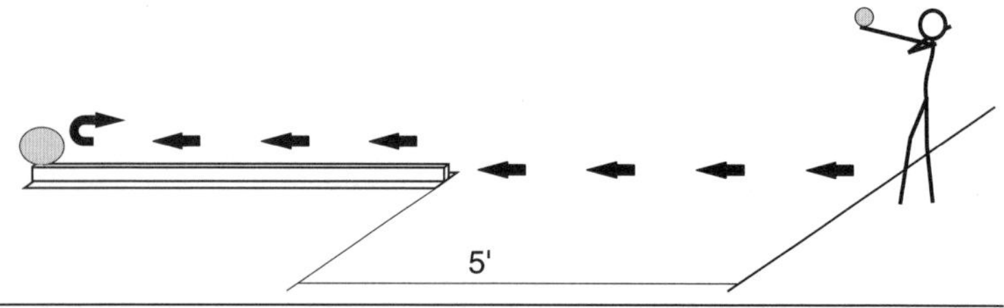

4. Kicking the ball off the bench (test of dynamic balance)

Equipment: gymnastic bench 4 meters (13 feet 4 inches) long, medicine ball 2 kg (4.4 lb), baseball or tennis ball, chalk

Place the gymnastic bench upside down (its narrow beam is up) on the floor. Draw a starting line perpendicular to the bench 1.5 meters (5 feet) from one end. Place the medicine ball on the other end of the bench. The athlete stands at the starting line, facing the bench, and grabs his or her right ear with his or her left hand from under his or her right armpit. The small ball is on the outstretched palm of the right hand. At a signal, the athlete runs along the beam to the medicine ball, kicks it off the bench, makes a turn at the end of the bench, and returns to the starting line.

During the attempt the position of the athlete's arms has to remain unchanged, otherwise the attempt does not count. If the athlete falls off the bench, the first time he or she steps back on the bench in the same spot and continues. Two falls stop the attempt. Record the time of the shorter attempt.

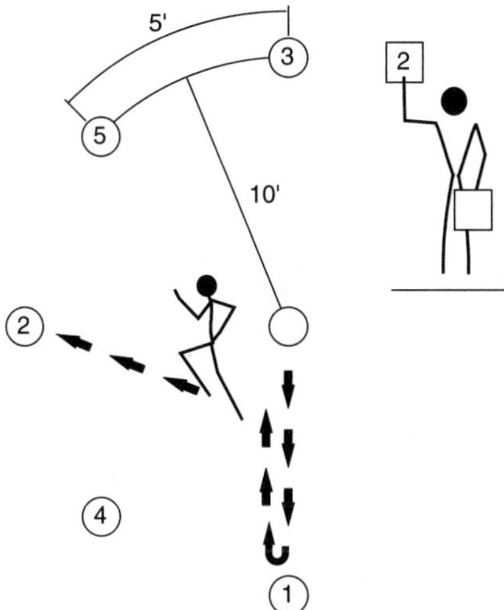

5. Sprinting to called-out numbers (test of spatial orientation)

Equipment: 1 big medicine ball, 5 smaller medicine balls numbered 1-5, numbers 15 cm (6 inches) tall, cards with numbers 1-5, 20 cm (8 inches) tall

Arrange five numbered medicine balls in a semicircle with a radius of 3 meters (10 feet) from the bigger ball. The distance between the smaller balls will be 1.5 meters (5 feet). The numbered balls should be arranged in random sequence. The athlete stands with his or her back to the balls and with one hand placed on the bigger ball. When the tester shows one of the numbered cards, the athlete turns and runs to the ball with that number, touches it, and runs back toward the starting position. Before the athlete can reach the starting position, the tester shows another numbered card and the athlete runs toward the ball with that number, touches it, and returns, and the whole action is repeated once again. After touching three balls, returning to the starting point and touching the bigger ball the attempt is completed. Each athlete is allowed two trials, and the time of the better one, from flashing of the card to the final touching of the bigger ball, is recorded.

7

ENDURANCE

Endurance refers to the ability to:

- continue work with assigned intensity;
- protect the functional integrity of the body in spite of internal and external stress; or
- tolerate fatigue.

Together with strength and speed, endurance is considered to be a conditioning ability, which means that it does not belong to coordination-related abilities.

Endurance is a complex ability. Hollman and Hettinger (1980) divide endurance according to the way muscles are involved, the predominant sources of energy, and the duration of effort, as you see in figure 27.

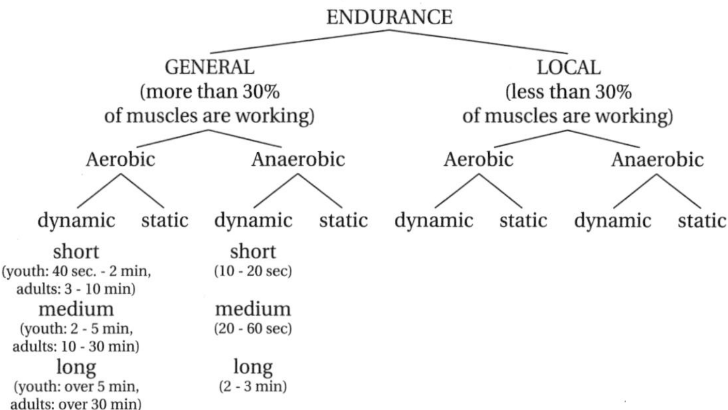

Figure 27. Types of endurance (Hollman and Hettinger 1980)

Another way to categorize endurance is according to duration and the kinds of demand the athlete places on his or her body.:

- Long duration endurance
- Intermediate duration endurance
- Short duration endurance
- Speed-endurance (15 to 45 sec.)
- Sprinter's endurance (up to 15 sec.)
- Strength-endurance (muscle endurance)

With regard to methodology of training, the following classification of types of endurance is useful:

General endurance is the ability to perform over a long time any physical effort involving numerous groups of muscles that has a positive influence on sports specialization.

Directed endurance is the ability, based on aerobic fitness, that creates the functional basis for special endurance. In training methods the structure of movement is identical and the character of an athlete's effort is similar to that of the sports specialization.

Special endurance is the ability to perform efforts typical in a given sports discipline, for the same duration as that required in the discipline, while preserving the necessary quality of techniques.

Endurance is related to a child's general physical efficiency, or aerobic fitness.[1] Aerobic fitness does not vary much between schoolchildren and school-age youth and is relatively constant. This fact allows the instructor to compare results of aerobic efforts in different age groups and to draw conclusions as to the effectiveness of endurance training.

In short efforts such as 600- to 800-meter runs, the results depend mainly on anaerobic-lactacid efficiency. Such efforts cause excessive oxygen debt, greater lactic acid concentration, and greater exhaustion than a 3000-meter run. This exhaustion is a consequence of the low economy of a child's muscular work in anaerobic efforts. Differences

---

1 The best measure of this efficiency is maximal oxygen intake per unit (kg) of body mass (VO_2max ml x kg^{-1} x min^{-1}).

among age-groups of children in anaerobic efforts—for example, 5 minutes of running interspersed with marching—on the average exceed 30%. Young children's anaerobic efforts cannot be safely or sanely compared to older children's efforts. A young child's low tolerance for anaerobic work may cause him or her to faint after an all-out effort in a 600-meter run, for example. With regard to sports training, this makes it impossible to sort out to what degree a child's achieved results are a consequence of training and to what degree a consequence of the natural increase of anaerobic efficiency associated with growing.

In light of the preceding, it should be obvious that aerobic fitness is what to work on. Specifically, and most important from a health-building point of view, work to develop general aerobic dynamic endurance (see figure 27, page 93). Concentrating on aerobic endurance for children shows a proper regard for the health and development of children, which is why the remainder of this chapter will be devoted to this type of endurance.

Main factors in development of endurance

There are several factors important to the development of endurance. These include considerations of: physiological and biochemical aspects; body type and build; coordination, technique, and other movement abilities; psychological aspects; and environmental aspects.

1. Physiological and biochemical aspects. Efficiency of the cardiorespiratory system, which is expressed by maximal oxygen intake (VO_2max), accounts for approximately 60% of children's aerobic endurance performance (Palgi 1980). Especially strong is the connection between endurance and efficiency in beginning athletes. With time, as VO_2max reaches its genetically determined upper limit for a given individual, the anaerobic threshold—the percentage of utilization of one's VO_2max—becomes more important.

Endurance is closely related to the efficiency of the circulatory system, which depends on two factors.

- The ability to bring oxygen in from the environment, where lung ventilation and the diffusion capacity of alveoli play a key role.

- The transportation of oxygen from the lungs to muscle fibers, where heart volume (per stroke and per minute), the volume of blood in circulation, and the oxygen-carrying capacity of blood (number of red cells, concentration of hemoglobin) play key roles.

How well the muscles use the oxygen delivered to them in turn influences the effectiveness of energy processes, and thus the aerobic fitness. As you recall, in endurance efforts up to 60% of VO_2max aerobic processes are the main source of energy for muscles. Efforts requiring 90% or more of VO_2max are based on anaerobic processes for production of energy. Efforts between 60% and 90% of VO_2max are hence of mixed aerobic-anaerobic character.

In spite of the great importance of maximal oxygen uptake in endurance, it is necessary to remember that the lower coefficient of correlation of an endurance run results with VO_2max in children suggests that in their case aerobic fitness is less important in endurance results than for adults. This fact should direct the attention of the coach to other factors in the development of endurance.

2. Body type and build. Among those other factors are body type and build, especially fat tissue and body mass. Absolute (total body fat, or TBF, expressed in kg) and relative (body fat, or BF, expressed as a percentage) fat content in the body are negatively correlated with the effectiveness of body movements. Approximately one-third of the differences in endurance performance between boys and girls is attributable to differences in fat tissues, which differences become greater between sexes than within the same sex as children age. The more overweight a child is, the worse is that child's endurance, the greater is the increase in the concentration of lactic acid, and the lower is the child's anaerobic threshold.

Overweight not only lowers work efficiency but also significantly and systematically lowers the distance possible in an endurance run, mainly because of the increased energy costs. Each 5% of overweight penalizes a child approximately 89 meters in a 12-minute run test (Cureton et al. 1978). In a 10-mile run each kg (2.2 lb) reduction of body mass improves performance by 30 seconds (Martin 1985).

It is obvious that of two children of the same sex, height, and aerobic capacity but of different body mass, the lighter one will have greater relative aerobic fitness. This example should prevent coaches from equating results in a run with function of the cardiorespiratory system only, especially in the case of overweight persons.

Although body mass and fat tissue have obvious influence on endurance potential, the role of body height is less clear. According to Kemper (1983) the influence of greater height on results in a 12-minute run can be estimated to be within few percent. According to Havel and Horkel (1985), however, the best results in this run are achieved by the shortest children. Results of other studies do not seem to point to any definite tendency, or to justify emphasizing this factor in developing norms in, for example, a 12-minute run (Drabik 1989).

3. Coordination, technique, and other movement abilities. Proper coordination of various parts of the body—one's arms and legs during a run, for example—affects economy and effectiveness of movement. Economy of movement, in turn, makes it possible to continue the effort longer, which is simply a description of endurance. Systematic perfection of technique—leading the thigh, placing the feet, and arm movements during a run, for example—leads to high economy of movement and protects an athlete from unnecessary losses of energy. Perfecting technique for endurance efforts permits improving endurance performance without increasing training loads at the initial stage of athletic training.

Strength and speed are also related to endurance. Too much strength resulting from excessive increase of lean body mass will be an obstacle in achieving good results in long-distance runs. On the other hand, too little will lead to quick fatigue.

A low level of speed will nullify chances of winning in competition, and in a workout the speed of movements determines, to a great degree, the energy sources used and thus the training effect.

4. Psychological aspects. The specific character of endurance efforts puts great demands on willpower. The general structure of willpower's elements in endurance sports is shown in figure 28.

Figure 28. Structure of willpower elements of endurance in an athlete according to Puni (1976) modified by Raczek (1987a)

The elements of willpower are closely connected to an athlete's motivation for systematic training and the drive to achieve a set goal. It is motivation that enables athletes to reach within for psycho-physical reserves that let them reach record results.

Develop elements of will purposefully, by confronting the athlete with tests (obstacles) that permit surfacing of these qualities. The most difficult tests are actual competitions.

5. Environmental aspects. Temperature, humidity, air resistance, and altitude above sea level all influence performance in endurance efforts.

Development of endurance in children and youth

At the preschool age (3-7 years) endurance is systematically increasing, probably due to the high mobility of a child at that age.

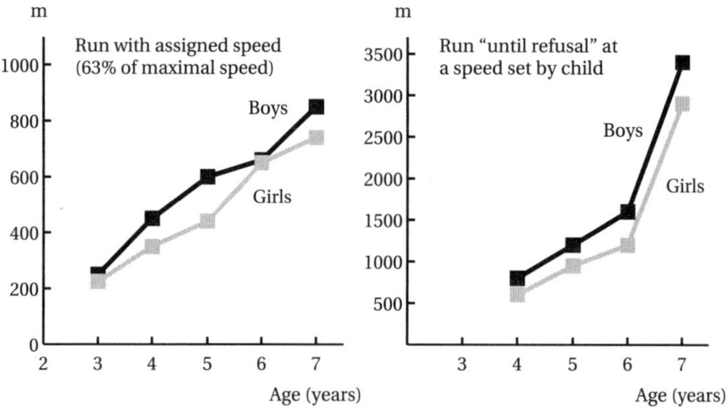

Figure 29. Development of endurance in preschoolers (Frolov, Yurko, and Kabachkova 1974; and Nadori 1979)

Note that results of girls and boys do not differ much. Six-year-old children can deliver impressive performance in efforts of long duration—10 minutes 48 seconds (boy) and 11 minutes 40 seconds (girl) on a 2.5-kilometer (1.5-mile) distance during National Runs in the U.S.A. (Fixx 1979). This same boy on Cooper's test (12-minute run) would be able to cover approximately 2800 meters (3062 yards) in 12 minutes, which is an excellent result for an adult (20-29 years old) man (Cooper 1981).

From ages 8 to 13 endurance continues to increase similarly for both boys and girls. At the end of this period (ages 12-13) nontraining girls usually reach their best endurance results, achieving approximately 110% of the endurance level of 18-year-old girls. Because girls are more advanced in endurance development, for them the period from ages 12 to 14 is decisive for endurance training.

In this age period of 8 to 13, endurance results of some children are truly magnificent.

- Boy, 9-year-old—6 km (3.6 miles) in 35 minutes (Travin and Diakonov 1983)

- Boy, 9-year-old—10 km (6 miles) in 39 minutes 5 seconds (Aaken 1979)
- Boy, 9-year-old—marathon (26 miles) in 3 hours 19 minutes (Aaken 1979)
- Girl, 11-year-old—marathon in 3 hours 1 minute (Aaken 1979); this result achieved in 1974 is 28 minutes better than the result of the male Olympic gold medalist in 1904.

After the ages of 12 to 13, development of endurance ceases to proceed similarly for both sexes. Boys' endurance continues to grow, with the greatest increases in endurance in nontraining boys occurring between ages 8-11 and then again between ages 15-16. The greatest increase of endurance in nontraining girls occurs between 8-10 years of age and their best results are achieved around the age of 13, which is followed by stagnation and regress. It is worth noting that as the duration of endurance effort is increased, the younger age groups of girls achieve better results (figures 30 and 31). This explains the necessity of beginning endurance training with long and middle distances.

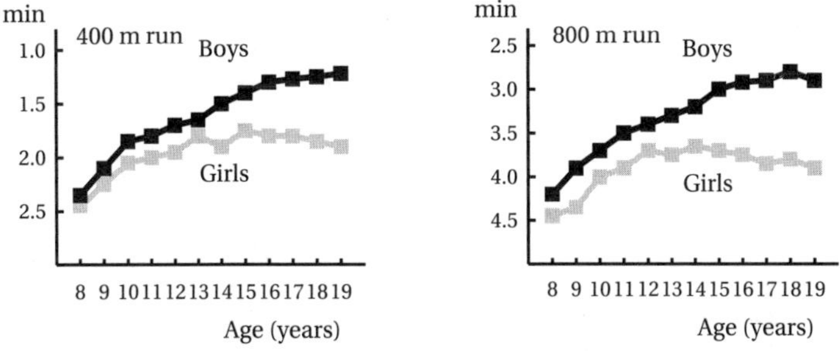

Figure 30. Development of children's and youths' endurance as shown by 400- and 800-meter runs (Raczek 1987a)

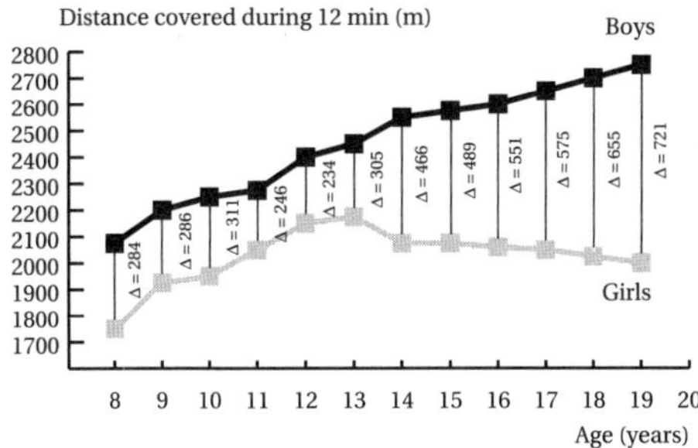

Figure 31. Development of children's and youths' endurance as shown by Cooper test (Drabik 1989)

Summing up the subject of the dynamics of endurance development during childhood and youth, there are also some trends. In Poland (Raczek 1987a), for example, and the U.S.A. (Gilbert, Montes, and Ross 1984), there are symptoms of regress of endurance in children of older school age (see figure 32).

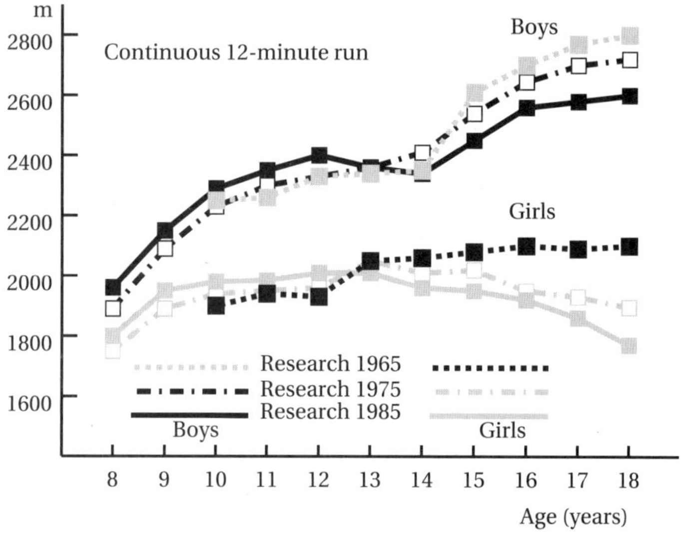

Figure 32. Changes in endurance development of two school populations

Research evidence from Poland also points to regressive trends in aerobic fitness, which is basic to endurance. These facts point to a younger generation whose fitness is going downhill, which may have a negative impact on sports if it proceeds unchecked.

Endurance training

The course of development of endurance in the athlete's life determines the coach's long-term plan and the means of endurance training he or she chooses. The fast pace of development for aerobic endurance between 8 and 12 years of age supports beginning "training" from the earliest age, not for its immediate athletic results, but as a means to improve the body and to prepare it to tolerate future efforts. In children, endurance training has to systematically stimulate the natural process of endurance development. Even four-year-old children who participated in one year of "training" consisting of hiking, games, and running improved their results in the run "until refusal" by 80% (boys) and 56% (girls). Control groups without any training experience an increase of endurance of 23% (boys) and 18% (girls)—see table 34.

Table 34. Endurance run (results of training and nontraining children, expressed in meters covered "until refusal" (Frolov, Yurko, and Kabachkova 1974)

				After 1 year		After 2 years	
Age	Sex	Training	Nontraining	Training	Nontraining	Training	Nontraining
3	M	258	254	740	476	1196	583
3	F	246	235	620	389	1121	572
4	M	466	460	1502	622	1776	716
4	F	370	384	1146	480	1479	711
5	M	608	594	1765	690	2656	787
5	F	458	452	1249	676	1865	786

In an endurance development program for children and youth it is necessary to take advantage of periods or growth stages during which their bodies are most susceptible, the so-called sensitive periods you first encountered in chapter 1. Concerning these sensitive periods, remember the individual differences caused by gender, variation in pace of growth, environmental influences, and factors related to the person's physiology: height, mass, lung capacity, body proportions and mass-height indexes. These all have a bearing on the continuing pace of endurance development.

In spite of the individual differences, there are certain general recommendations regarding the best ages for starting and intensifying aerobic and anaerobic endurance training (see table 35).

Table 35. Recommended ages for starting and intensifying aerobic and anaerobic endurance training

Endurance	Sex	Age				
		8-10	10-12	12-14	14-16	16-18
Aerobic	M	+	+	+	+	+++
Aerobic	F	+	+	+	+	+++
Anaerobic	M				+	+
Anaerobic	F			+	+	+++

+ start of training; ++ intensive training; +++ sport specialization

These recommendations also agree with the general model of correct training procedure (see figure 33). As the pace of changes associated with the growth of an individual decrease, you should increase the training.

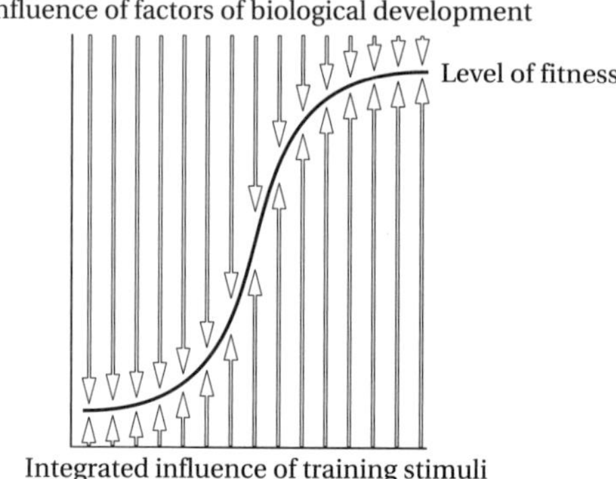

Figure 33. Changes of the level of the ability treated as an effect of interaction between biological development and the influence of training (Sozanski 1984)

Girls should begin endurance training earlier than boys. Girls mature sooner and thus have a shorter sensitive period for developing endurance than boys. Girls past puberty undertake major endurance efforts only reluctantly.

Conduct endurance training in accordance with the natural rhythm and direction of developmental changes. The scope and sequence of types of training is well-described using the model of "the training pyramid." (See figure 34.)

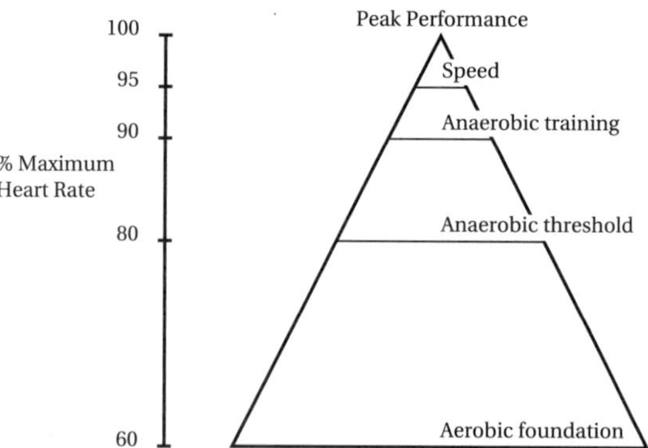

Figure 34. The Training Pyramid (Sharkey 1986)

Aerobic training, which should dominate in the training of children and youth, forms the base of the pyramid. Suggested amounts of aerobic training in sports that demand a constant effort lasting from 10 seconds to 30 minutes are as follows.

- Efforts lasting from 10 seconds to 2 minutes—aerobic training 2-3 hours per week
- Efforts lasting from 2 minutes to 15 minutes—aerobic training 3-5 hours per week
- Efforts lasting from 15 minutes to 30 minutes—aerobic training 5-7 hours per week

Table 36 shows the relative importance of various types of energy-generating processes in maximal efforts of various duration according to MacDougall, Wenger, and Green (1982).

Table 36. Share (in %) of various types of energy processes in maximal efforts of various duration

Duration	Anaerobic-alactacid (%)	Anaerobic-lactacid (%)	Aerobic (%)
5 sec	85%	10%	5%
10 sec	50%	35%	15%
30 sec	15%	65%	20%
1 min	8%	62%	30%
2 min	4%	46%	50%
4 min	2%	28%	70%
10 min	1%	9%	90%
30 min	1%	5%	94%
1 hour	1%	2%	97%
2 hours	1%	1%	98%

Principles of endurance training

Besides observing the basic principles of physical training, there are thirteen specific principles essential to the proper conduct of endurance training.

1. Begin endurance training with general aerobic endurance. Base this beginning training firmly on the child's physiological potential. Aerobic fitness is important to health and also to improved sports performance because it raises the anaerobic threshold or postpones having to use anaerobic sources of energy in an exercise. Furthermore, aerobic fitness improves the ability to eliminate oxygen debt.

2. Train year-round, with seasonal changes of the means of training. Changing the means of training (skiing or skating in winter, running and rowing in spring and fall, swimming in summer) makes training less monotonous and enlarges the child's store of movement skills, thus improving coordination.

3. Get in shape gradually. Starting new exercises at low levels of intensity and volume (e.g., mileage) prevents injury and thus permits systematic and continuous training.

4. Maintain training regimen. A few weeks of not working out requires several months of work to regain the athlete's previous level of endurance.

5. Teach children to listen to their body. From the very beginning of training children should be taught to "listen to" their body's reactions to effort, such as muscle pains, arrhythmic breathing, a stitch in their side, or chest pains, for example.

6. Increase the volume (duration) of exercises first; do not rush to increase their intensity. You recall that intensity is reflected in the heart rate of the athlete, and relates to the frequency of movements within the same time period. (See pages 41-45 in chapter 4.)

7. Leave enough energy for the child's healthy growing and maturing. Your first concern is always the well-being of the child and his or her development. Always.

8. Vary the conditions of training. You will guarantee progress if you change the conditions, as for example, changing the running surface (sand, shallow water, forest trails), or changing exercise partners.

9. Divert attention from fatigue. One of the methods of diverting attention from fatigue is frequent change of the conditions of training, as you read in the eighth principle. Other methods could be discussions or even telling jokes during aerobic exercises, or in the case of children, running along shapes of geometric figures or shapes of animals.

10. Take advantage of the sensitive periods in an individual's development of endurance. Doing physical training when the endurance naturally develops at a greater rate improves the effectiveness of training and allows the child to reach a higher level than otherwise.

11. Incorporate cycles of loading, peaking, and recovery in the training. A continuous increase of training loads leads to overtraining, so after the young athlete reaches a level at which smaller gains come with increasingly greater effort, partially reduce the loads to let the body recover and recharge for reaching new goals starting from a higher level.

12. Train the mind and body simultaneously. This principle applies to developing elements of willpower, as well as to learning about training and its effects on one's body.

13. Keep sport in its proper place. Not everybody will achieve success in sports, fewer still will make a living at it, and only a very few will be able to do nothing else. The consequence of this principle? Do not neglect education and certainly do not neglect health. Health problems resulting from overdoing sports (injuries, bad posture, chronic overstrain of internal organs) limit one's performance level and can last a lifetime.

Training loads in endurance training

In sports, *training load* refers to the duration of effort in a given zone of intensity. Loads can be classified as follows:

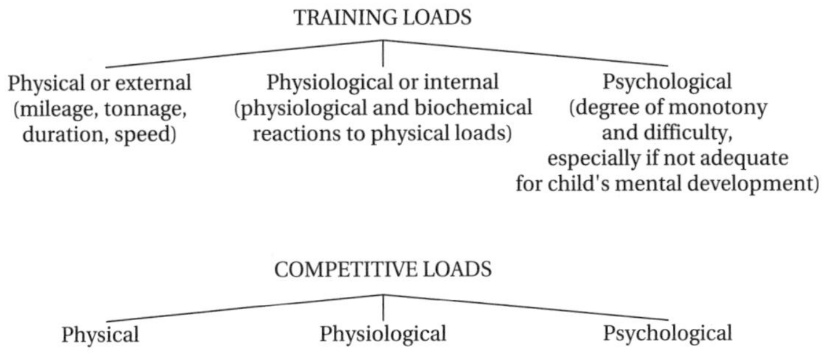

Figure 35. Classification of loads

The intensity of the body's reactions (internal load) depends on the magnitude of the external load, changes in its components, and on the shape the athlete is in.

Training loads determine the body's adaptation to effort. This adaptation can occur only at a certain magnitude of the load in relation to the current shape of an athlete. This zone of effective training adaptation varies from one individual to another. In young and in beginning athletes it is much wider than in advanced athletes, which allows for making progress while using relatively low endurance loads with youth.

The effectiveness of loads depends on their volume and intensity, on the body's internal reactions, and also on the athlete's psychological tension and emotions during exercising. Making workouts attractive lowers psychological tensions and makes it possible to perform more and better work.

Training loads have the following components:

- Volume (e.g., number of exercises, duration, mileage, tonnage) determines the general development of the athlete and maintenance of an achieved endurance level.

- Intensity (e.g., speed of performing exercises, frequency of movements, power output) determines the athlete's reaching an adequately high level of endurance.

- Rest breaks determine the body's recovery and readiness for renewed effort.

According to the sixth principle of endurance training, increasing the volume of exercises is the first step in developing endurance. Here is the sequence to follow to increase the volume of various elements of training.

1. Increase the frequency of workouts.

2. Increase the duration of workouts.

a. Increase the duration of particular exercises (e.g., covering longer distance with the same speed).

b. Increase the number of repetitions (e.g., number of runs).

c. Increase the number of exercises (e.g., more of various distances, more forms of movement during a single workout).

The effectiveness of increasing only the volume of work is limited. (See figure 36.)

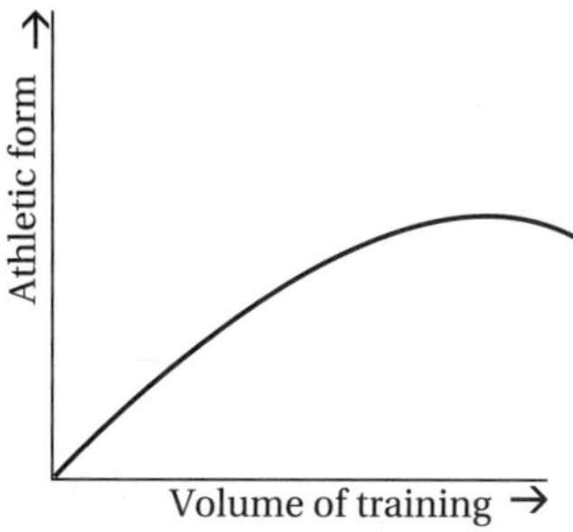

Figure 36. Relations between volume and athletic form or condition

When you have exhausted the means of increasing the volume of training and the level of endurance remains the same, it is time to start increasing the intensity of exercises. In the years following, for a steady increase in the training level, both the volume and the intensity of training have to be increased. Finding the optimal ratio of volume to intensity of the load is difficult. The data in table 37 set guidelines for establishing endurance training loads for children and youth **who are not specializing in endurance sports.**

Table 37. Volume of endurance loads in a workout (Raczek 1989)

Volume of the load	Age in years		
	10-12	13-15	16-18
	Volume in minutes		
high	15-20	20-30	30-40
medium	10-15	15-20	20-30
low	5-10	10-15	15-20

The duration of exercises depends on age, sex, and level of aerobic fitness. For children with low fitness the volume of exercises has to be several times lower than for the highly fit—10 minutes instead of 40 as an example. The number of workouts per week also has to be lower for the less fit. Frequency of workouts in a weekly microcycle is of great importance in realizing the assigned volume of work. Three workouts per week are a minimum for beginners. As the level of fitness increases, gradually increase the number of workouts. This allows for increasing the total volume of exercises in a microcycle without drastic increases in the load volume for single workouts. An excessive increase of the volume of loads in single workouts, rather than increasing the frequency of workouts in a week, lowers the total effectiveness of the loads because it causes excessive fatigue. In a school setting dedicate approximately 30% of the p. e. lessons in a year to endurance, from 3 to 20 minutes per lesson. In the total amount of time dedicated to endurance, devote 60-70% to endurance in long efforts (more than 10 minutes).

More difficult than setting a beneficial exercise volume is setting the intensity of exercises in endurance training. The appropriate intensity varies depending on the individual's age and aerobic fitness. Heart rate values define zones of various intensity. (See table 38.)

Table 38. Values of heart rate and zones of intensity (Raczek 1989)

Intensity	Age	Heart rate	
		girls	boys
low	12-15 16-19	<138 <132	<132 <126
moderate	12-15 16-19	138-150 132-144	132-144 126-138
high	12-15 16-19	156-180 150-174	150-174 144-168
very high	12-15 16-19	186-204 180-198	180-198 174-192
maximal	12-15 16-19	210-more 204-more	204-more 198-more

Heart rate during a given effort should be somewhere between 150 to 180 beats per minute for the intensity to be sufficient in developing endurance. The athlete should perform most efforts in a "steady state," i.e. at an intensity such that functions of the body can continue without discomfort as long as there are adequate energy stores or when oxygen supply equals oxygen demand and when the removal of carbon dioxide (CO_2) equals its production. Children can maintain effort of that intensity for over an hour. With the increase of fitness, the athlete's volume of work that can be performed in a steady state increases too. A child's body, even when its heart rate reaches 200 per minute, still derives energy from aerobic reactions.

For any endurance effect, the young athlete must perform efforts longer with a heart rate lower than 150 per minute. To avoid lowering the effectiveness of training associated with a lower intensity of work, the athlete must perform a greater volume of work over a longer time.

The indicator for setting the target training heart rate is an individual's maximal heart rate. Practical considerations justify using the following method of calculating the target heart rate:

HR_{max} = 220 - age in years.

To improve the aerobic fitness of persons in poor shape, an exercise intensity eliciting 60%-70% of HR_{max} (equivalent to 50-55% of VO_2max) is best; for persons in good shape, 80%-90% of HR_{max} is best (equivalent to 70-80% of VO_2max). Another way to establish the target training heart rate is to calculate 60% or 70% of the difference between HR_{max} and HR_{rest}, and add HR_{rest} (Karvonen's formula). According to this formula (Karvonen et al. 1957), you would calculate the target heart rate for two boys of different age as follows:

Age	HR_{max}	HR_{rest}	70% (HR_{max} - HR_{rest}) + HR_{rest} = HR_{target}
8	212	90	70% (212 - 90)+ 90 = 175
14	206	80	70% (206 - 80)+ 80 = 168

Methods of endurance training

You can apply the described training loads within various training methods as you see in figure 37.

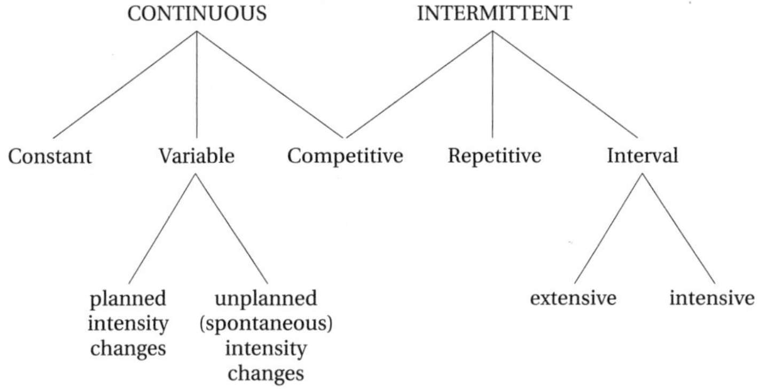

Figure 37. Methods of endurance training

A brief description of these methods is shown in table 39.

Table 39. Basic methods of applying loads in endurance training

Elements of the load in single exercises	Continuous methods: uniform ① variable ②	Extensive interval method	Intensive interval method	Repetitive method
INTENSITY (%) 100 80 60 40 20	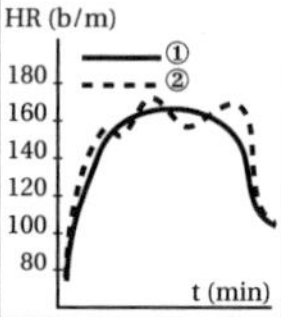 HR (b/m) 180 160 140 120 100 80 ① ② t (min)	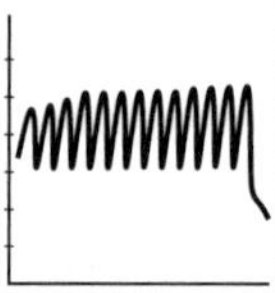	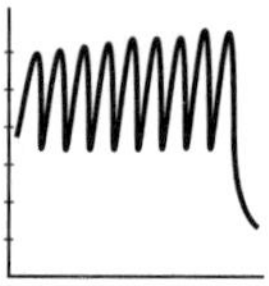	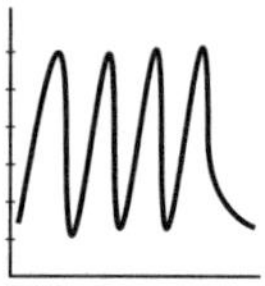
INTENSITY Endurance Speed, Strength	 40-60% 30-50%	 60-80% 50-60%	 80-90% 65-75%	 90-100% 80-100%
VOLUME Endurance Speed, Strength	 very high very high	 12-30intervals 20-30 reps/set	 6-12 intervals 8-12 reps /set	 1-6 repetitions 6-13 reps/set
REST BREAK	no break	short	incomplete;	HR—120/min
DURATION Endurance Speed, Strength	 very long many brief exercises	 medium 15-30 sec.	 medium to short 8-15 sec.	 short short
TRAINING EFFECTS	—directed endurance —general endurance —strength endurance	—directed endurance —general endurance —strength-endurance —speed-endurance —strength	—speed-endurance —special endurance —speed —strength-endurance —speed-strength —maximal strength	—speed-endurance —special endurance —speed —strength-endurance —speed-strength —maximal strength
PHYSIOLOGICAL EFFECTS	—economization of metabolic processes —regulation of cardiovascular system —improved aerobic fitness	—regulation of cardiovascular system —economization of metabolic processes —improved aerobic fitness —increased muscle mass	—regulation of cardiovascular system —economization of metabolic processes —increased reserves of energy sources —improved anaerobic fitness —improved sensorimotor coordination	—economization of metabolic processes —increased reserves of energy sources —improved anaerobic fitness —increased muscle mass —improved sensorimotor coordination

In endurance training of children and youth continuous methods are particularly beneficial. The energy-generating mechanisms (mainly aerobic) that are engaged during continuous efforts best fit the potential of a child's developing body. The level of endurance achieved by these methods lasts longer than in the case of intermittent methods.

Each training method has its limitations, which is why you should combine different methods in training. But remember: Children before puberty have a low ability to perform anaerobic efforts. You won't be developing endurance with methods that are too intensive. You should only be using interval methods, and especially their intensive varieties, after a long period of systematic preparation of the child's body by continuous methods. Combining different methods can be complex, ranging from using different methods in one microcycle or mesocycle but only one method in any single workout, to integrating—using more than one method in any single workout.

Endurance training exercises

Exercises in endurance training can be divided as follows:

1. Exercises with a complex influence on the body. Obstacle courses indoors and outdoors (e.g., running, crawling, jumps, climbing); circuits consisting of 8-12 stations with exercises for major muscle groups; movement complexes (e.g., dancing routines, or routines consisting of various forms of walking, running, and jumps performed in a variable rhythm, continuous gymnastic routines performed in one spot or over a large area), playing games involving multiple repetitions of racing or relays, sports team games (ball games, hockey), elements of individual contact sports (e.g., wrestling or judo—grappling; boxing—shadow boxing; karate or taekwondo—shadow fighting)

2. Exercises developing general endurance for running. Hikes, marches, jogging, continuous and variable runs, easy intervals, cross-country runs, *fartlek*, orienteering, small running games (e.g., warm-up while jogging, perfecting pace in several repetitions of a 50- to 150-meter distance with high to very high intensity and jogging during rest breaks, flexibility exercises, cool-down by jogging and marching while performing exercises that loosen up the muscles and calm one down)

Running exercises especially require variety. To make them less monotonous, you can have children run along geometric figures:

a. Square, varying the pace
b. Triangle with one point (a coach or teacher) constantly moving
c. Thunderbolt
d. Labyrinth
e. Animal shapes

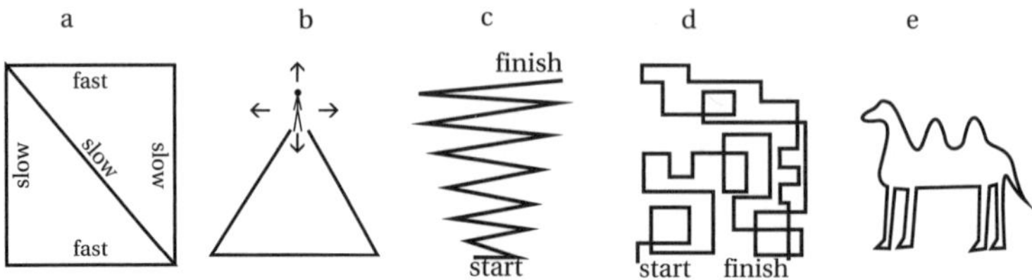

Figure 38. Varying running exercises to reduce boredom

You can also vary the time of work and rest, for example:

f. Pyramid run—1 minute running, 1 minute jogging, 2 minutes running, 1 minute jogging, 3 minutes running, 1 minute jogging, 2 minutes running, 1 minute jogging, 1 minute running, 1 minute jogging

g. Run interspersed with jogging

consecutive minutes of the effort	1	2	3	4	5	6	7	8	9	10	11	12
r—running j—jogging	r	j	j	r	j	j	r	j	j	r	r	j

3. Exercises developing special endurance. Repeating special exercises with high frequency; performing special exercises at a high intensity; performing special exercises in difficult conditions (e.g., on the snow, in sand); tests and competitions

4. Exercises dependent on a given school's resources. skiing, skating, roller-skating, swimming, bicycling, kayaking, hiking over difficult terrain or trails

Sharkey (1986) recommends that children from 6 to 10 years old develop endurance by spending up to four hours per week playing simplified team games. They should have fun and formal endurance exercises are to be avoided. From ages 11 to 14 Sharkey recommends continuing the use of team games and the introduction of formal endurance exercises such as long, easy intervals. Endurance exercises in a continuous mode, with constant and variable intensity, are better suited to children and early adolescents, Sharkey points out. Thus, they should be used more than intervals. The amount of time dedicated to endurance training is 4-6 hours per week. From ages 15 to 19 he recommends increasing the intensity and volume (between 6 and 8 hours per week) of endurance training, combining long and short intervals, and exercising at the anaerobic threshold (170-180 HR). To Sharkey's recommendations add this caution: The young athlete should do intervals together with exercises done in the continuous method.

Important note for coaches in sports that require high speed and quick reaction: Exercises of long duration, such as those used to develop aerobic endurance, increase the tension of the parasympathetic nervous system. If the tension of the parasympathetic system is too high, an athlete's speed and reaction time suffer. The excessive tension of this system may result either from using only high-volume but low-intensity exercises (extensive training methods), or from a lack of balance between the volume and the intensity of training loads. To determine the right balance between the intensity and the volume of training loads, a coach should monitor speed and reaction time. A method of determining the proper balance of intensity and volume of the loads through monitoring an athlete's pulse rate is described in appendix A.

Training tips for running technique

Running is the most commonly used form of movement in developing general aerobic endurance. It is a simple, natural movement yet athletes can do it wrong. Here is a description of the correct running technique.

Keep the trunk straight, leaning slightly forward. Arms, bent at elbows, move forward and backward. Moving the arms across the front of the trunk causes swaying of the trunk, which stresses the knees and can injure them. Hands, arms, the upper part of the trunk, and facial muscles are fully relaxed. At low speeds the foot contacts the ground with the outer side of the foot close to the heel and rolls toward the front; or, at higher speeds or when running uphill, with the outer side of the front of foot. The toes point slightly inward. To find out how much, tell the athlete to suspend his or her foot above the ground and relax it. The toes will turn slightly inward. This will be the correct position. Steps, at the beginning of the running program, should be short—1 or 2 foot lengths. Direct the push-off forward, not up as in jogging. If the child runs too slow to push off forward—i.e., jogs—the push-off is directed up, which causes injuries to the muscles and joints of the legs and the joints of one's back.

In the first month of running workouts, the child should breathe through the nose only. When a person breathes through the nose it means that the effort is adequate to his or her fitness. There is an exception to this rule—some people have trouble breathing only through the nose, even at a slow running pace. They should not force themselves to breathe only through the nose.

Evaluation of endurance

Evaluation is an inseparable element of sports training. The most common form of evaluation of endurance are test runs at various distances (minimum time on a standard distance) or of various duration (maximum distance during standard time). Endurance is determined by various factors, but evaluation by the result of a run—its duration or distance—represents an expression of the integration of endurance's elements and of the relations among them. Because of that, tests consisting of running are a reliable tool in evaluating endurance.

Cooper's run-walk test is applied in several countries. It consists of measuring the maximum distance covered during 12 minutes. The percentile values shown in table 40 suggest possible goals for aspiring champions. Tables 41 through 44 show norms in other endurance tests.

Table 40. Norms (in percentiles) for school children for 9- and 12-minute run (Roche 1980).

Percentile	Age										
	7	8	9	10	11	12	13	14	15	16	17
	9-minute run (in m)				12-minute run (in m)						
95 boys	2055	1958	2033	2163	2647	2734	2875	3030	3125	3171	3196
95 girls	1710	1800	1838	1800	2250	2350	2548	2450	2681	2875	2573
75 boys	1616	1631	1828	1817	2358	2468	2577	2800	2800	2892	2870
75 girls	1410	1535	1635	1653	1998	2104	2178	2230	2288	2335	2205
50 boys	1440	1410	1683	1644	2036	2261	2397	2577	2605	2675	2724
50 girls	1245	1319	1420	1450	1730	1920	1910	2050	2035	2053	2046
25 boys	1304	1275	1480	1530	1685	1999	2161	2368	2423	2445	2432
25 girls	1154	1172	1285	1297	1516	1700	1657	1795	1805	1827	1787
5 boys	948	998	1227	826	992	1564	1716	1955	1993	2089	2000
5 girls	550	970	845	675	1025	1323	1277	1400	1560	1361	1374

Table 41. Aerobic fitness rating for females as estimated from time (in minutes and seconds) of the 1-mile run (Sharkey 1986)

Age	Low	Average	High
10	11:42	10:29	8:22
11	11:11	9:58	7:51
12		9:24	7:17

Table 42. Aerobic fitness rating for males as estimated from time (in minutes and seconds) of the 1-mile run (Sharkey 1986)

Age	Low	Average	High
10	10:25	9:07	6:52
11	10:02	8:44	6:31
12	9:39	8:21	6:06

Table 43. Aerobic fitness rating for females and males as estimated from time (in minutes and seconds) of the 1.5-mile run (Sharkey 1986)

Age	Low	Average	High
Females 13+	18:50	16:57	13:38
Males 13+	12:39	11:29	9:29

Table 44. Results (in meters) of the 15-minute run qualifying as good (B grade) according to various authors: 1—boys, 2—girls

	Auerbach 1978		Peters 1985		Drabik 1989	
Age	1	2	1	2	1	2
8			2700	2400	2386-2800	2090-2438
9			2800	2500	2560-3064	2236-2640
10	2800	2600	2900	2600	2569-3022	2309-2725
11	3000	2700	3000	2700	2684-3207	2395-2811
12	3100	2800	3100	2800	2811-3229	2512-2880
13	3250	2900	3200	2800	2934-3377	2535-2957
14	3400	2900	3300	2800	3017-3444	2439-2836
15	3550	2900	3400	2800	3047-3422	2483-2868
16			3500	2800	3157-3583	2484-2835
17			3500	2800	3190-3583	2502-2902
18			3500	2800	3195-3641	2474-2878
19			3500	2800	3259-3687	2465-2761

A test consisting of running with constant speed equal to 60% of the subject's maximal speed has been developed in the former Soviet Union. Evaluation is based on the distance covered. The duration of the run is also registered. An athlete's maximal speed is figured from the result of a 30-meter run from a flying start (15-meter fast walk). After determining the athletes' maximal speed, athletes with similar speed (difference of 0.2 second is admissible) are divided into groups of 3 or 4. Next the average time and thus speed (in meters per second) on the 30-meter distance and then 60% of the maximal speed for each group is figured out. For example, if the average time of a 30-meter run is 5 seconds—the speed is 30 m÷5 s = 6 m/s; 60% of this maximal speed—6 m/s x 60% = 3.6 m/s.

Next, calculate the time subjects are expected to cover 400 meters in—400 m÷3.6 m/s = 111 s (1 minute 51 seconds).

During the endurance test the permissible variation for covering each 400-meter lap is plus 2 seconds. If the time for a subsequent 400-meter lap is longer than that by more than the 2 seconds—the test is over.

Results are graded as follows: less than 800 meters—low; 800-2000 meters—average; over 2000 meters—high endurance.

8

SPEED

As a motor ability speed is mentioned in every conceptualization of physical fitness. Speed to a great degree is determined by heredity. Professor Astrand's saying, "If you want to be a [sports] master you must pick your parents carefully," applies to speed more than to other abilities. Speed refers to the ability to:

- perform movements in the shortest time possible in the given circumstances (Ulatowski 1981);
- displace oneself fast—from a mechanical point of view speed is expressed as a ratio of distance to time (Bompa 1985); or
- maximally accelerate and to perform single movements with maximal speed, or to perform several successive movements with maximal frequency (Harre and Hauptmann 1988).

Harre and Hauptmann go on to assert that speed in its pure form occurs only in those movements in which external resistance is very small, as for example, in hitting a ball in table tennis.

There are three elements of speed to concern yourself with.

1. Reaction time (maximal speed of reacting to a signal)

2. Speed in a single simple movement (the minimal time of one movement)

3. Frequency of movements, determined in movement cycles per time units

The first element of speed—reaction time—depends on many factors, as figure 39 suggests.

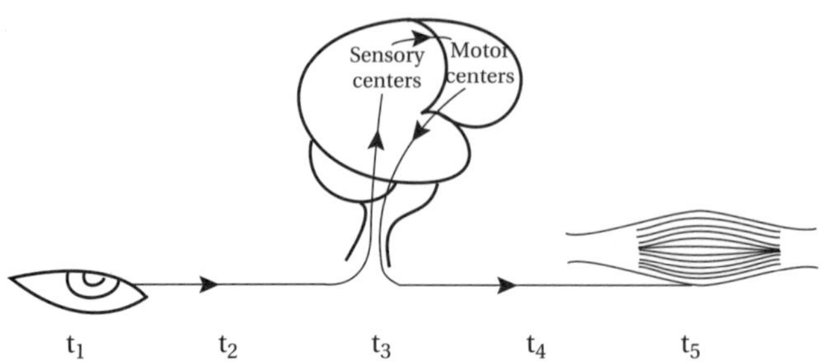

Figure 39. Components of reaction time

t_1—time it takes for a stimulus to excite a receptor, which depends mainly on the state of the receptor and on one's concentration. It can be shortened by concentration exercises.

t_2—time it takes for an impulse to travel to the central nervous system, which depends on the length of the sensory neuron. It cannot be shortened by training.

t_3—time it takes to transmit impulses through the nervous path from sensory to motor centers and produce an effector signal, which depends on the mobility of nervous processes. It is the longest time, and it can be shortened by repetition of the task.

t_4—time it takes to transmit the effector signal from the central nervous system to the muscle, which depends on the length of the motor neuron. It cannot be shortened by training.

t_5—time that elapses between the arrival of the stimuli at the muscle's motor plate (where the motor neuron ends on the muscle) and the beginning of the muscle's contraction, which depends on the contractibility of muscle fibers. It can be shortened by exercises that improve muscle elasticity.

Generally reaction time depends on the:

- kind of stimuli or signal (shorter time for sound than for light signal);
- state of the receptor;
- age (for example, t_4 is shortest from 8 to 29 years);
- sex (in girls, reaction time is usually longer [Geblewiczowa 1973]);

- body height (because of the length of nerve fibers);
- state of mind;
- starting position (reaction time is shorter when body weight is distributed equally between both feet, with feet about shoulder width apart [Sozanski and Witczak 1981]);
- level of training and athletic experience;
- external conditions; and
- type of reaction (shorter in simple reactions and longer in complex reactions when one has to choose how to react to various signals).

The second element, speed in a single simple movement, refers to the time it takes for a given body part to cover a certain distance. Duration of the simple single movement depends mainly on the amount of resistance to overcome, and thus it is related to strength. Strength is one of the main factors influencing speed of movement (Bompa 1985).

The third element, frequency of movements, has little susceptibility to improvement by training. It is determined genetically (Sozanski and Witczak 1981). At least as far as sprinting (running) is concerned, however, an individual's stride frequency potential is much higher than is ever used in competition (Wilmore 1982). For a sprinters' coach this suggests concentrating on improving reaction time and speed of single movements rather than on stride frequency. In the performance of sets of movements at high speed (e.g., sprints), there is an acceleration phase and a phase of maintaining maximal speed. Maximal speed can be maintained for only a short time—6-8 seconds. After that, mental and physical fatigue cause lowering of the speed. Increasing the phase of maintaining the maximal speed leads to development of speed-endurance and conversely, improving speed-endurance increases the phase of maintaining maximal speed.

These three elements make up the whole complex of speed. Various proportions of these elements make up forms of speed specific to particular sports—in some, reaction time is the most important of these elements (e.g., skeet shooting/trapshooting); in some, speed of a single movement (e.g., baseball pitching, shot put); in some, frequency of movements (e.g., kayaking). Some sports require a high level of two of the elements (e.g., reaction time and single movement speed in wrestling, table tennis); and in some all three elements are equally important (e.g., sprinting, boxing).

Preconditions of speed

1. **Morphological.** The proportion of fast-twitch fibers in a muscle is an essential factor determining one's speed. Their decisive predominance means great speed potential. A high amount of connective tissue in a muscle reduces speed potential, as do the high internal viscosity of a muscle and low capillarization of a muscle (Bompa 1985).

2. **Energetical.** Speed depends mostly on anaerobic-alactacid processes when resynthesis of ATP is ensured by the breakdown of phosphocreatine. These processes can provide energy for approximately 6-8 seconds. Later anaerobic-lactacid (anaerobic glycolytic) processes play an increasingly important role.

3. **Psychological.** Willpower, knowledge of the purpose of exercises, and concentration of attention are the most essential psychological factors in achieving high speed (Harre and Hauptmann 1988).

4. **Technique and coordination.** Improving technique is the key to increasing speed. This applies mainly to technically complex sports such as gymnastics, figure skating, or judo. Mastering technique depends on coordination. Developing coordination improves technique and thus speed.

5. **Level of strength, endurance, and flexibility.** A high level of strength as a rule has a positive influence on acceleration and reaching maximal speed of movements. When movements have to be not only fast, but also performed repeatedly for a prolonged time, that requires speed-endurance, which increases acceleration by prolonging the phase of accelerating and increases the time of maintaining maximal speed by postponing fatigue. Good flexibility, by permitting greater reach of movements, ensures the best achievable acceleration and reduces loss of speed caused by tension of the antagonistic muscles (Harre and Hauptmann 1988). Great elasticity of muscles and an ability to relax them on demand are specially needed for speed, and these are two aspects of flexibility.

Development of speed in stages of growth

The dynamics of the development of speed in boys and girls are very similar. (See Figure 40.) The sensitive periods for developing speed are between the ages of 7 and 9 for both sexes and additionally for girls between 10 and 11 (Guzalowski 1977).

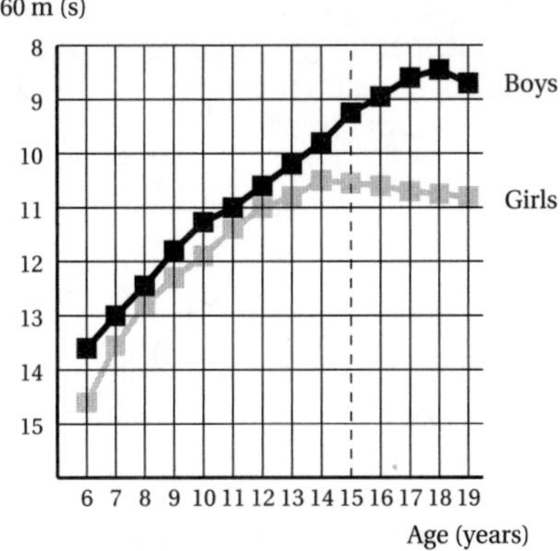

Figure 40. Development of speed (until age of 15 years according to Barabas [1989], and from age 16 to 19 according to Sozanski [1972])

The curve of speed development varies, as figure 39 suggests, depending on the age of the child.

- Early childhood—Speed is little developed, for example reaction time until age 7 is longer than 0.5 of a second (Sozanski and Witczak 1981).

- Younger school age (7-12)—Around the ages of 8-10, speed reaches more substantial values. During these years 69% of girls' and 30% of boys' speed increase occurs (Denisiuk and Milicerowa 1969). Reaction time improves most from ages 7 to 11, the greatest improvement of frequency of movements occurs between the ages of 7-9, and big increases of speed occur between 10 and 12.

- Older school age (12-15)—Increasingly improving nervous and muscular systems provide the basis for the further development of speed, reaching very high results.

Around age 14 the roads of speed development for boys and girls divide. Boys' speed keeps increasing until 18 while girls' speed results after age 15 as a rule are progressively worse. Girls have their last acceleration of speed improvement at age 13 or 14 (MacDougall et al. 1983). During the period from age 11-19 70% of boys' speed increases and 31% of girls' speed increases occurs (Denisiuk and Milicerowa 1969).

Speed training

The strategy of long-term speed training is determined by the curve of speed development, based on the changing biological properties of the child's body. These biological properties are the predominant type of muscle fibers and specifics of energy processes. Anaerobic efficiency—its development reflected by maximal anaerobic work (MAW) shown in figure 40—depends on several factors.

- Amount of glycogen stored in muscles—less in children than in adults
- Ability to produce energy without an adequate supply of oxygen
- Ability to produce energy with an adequate supply of oxygen—for children there is a strong correlation between VO_2max and speed of running (MacDougall et al. 1983): for 7-9 years old, r=0.72; for 10-12 years old, r=0.68; for 13-16 years old, r=0.77, which means that increasing aerobic endurance also improves speed
- Ability to perform efforts while internal environment is disturbed—e.g., despite fatigue, oxygen deficit, high body temperature

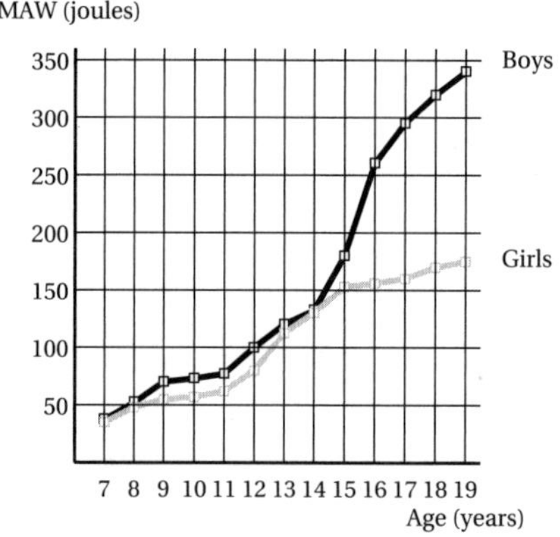

Figure 41. Maximal Anaerobic Work from ages 7 to 19 (Szopa 1989b)

Your long-term plan of speed training for children and youth should take into account those sensitive periods of life during which the elements of speed most dynamically develop. (See table 45.)

Table 45. Sensitive periods in the development of speed

	boys (ages)	girls (ages)
speed of single movements	7-9	7-9, 10-11, 13-14
speed of locomotion	14.5-15.5	10.5-11.5, 11.5-12.5

In girls acceleration of the development of the three elements of speed occurs earlier than in boys. Girls' speed predispositions are especially actively formed during younger school age (7-12). During this period, girls' speed increases most (Weineck 1983). At this age body proportions are such that children have good leverages for fast movements, which you should take advantage of by stressing speed in children's exercises.

In adolescence, ages 12-15, a big increase in maximal strength and anaerobic efficiency make it possible to do all kinds of speed exercises, including anaerobic work and speed-strength exercises (Weineck 1983).

Principles of speed training

1. Practice mastered movements faster than the individual's currently normal speeds (Sharkey 1986). This is the key to improving speed.

2. Practice first at less than maximal speeds. Only when the technique of the movements is truly mastered should the athlete attempt maximal speed.

3. Go from simple movements to complex, from easy to difficult, from the known to the new. This general teaching principle holds true for all training.

4. Combine speed exercises with techniques of the sport. If the young athlete perfects each technique, it will reduce any time losses due to biomechanically unsound forms of movement.

5. Vary the exercises you choose to develop speed. Include among them coordination exercises.

6. Vary the conditions in which speed exercises are done. Do them in more difficult, in easier, and in constantly changing situations.

7. Prefer doing more sets to increasing the duration of one set. The duration of one speed exercise or one set of repetitions should be such that speed is not reduced by fatigue—approximately 4-5 seconds.

8. Schedule long rest breaks. Make rest breaks from 1 to 2 minutes long and fill them with light activity.

9. Schedule long, thorough warm-ups of all muscles. In a workout speed exercises should immediately follow warm-ups of 15-20 minutes. These warm-ups should not be strenuous and not be fatiguing! In a microcycle, do the speed workout after the day of rest and not after days with strength or endurance workouts.

10. Take advantage of the sensitive periods in development of speed. Develop reaction time and frequency of movements earlier in life, and the forms of speed based on strength and anaerobic capability later.

Methods of speed training

Long-term speed training should follow the sequence of methods recommended by Raczek (1989).

- Develop speed by means of play and games and simplified team sports.
- Develop speed within a framework of general fitness preparation (performing a majority of exercises stressing speed).
- Develop directed and specific speed using speed-strength exercises such as sprints, jumps, throws, lifting light and medium weights with maximal speed. Which exercise you choose depends on the sport you are training for.
- Use teaching methods that form technical habits leading to reaching high speed in techniques.
- Develop sufficient strength to overcome resistance in speed exercises and to protect from injuries.
- Develop speed-endurance required for a given sport, so that athletes can move fast for as long as it is needed.
- Develop other motor abilities to an optimal level that supports the athlete's speed.

In training for speed you will mainly use the repetitive method, and for beginners offer exercises mainly with less then the highest intensity. An athlete who performs more repetitions of competitive exercises in their strict form and at maximal speed rather than at somewhat reduced speed will develop a quick stabilization of speed—the formation of a "speed barrier." Only 4% to 20% of the total number of jumps in training by the best Polish long jumpers is performed with a full prerun at maximal speed (Ulatowski 1981). For other jumps, the situation is similar. In the case of beginners, apart from limiting the amount of exercises they do at maximal speed, you should postpone introducing specialized and competitive speed exercises, e.g., sprints and jumps in strict competitive form, with a full prerun. This will lay the foundation for a high level of future achievements.

If at the beginning stages of training you have children practice sprints, for example, at full speed, there is a great likelihood of their forming a speed barrier. You are also likely to make specialized exercises ineffective in the future no matter how much the athletes improve in general strength, reaction time, coordination, endurance, and the like.

On the other hand, if you provide beginners with general and versatile training, including a high proportion of general speed-strength exercises, you will avoid formation of a speed barrier. The athlete who follows this regimen will acquire all that general exercise can give and be ready to benefit from directed and specialized exercises.

A case in point (Ulatowski 1981): In Poland a group of twenty-one girls did only general speed-strength training without stressing specialized speed up to age 14.5. None showed unusual promise. After advancing to specialized training, most of them had outstanding results in track and field speed events at the ages of 16-17. Three of them won national championships in Poland!

The general structure of speed training is diagrammed in figure 42 (Sozanski and Witczak 1981).

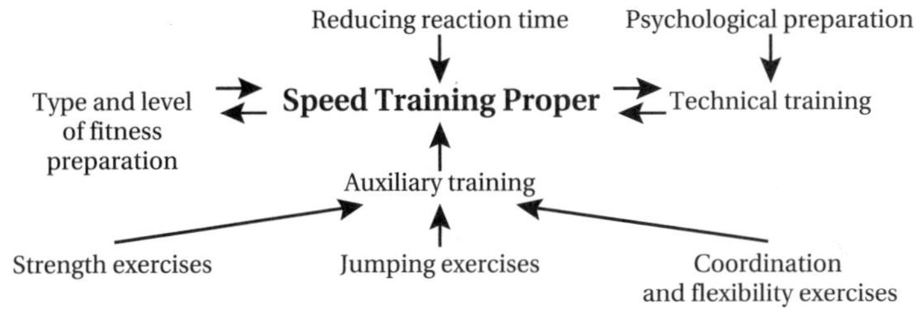

Figure 42. General structure of speed training

General speed training exercises

In general speed training exercises, for the most part, young children should be having fun.

1. Involve children in all kinds of play involving running, races, and relays.

2. Encourage children to play orientation games:

a. Day and Night—Gather children in two teams, with some way to distinguish the teams (scarves of the same color, armbands, shirts and skins); one team is "day," the other "night." On a signal, day chases night, then vice versa.

b. Flood—Children run around the playground, and at a signal must escape the flood by stepping on or climbing objects above the ground.

c. Spud—All players get a number (counting off). They stand in a circle around the one who is It, who throws a ball high into the air and calls a number. The child with that number catches the ball while all other players scatter. As soon as the ball is caught, the catcher yells "Spud!" and the others must freeze where they are. The catcher then chooses one player, is allowed three giant steps (from a flying start) toward him or her, and throws a ball. The other player can bob, weave, and feint, but cannot move both feet from where they are positioned. If hit, the player receives an *S*, and is it. When a person has *spud* spelled out, he or she is out of the game.

3. Games involving jumps

4. Reaction exercises with one type of signal (quick start on the clap)

5. Reaction exercises with choice (quick start on one chosen signal from among many other signals, for example, on a whistle but not on a clap, rap, ring, or shout)

6. Reaction exercises with choice while diverting children's attention

7. Quick start or other quick movement against active resistance of a partner

8. Running in lightened conditions (downhill, with the wind)

9. Running and following a leader (mechanical hare)

10. Running on a treadmill

11. Elements of individual contact sports (wrestling, judo, fencing, boxing) in reduced space, or shortened round duration

12. Auxiliary exercises such as coordination, flexibility, jumping ability, and strength exercises; the more resistance that has to be overcome in a given movement, the more improvement of the speed depends on strength exercises

13. Gymnastic exercises because they improve coordination, flexibility, and strength

Evaluation of speed

1. Measure reaction time. Use electronic equipment that gives a signal and then measures time elapsed from the signal to, for example, pressing a button; or by such simple means as a relay stick with strips one centimeter (0.4 inch) wide and placed one centimeter apart, that has to be caught as soon as a tester releases it without a warning. (See figure 43.)

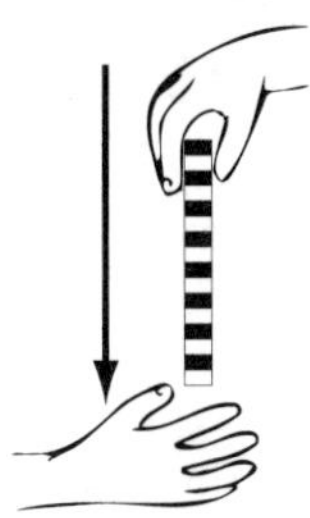

Figure 43. Reaction time test

2. Measure time of a single movement. The movement should be simple but at the same time typical for and useful in a given sport.

3. Measure running speed. Have boys and girls run distances from 20 to 60 meters from a high start, or distances of 50 yards. (See table 46.)

Table 46. Speed rating for boys and girls as estimated from time in seconds on a 50-yard dash (Sharkey 1986)

	LOW		AVERAGE		HIGH	
Age	boys	girls	boys	girls	boys	girls
9-10	8.9	9.15	8.2	8.6	7.5	7.7
11	8.6	9.0	8.0	8.3	7.3	7.6
12	8.3	8.7	7.8	8.1	7.1	7.3
13	8.0	8.5	7.5	8.0	6.7	7.1
14	7.7	8.3	7.2	7.8	6.5	7.0
15	7.3	8.2	6.9	7.8	6.2	7.1
16	7.0	8.3	6.7	7.9	6.2	7.2
17	7.0	8.4	6.6	7.9	6.1	7.1

4. Measure speed of upper limb movements. Use plate tapping as a means of measurement. Start with arms crossed, the preferred hand over the weak hand resting on the square. Measure the time to make twenty-five cycles of touching each round plate.

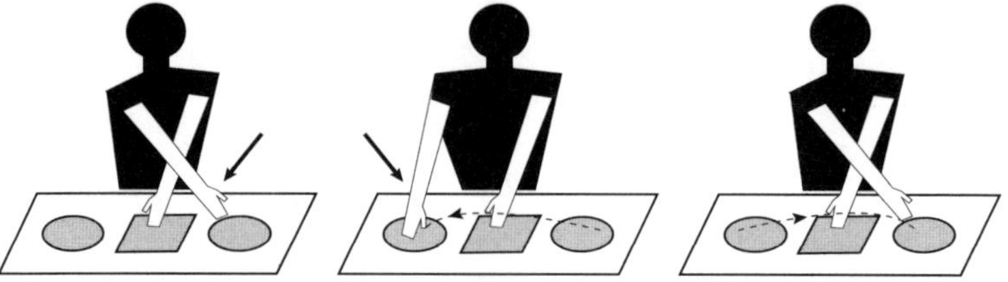

Figure 44. Plate tapping

5. Measure running speed and agility. Use a shuttle run. Two lines 4 feet long (1.2 meter) long and 16.5 feet (5 meters) apart. Both feet have to cross the line each time. Measure the time of five cycles. Subject starts with both feet behind the line and ends when one foot crosses the line after the fifth cycle.

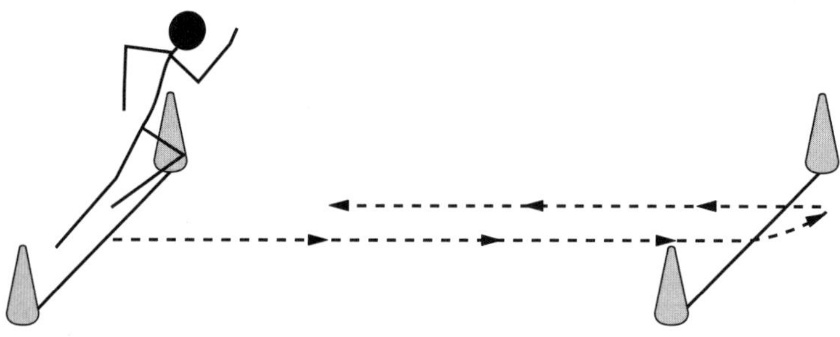

Figure 45. Shuttle run

9

STRENGTH

Strength refers to the ability to overcome resistance or to resist force (Zaciorski 1970). It can be expressed as a product (F = ma) of moved or stopped mass (m) and its acceleration or deceleration (a). Muscular strength refers to the maximal force that a muscle can exert in its single voluntary contraction (Sharkey 1984).

Types of strength

There are two types of strength:

1. Isometric or static strength, used when the tension of a muscle increases while its length remains constant

2. Isotonic or dynamic strength, used where the tension of a muscle is constant while its length changes: dynamic strength is divided into slow strength, fast strength, and explosive strength.

Slow strength (F_s) is used when maximal mass (m_{max}) is given minimal acceleration (a_{min}), for example, when slowly lifting a barbell.

$$F_s = m_{max}a_{min}$$

Fast strength (F_f) is used when less than maximal mass (m_{sub}) is given less than maximal acceleration (a_{sub}), for example, while running or rowing.

$$F_f = m_{sub}a_{sub}$$

Explosive strength (F_e) is used when less than maximal mass (m_{sub}) is given maximal acceleration (a_{max}), for example, in shot put, long jump, or low start for sprints.

$$F_e = m_{sub}a_{max}$$

There is an even more precise definition of explosive strength—it is the ability to apply as much force as possible in the shortest time.

To evaluate the explosiveness of a movement, use this equation:

$E_i = F_{max} \div T$

E_i—index of explosive strength

F_{max}—maximum force reached in a given movement

T—amount of time it took to reach maximal force in this movement

Sharkey distinguishes one more type of strength—isokinetic strength—supposedly used when a muscle contracts with a constant speed against variable resistance, but these are actually isokinetic expressions of dynamic strength. Isokinetic expressions of dynamic strength are both developed and displayed mainly, if not exclusively, in special isokinetic exercise devices.

There are four more concepts related to strength: absolute strength of a muscle, relative strength of a muscle, absolute muscular strength, and relative muscular strength (Wazny 1977).

Absolute strength of a muscle is measured by the minimal resistance that makes it impossible for a muscle stimulated with maximal intensity to contract.

Relative strength of a muscle equals the absolute strength of this muscle divided by the surface of a cross section of its muscle fibers.

Absolute muscular strength (of an individual) is the greatest amount of force that an individual can display in a given movement.

Relative muscular strength (of an individual) is an individual's absolute muscular strength divided by his or her body weight.

Development of strength in stages of growth

Particular muscle groups differ from each other in their absolute and relative strength as well as in the pace at which they develop.

In boys absolute muscular strength grows constantly during their school age (7-19), while their relative strength increases most between 13 and 14 years. In the period between ages 12 to 15, the muscular strength of boys increases significantly faster than the muscular strength of girls (Hettinger 1964). There is a particularly high difference between the sexes in the static strength of the shoulders and back. Dynamic strength develops mostly until puberty and until then there are no big differences in strength between sexes. Later, strength development in girls stagnates while boys' strength further grows to be 50% higher than girls'. The strength of those muscle groups that are constantly used (for example, muscles of the hand) develops longer (Wolanski and Parizkowa 1976).

Figure 46 tracks the development of strength measured by pull-ups (boys) and arm hangs (girls) on a high bar. You can observe the systematic increase of arm strength in boys while in girls this increase occurs only up to 15 years of age.

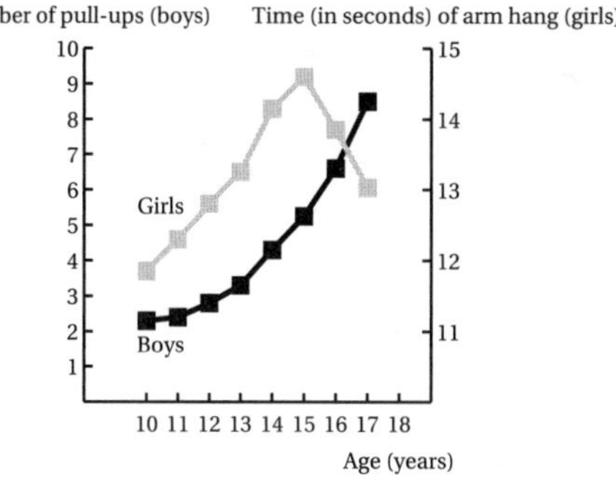

Figure 46. Development of strength

Table 47 shows the data points that plot the lines for figure 45.

Table 47. Average values of pull-up and arm hang (Gilbert, Montes, and Ross 1984)

Age	Pull-up in number of repetitions (boys)	Flexed arm hang in seconds (girls)
10	2.4	11.9
11	2.5	12.4
12	2.9	12.7
13	3.4	13.3
14	4.4	14.2
15	5.3	14.7
16	6.8	13.9
17	8.6	13.1

Preconditions of strength training

1. **Maturity of the central nervous system—adaptability of nervous excitations.** Strength exercises require rapid changes in the level and location of excitation in the central nervous system and this depends on the stage of a child's development.

2. **Physiological cross section of a muscle.** A greater cross section means greater strength potential.

3. **Type of muscle fibers.** For strength, a predominance of fast-twitch fibers is best.

4. **Number of, and quality of synchronization of, active muscle fibers.** The more fibers are active and the better their synchronization in a movement, the more force the athlete can apply.

5. **Biological maturity.** The amount and the kind of resistance beneficial for a child depends on the child's stage of biological development—especially on the degree of bone development, the ability of the cardiovascular system to handle increased pressure, and, in the case of strength-endurance exercises, on anaerobic fitness (Astrand 1970).

6. **Hormonal activity.** Although a low level of androgens does not prevent prepubescent children from gaining strength, a high level of those hormones does help (Duda 1986).

7. **Technique.** Knowing how to do strength exercises prevents injury and helps in overcoming greater resistance.

An early start in developing strength is decisive for physical fitness and children can benefit from strength training (Duda 1986). One study showed over 40% increase of strength in boys and girls aged 10 and 11 after training for nine weeks (Sewall and Micheli 1986). Keep in mind that the very elasticity of the young skeleton makes it less resistant to pressure, and it may be easily deformed. The danger to young athletes in strength training is nearly exclusively to the bones and ligaments rather than to the muscles. Even intensive training should not damage young muscles because they are protected by the ease with which they tire.

Children's bones are intensely reshaped during the processes of growth. The bones of adults change much slower in response to any stress, as for example the stress of strength training. Chronic or sudden stress that causes a strain or sprain in an adult may cause an epiphyseal (growth plate) fracture in a child. Growth plates are weaker than the ligaments attached to them, and many children's growth plate injuries are misdiagnosed as sprained ligaments. The consequences of growth plate injury may be deformed bones (leg, arm, back), uneven length of arms or legs, or stunted growth. However, systematic and rational strength training has a positive effect on bone growth. For example, the bones in a tennis player's racquet hand grow longer and stronger than those in the other hand (Dick 1977). Muscle pull is the fundamental stimulus for the thickening of bone, and intermittent use of submaximal resistance (80%-90%) stimulates height growth (Dick 1977).

Excessive loading (compressing) of the spine may cause Scheuermann's disease in which the lumbar vertebrae become wedge-shaped, herniating the nuclei of the intervertebral discs into the bone in places. Postpone loading of the spine, as in standard weightlifting exercises, until the spine's musculature is well developed (ages 18 to 20).

Preschool age. The task of strength training at this age is to satisfy children's movement needs by providing a broad array of stimulation sufficient for skeletal and muscular development: marching, running over varied terrain, throwing, games involving jumps, and crawling are examples.

Younger school age. Offer further versatile strength exercises suited to children's abilities and their natural movement needs.

Sharkey (1986) recommends strength exercises 3 times per week at the ages of 6-10, each time for up to 15 minutes. The child's body provides sufficient resistance in movements such as sprints, jumps, crawling, climbing, supports on bars, and pull-ups. Pull-ups seem to be a strenuous exercise, providing resistance exceeding the recommended percentages of a child's body weight because only the arms are lifting the whole weight of the body. There are mitigating circumstances, however: a) children will not persist in doing something their bones, muscles, or nerves are not ready for, so long as they are not being pushed by adults or older children; and b) lifting 100% of one's body weight in a pull-up is not the same as lifting a barbell with the same load—the spine, pelvis, thighs, legs, and feet are not compressed in a pull-up.

Dr. Michael A. Nelson, chairman of the American Academy of Pediatrics' Committee on Sports Medicine and Fitness, said that children as young as 7 or 8 year can lift weights that can be lifted 12 to 15 times per set. Lifting loads that do not permit such a high number of repetitions could damage growth plates, thus stunting the growth. Bodybuilding or competitive weightlifting should wait until the peak growth period is over—usually around 15 for both girls and boys (American Academy of Pediatrics 1990).

At the age of 10 children can start learning the techniques of high and long jumps for track and field. Teach the natural technique (approach on a straight line at an angle to the bar with scissorlike movement of the legs while clearing the bar) for a high jump at this age. The same goes for a long jump—teach the natural technique, or "bent legs," with legs bent in all joints after the takeoff, no additional leg movements in flight, and arms stretched out in front.

Uneven stress on legs and shocks from landings can displace pelvic bones, and a large number of jumps and landings on a hard surface can cause flat feet (Roshchupkin and Gogin 1989). To prevent these problems Roshchupkin and Gogin recommend that up to age 9, before children feel like serious jumping—long jump, depth jumps, high jump rather than just little hops—they should start doing exercises that strengthen their feet and lower legs.

Older school age and puberty. Because of the growth of young bodies at these ages, there is a susceptibility to deformations of bones, particularly of the spine. Avoid exercises putting considerable stress on the spine. If such stress occurs anyway, do some exercises in suspension after those exercises.

At these ages (11-14), children should mainly do strength-endurance exercises: over 10 repetitions per set in 2-3 sets. Only later, during the second phase of puberty, may strength training start resembling that of adults, but with a greater emphasis on volume than on intensity. The resistance then is increased so the athlete can lift the weights up to 10 times in a set.

Speed-strength exercises such as jumps are suitable for 11- to 14-year-old children because this is the period when speed-strength increases rapidly and naturally (Roshchupkin and Gogin 1989). As soon as girls finish their adolescent growth spurt and before reaching sexual maturity, they should undertake regular strength training because at this stage of life their androgenic hormones reach the highest levels. The speed-strength of girls stabilizes or even deteriorates when they reach age 14. Boys' explosive strength (a more advanced form of speed-strength) increases with age and reaches its maximum rate of increase at ages 15-17. Explosive strength increases in males until age 25 and until age 14 in females.

Until the ages of 11 or 12, boys and girls develop similarly. Up to that age, body height increases faster than muscle mass and, because of that, running and jumping (both requiring speed-strength) are recommended rather than standard strength exercises. After that age girls' weight and height surpasses that of boys because of girls' earlier sexual maturation. During the period of sexual maturation strength efforts involving straining, such as lifting weights, jumping with weights, or depth jumps, may harm girls' reproductive organs.

Children 9 to 11 years old can do one strength exercise in a workout per body part, in two sets each consisting of 12-15 repetitions, with resistance up to 50% 1RM (1 Repetition Maximum) of the child (Micheli 1990). This can be increased when children can do two sets of 15 repetitions for four consecutive workouts. Children 12 to 14 years old can also do only one strength exercise per body part, in three sets of 10-12 repetitions each, with resistance between 50% and 60% of a child's 1RM. This can be increased when they can do three sets of 12 repetitions in three consecutive workouts. Young athletes 15 and 16 years old can do two strength exercises per body part, in 3-4 sets of 7-11 repetitions each, with resistance between 50% and 70% of the individual's 1RM. This can be increased when they can do three sets of 12 repetitions in three consecutive workouts. Young athletes 17 years old and older can do two strength exercises per body part, in 4-6 sets of 6-10 repetitions each, with resistance between 50% and 80% of the individual's 1RM. This can be increased after doing four sets of 10 repetitions for two consecutive workouts.

According to Sharkey, children 11-14 years old should do strength exercises 3 times per week, each time for 30 minutes (Sharkey 1986). Youth 15-19 years old should do 3 strength workouts per week, each workout up to 45 minutes. During the second phase of puberty introduce directed strength exercises into strength training of youth.

Principles of strength training

1. Precede all strength training with an orthopedic examination. Strength training can aggravate existing posture defects if it is not preceded by a program of corrective exercises and is not designed with an individual's limitations in mind.

2. Emphasize versatile development of muscular fitness, focusing on those muscles that maintain posture. The muscles of the abdomen, lower and upper back, hips, and thighs are the ones to concentrate on. If unguided, children will usually concentrate on developing their arms, chest, and legs instead. The type and amount of strength exercises should lead to a harmonious development of all muscle groups.

3. Provide strength training in stages, none of which can be skipped or rushed. Figure 46 shows the proper division.

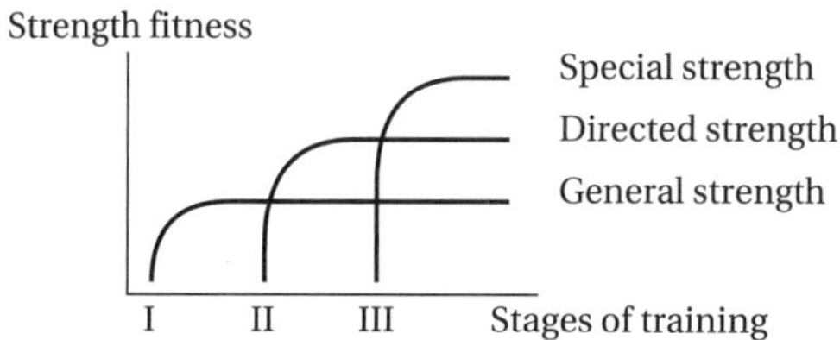

Figure 47. Stages of strength training (Wazny 1977)

4. Sequence strength exercises appropriately. The correct sequence in a long-term strength training program is to be: speed-strength exercises, strength-endurance exercises, strength exercises. In all cases dynamic concentric contractions should dominate.

5. Place strength exercises appropriately within a workout. During general fitness lessons or workouts, schedule strength exercises at the end of the main part of the workout or lesson, right before endurance exercises.

6. Switch the exercised body part after each type of exercise. Jumps may be followed by throws, for example, then throws by running. Immediately following jumps with running is too fatiguing for children's legs.

7. Teach the proper form of an exercise first; then add resistance. The amount of resistance or the number of repetitions, or both, should be such as to make a few extra repetitions possible. Using so much resistance that the child cannot repeat the exercise due to lack of strength or to fatigue interferes with healthy growth. Both excessive volume and excessive intensity of resistance in exercises inhibits height growth. Resistance should permit the full range of motion in strength exercises. A prepubescent strength-training workshop held by the American Orthopaedic Society for Sports Medicine in August 1985 resulted in the following recommendations: 2-3 strength workouts per week, each workout to last 20-30 minutes, exercises to be done in 1-3 sets of 6-15 repetitions each, resistance to be increased by .5 to 1.5 kg (1-3 lbs) after the prepubescent child can do 15 repetitions in the proper form (Duda 1986).

8. Provide adequate recovery periods between workouts. Children are growing (which can be exhausting in itself) and learning, and some are working in addition to working out. They need sufficient and proper rest.

Types and methods of strength training

General strength exercises have the task of ensuring an all-round development of the strength of the athlete so his or her muscles, ligaments, and bones can withstand the more intensive directed and specialized strength exercises. Usually the athlete does general strength exercises more slowly than the sports technique requires, with a resistance that develops a different type of strength than that used in the sports technique. For example, children and youth would start with a smaller weight in doing 15 slow repetitions. Then, if they were looking to specialize in shot put, they would progress to deadlifts with a weight permitting 6-8 slow repetitions. These would strengthen the back and thighs of shot-putters, so they can take the stress of heavy squats with weight permitting 8 or more repetitions. Eventually a shot putter can safely do explosive squats that are duplicating the action of the lower body in a shot put.

Directed strength exercises involve all or some of the muscle groups that are the main participants in the actual sports technique. Their dynamics (speed, rhythm) are similar to the dynamics of the actual sports technique, so they use the same energy source as the technique. They differ from the technique in their reach of the movement and its trajectory. Various throws with medicine balls, with shots, and explosive squats are the directed exercises for shot-putters, for example; various jumps, other than the competitive one, are the directed exercises for jumpers.

Special strength exercises are those that have similar spatial form (trajectory and range of motion) to the actual competitive technique; they have similar temporal form (speed and rhythm) as the actual technique; and the maximal force in those exercises is developed in the same spot and instance as in the actual technique.

In strength training for children and youth, only dynamic strength should be developed and only through repetitive methods:

1. Method of small loads permitting a high number (approximately 30) of repetitions. The goal is to improve resistance to fatigue.

2. Method of moderate loads, in the form of circuit training (moving from station to station) consisting of up to ten exercises, up to 20 repetitions per exercise.

3. Method of big loads permitting 10 repetitions, doing 8-10 exercises per workout.

Exercises for strength training

Recommended strength exercises arranged in the order of difficulty and intensity.

1. Obstacle courses, climbing, half-hangs, rope pulling

2. Climbing, vertical supports (as in standing push-ups), hangs

3. Exercises involving overcoming one's body weight, exercises with an additional load (medicine balls)

4. Horizontal supports (as in push-ups), pull-ups

5. Exercises with a partner, with dumbbells, with a barbell; dumbbells are preferred to a barbell because they permit applying equal resistance to each arm. Since usually the total weight a child can lift on two separate dumbbells is less than he or she could lift on a barbell, using dumbbells reduces the compression of the spine. The child can also use only one

dumbbell—switching it from hand to hand, which exercises each side of the upper body while cutting at least by half the compression of the spine (provided that the spine is kept straight during such an exercise—because lifting a dumbbell while bending or twisting the spine can be more harmful than barbell lifts).

One-legged squats or step-ups place the same load on the exercised leg as adding a barbell equal to the child's body weight in a normal two-legged squat. Squats with a heavy barbell on the child's shoulders place a heavy load on the spine and can cause dystrophic changes to vertebrae and intervertebral disks. Exercise muscles of the back by doing back extensions on the bench, deadlifts, and "good mornings," for example, performing movements slowly to avoid fractures of vertebrae and without unnecessarily compressing the spine.

Exercises to avoid

There are some exercises a wise coach will avoid.

- Straight-leg sit-ups are supposed to strengthen the abdomen, but instead they stress hip flexor muscles, which in turn stresses the lower back. Abdomen muscles are active in this exercise for approximately one third of the movement's time. Preferred exercises: Bent-leg sit-ups, abdomen crunch (curl-up).

- Double-leg lifts and scissors (whether lying on the floor or hanging from the bar) are supposed to strengthen the abdomen, but instead they stress hip flexors and can cause lower back problems. Preferred exercise: Single-leg lifts.

- Simultaneous leg and arm raises lying on the stomach are supposed to strengthen lower back muscles but can hurt lumbar vertebrae. Preferred exercise: Alternate leg and arm raises.

- Push-ups strengthen triceps and chest, but in the case of weak abdominal and lower back muscles they can increase lumbar lordosis. Supporting oneself on open hands can damage wrists. Preferred exercise: Moving trunk forward and back while kneeling, head low above the floor, hands clenched in fists.

- Partial squats (in which the thighs are parallel to the floor) strengthen the thighs, but at this angle, patellofemoral stress peaks for both eccentric and concentric muscle contractions (Huberti and Hayes 1984). Preferred exercise: Full squat (legs bent until hamstrings make contact with the calves).

- Jumps or hops in full squat strengthen the thighs but can stretch the knee ligaments and damage the menisci. Preferred exercise: Natural jumps or hops.

- The duck walk strengthens the legs, but taking steps in a straight line entails bouncing and so places high compressive forces on the patella. If done with a flexed spine it may also reinforce bad postural habits. Preferred exercise: The squat creep.

- Back bridging on one's head strengthens the muscles of the neck, but if done with poor form (too much bending in the lumbar spine and not enough in the thoracic spine and hips), it also compresses and may damage the cervical discs. Preferred exercise: Pushing one's head against one's hands while standing or sitting.

These recommendations are not absolute. Wrestlers must do back bridging on their heads, for example. Only a professional coach, however, knows enough to decide what exercises an individual athlete can do, in what manner, how much, and when so as to maximize the benefits and minimize the harmful effects of the exercises.

Evaluation of strength

Equipment: A bar 38 mm (1.5 in) in diameter. For pull-ups it has to be suspended at a height greater than an athlete can reach with his or her arms while standing on tiptoe so he or she can hang from it with arms and legs fully extended and feet off the floor). For flexed-arm hangs this bar has to be suspended at a height level with the athlete's standing height.

1. Pull-ups

The athlete grips the bar with palms facing the body and performs as many pull-ups as possible, without moving the legs or swinging the body. Only correctly performed complete pull-ups count.

Table 48. Strength scores as estimated from the number of pull-ups performed (Sharkey 1986)

	Number of pull-ups		
Age/Score	Low	Average	High
9-10	0	1	6
11	0	2	6
12	0	2	7

Continued on next page

Table 48—continued

	Number of pull-ups		
Age/Score	Low	Average	High
13	1	3	8
14	2	4	10
15	3	6	12
16	4	7	12
17+	4	7	13

Table 49. Pull-ups (boys) (Leeds Education Department and Carnegie School of Physical Education 1981)

			Age		
Score	9	9.01-10	10.01-11	13.01-14	14.01-15
good	3-up	4-up	4-up	5-up	5-up
average	2	2-3	2-3	2-4	2-4
poor	0-1	0-1	0-1	0-1	0-1

2. Flexed-arm hang

The athlete grips the bar with palms facing the body, flexes her arms to lift her body so her chin is above the bar, and holds this position as long as possible. Begin timing as soon as the athlete is in the correct position and stop the watch as soon as her chin touches the bar, falls below it, or is tilted backward. Round the time to the nearest second.

Table 50. Strength scores as estimated from time in flexed-arm hang (Sharkey 1986)

	Time in seconds		
Age/Score	Low	Average	High
9-10	3	9	30
11	3	10	30
12	3	9	26
13	3	8	25

Continued on next page

Table 50—continued

	Time in seconds		
Age/Score	Low	Average	High
14	3	9	28
15	4	9	27
16	3	7	23
17+	3	8	26

Table 51. Flexed-arm hang in seconds (girls) (Leeds Education Department and Carnegie School of Physical Education 1981)

			Age		
Score	9	9.01-10	10.01-11	13.01-14	14.01-15
good	8-up	11-up	17-up	15-up	15-up
average	3-7	5-10	6-16	5-14	5-14
poor	0-2	0-4	0-5	0-4	0-4

Current knowledge of children's physiology indicates that lifting heavy weights and competitive weightlifting is bad for them before the end of bone development (19-20). In spite of this in 1990 the International Weightlifting Tournament for Schoolchildren took place in Moscow. Young weightlifters—120 of them—from Bulgaria, China, Cuba, Czechoslovakia, East Germany, Finland, Great Britain, Hungary, Romania, the Soviet Union, and Sweden competed. The weightlifters were 14 to 16 years old. The results were impressive: in the 60 kilogram weight class Ing Weizhung (China) lifted 120 kilograms (264 lbs) in snatch and 150 kg (330 lbs) in pull and jerk; in the 67.5 kilogram class Alexiey Petrov (Soviet Union) lifted 125 kg (275 lbs) in snatch and 152.5 kg (335.5 lbs) jerk; in the 75 kilogram class Karen Izitian (Soviet Union) snatched 130 kg (286 lbs) and lifted 172.5 kg (379.5 lbs) in the pull and jerk (Sergeev 1990). This is an example of disregarding the whole knowledge of children's physiology and giving greater priority to propaganda needs than to the health needs of children. There is no justification for such tournaments. They violate children's bodies and rights.

10

FLEXIBILITY

Flexibility refers to the ability to perform movements in a joint or in a series of joints. The greater the amplitude of these movements, the greater the flexibility. The main factors determining flexibility are:

- Elasticity and length of muscles and ligaments
- Normal structure of joints
- Good coordination
- Efficiency of energy processes
- Optimal emotional state

The level of flexibility in a given joint is determined by the joint's mobility and the length, elasticity, and tonus of muscles crossing this joint. The length of muscles is determined genetically but can be affected by strength training. The elasticity of muscles diminishes with age but can be improved by strength training. Muscle tonus depends on an individual's nervous system, fatigue, and emotional state. The mobility of a joint depends on the shape of its surfaces and the length of its ligaments, both determined genetically and better left alone. Stretching ligaments leads to loose-jointedness that, in the case of some joints, may lead to bad posture and also forces muscles crossing the joint to work harder at stabilizing it. Improving flexibility by affecting the muscles and the nervous system is safer (Kurz 1991).

There are three kinds of flexibility: dynamic, static passive, and static active.

Dynamic flexibility is the ability to perform dynamic movements within a full range of motion in the joint.

Static passive flexibility is the ability to maintain a stretched position, of the legs, for example, using one's body weight such as in splits, bridges, or piked positions; or using strength not coming from the stretched limbs, as for example lifting and holding a leg with an arm.

Static active flexibility is the ability to assume and maintain a stretched position using the strength of the stretched limb. The athlete is using the tension of the agonists and the synergists to maintain the stretch, while the antagonists are being stretched. Lifting the leg and holding it up, using the strength of the hip flexors and quadriceps of that leg while its hamstrings are being stretched, is an example of static active flexibility.

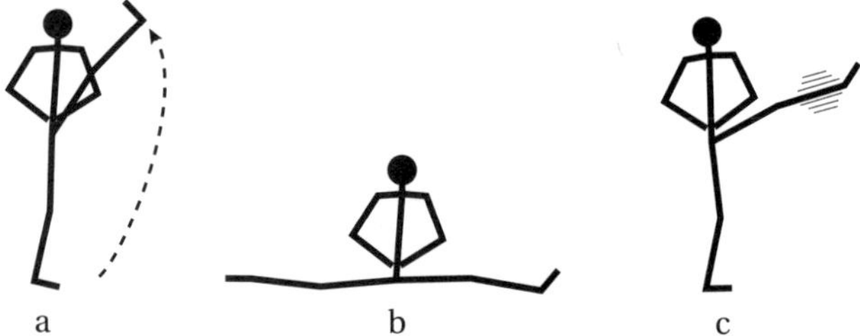

Figure 48. Kinds of flexibility: a) dynamic, b) static passive, and c) static active

Such stretches—especially lifting the leg and holding it high without any support—compress the spine and may increase lordosis because they bend and twist the spine while the hip flexor (iliopsoas) of that lifted thigh is pulling at the lumbar vertebrae. If such leg lifts have to be done—for example, in gymnastics—they should be immediately followed by exercises and stretches that correct lordosis (pelvic tilts, forward bends). In fact, any exercise that increases lordosis should be followed by corrective exercises.

Development of flexibility in stages of growth

Preschool age. Preschool children (ages 2 to 5) do not need to dedicate as much time to flexibility exercises as older children and adults, who may have to spend as much as 5-15 minutes per workout on flexibility. Preschoolers' bodies are so elastic that, in the course of natural play, they will put their joints through the full range of motion.

Younger school age. From the ages of 6 to 10, the mobility of shoulder and hip joints is reduced. To prevent this reduction of mobility, children in this age range must do dynamic stretches for the shoulders (arm raises and arm rotations in all directions) and hips (leg raises in all directions). Flexibility of the spine reaches its natural maximum at age 8 or 9, but the spine's flexibility can be increased beyond the natural range of motion until 15. Trying to increase the spine's natural range of motion, as well as repetitive bending and twisting of the spine, causes stress fractures to the growth plates of the vertebrae, spondylolysis, spondylolisthesis, and slipped discs, resulting in lifelong back problems. Many gymnasts pay for their spine's great flexibility by wearing body braces and spending the rest of their life in pain.

Avoid static stretches of all kinds (passive, active, isometric) in training preadolescent children because excitation dominates over inhibition in a child's nervous system. This means that it is hard for children to stay still, relax, and concentrate properly on feedback from their muscles for periods as long as static stretches require.

Isometric stretches (isometric tensions of stretched muscles) require concentration and body consciousness to interpret properly the sensations coming from the stretched and strongly tensing muscles so as not to injure them. Like all isometric exercises, isometric stretches may increase the resting tonus of muscles, which adversely affects movement coordination—something to be avoided during the limited period in life when one's coordination can be developed. Trainers should not use isometric or passive (relaxed) stretches before the second stage of sexual maturation because children's muscles do not resist stretching as much as those of adults and this causes their ligaments to be stretched. Ballistic stretches, in which one bounces to increase maximum stretch, are total idiocy, and a good trainer will never use them.

Older school age and puberty. Ages 10 to 13 (before the growth spurt) is when to intensify flexibility training because children, by gaining mass faster than height, get stronger and more active. Increased activity without an increased amount and intensity of stretches may cause bad habits—not using the full range of motion—and thus reduce children's range of motion.

During the growth spurt (13 to 15), height may increase nearly one inch in a month. Muscles and tendons do not elongate as quickly as growing bones. Excessive lumbar lordosis (swayback), leading to back injuries, results from the bones of the spine growing faster than its muscles. Pain in the kneecap, and eventual destruction of its cartilage, is caused by doing too much knee-bending when the quadriceps and hamstrings are tightened by the rapid growth of thigh bones. Stretches should target these muscles that are made tight by the rapid growth of bones, otherwise the child will develop bad posture or get injured. During this first stage of sexual maturation, all bones, ligaments, and muscles are weakened and the trainer should therefore avoid stressing the trunk by many repetitions of bends and twists.

In the second stage of maturation, after the growth spurt (15 to 19), you can intensify flexibility training once again and do sport-specific stretches similar in quality and quantity to those for adults: shoulder stretches for throwers (dynamic and static stretches), for example, or splits and bridges for gymnasts (static stretches).

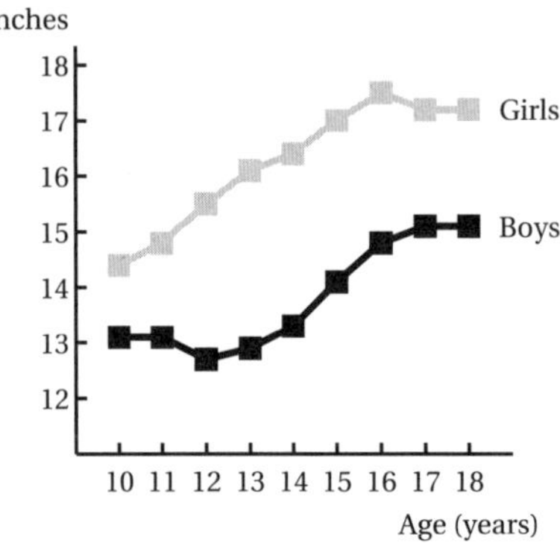

Figure 49. Development of flexibility as measured by the sit and reach test (Gilbert, Montes, and Ross 1984)

Principles of children's flexibility training

1. Use moderation. Overdoing flexibility exercises leads to bad posture and injuries in children and youth, but especially in children. Do not attempt to increase the mobility of the cervical and lumbar spine (neck and lower back) beyond the natural range of motion. And for all stretches—do not continue stretching (or any exercise) if it causes pain.

2. Combine flexibility with strength. Increasing flexibility without increasing strength in the new, greater ranges of motion is without advantage in sports and can cause injuries. A child's muscles must be strengthened in cases of excessive flexibility to prevent injuries and posture defects.

3. Work on specific joints. Development of flexibility does not progress evenly in all joints. Some joints require more work than others.

4. Prefer dynamic flexibility exercises with young children. Do not use static passive flexibility exercises before the second stage of sexual maturation. School-age children should do dynamic flexibility exercises (such as arm raises and circles, leg raises) daily in a few sets, each set consisting of approximately 10 repetitions. Generally, active exercises such as dynamic stretches are preferred over static stretches. Don't use bouncing (ballistic) stretches.

Methods of flexibility training

Flexibility of children as well as of adults is developed by the repetitive method, using several sets of an exercise for approximately 10 repetitions each.

Exercises for flexibility training

Exercises used with children: various mobile games, exercises that require a high range of movements, and play forms of gymnastic exercises.

Sharkey (1986) recommends that children from 6 to 10 years old and adolescents from 11 to 19 should do flexibility exercises only three times per week. Researchers of the former Soviet Union, however, recommend doing dynamic flexibility exercises every day and Matvieyev (1977) cites an experiment in which results of dynamic stretching for five days, twice a day, were twice as great as the results of doing the same total number of repetitions every other day, also twice a day.

Exercises to avoid

As was also true in strength training, there are some types of exercises that a wise coach will avoid.

- Avoid suggesting fast circular movements of the head or trunk in which the vertebrae are an axis of movement. This can cause compression of the nerve roots, and if neck circles are performed quickly they can damage arteries of the neck. Slow movements are safer.

- Hyperextension (bending backward) of the lower back overstretches the muscles of the abdomen, increases lordosis, and damages joint capsules and the ligaments that surround the discs, resulting in disc protrusion. Hyperextending the neck can jam the cervical vertebrae together and cause permanent damage because neck extension is limited by bone, not by soft tissues.

- Simultaneous raising of the arms and legs while lying on the stomach causes the same lower back problems as hyperextension. Raising and lowering either legs or arms is safer.

- Doing a standing toe touch with straight legs can damage the sciatic nerve. Bending the knees slightly is safer.

- Back bridging, if done with poor form (too much bending in the lumbar spine and not enough in the thoracic spine and hips), causes the same problems as hyperextension, and if done with poor form on one's head and feet rather than on the hands and feet, it may also cause compression and damage of the cervical discs.

Evaluation of flexibility

Sit and reach is the most popular test of flexibility. It accurately evaluates flexibility only for people of average, proportional build. Its usefulness is dubious for people with other types of build and during adolescence when disproportions between legs and trunk occur commonly.

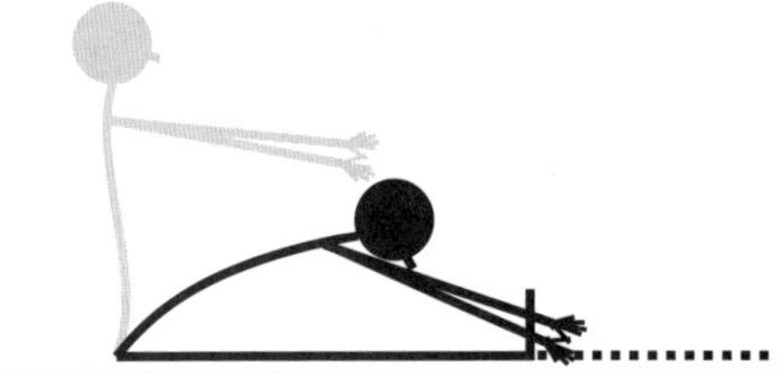

Figure 50. Sit and reach test

1. Have the athlete sit upright with knees straight, feet about shoulder-width apart, pointing up at about a 90° angle from the shin. Heels should be positioned just behind the 50-centimeter mark of a tape placed between legs.

2. The athlete places outstretched hands together in front, with thumbs locked and index fingers touching side to side.

3. Have the athlete reach forward as far as possible, sliding fingertips along the tape. Tell him or her not bend knees or ankles, and not to jerk. He or she holds position for at least two seconds. Note furthest distance, to the nearest centimeter.

A sit and reach test does not measure flexibility in one joint or of one body part, so other tests that are joint and muscle specific, and thus more informative, are preferable. Here are some more specific ways of measuring flexibility, in figures 51-57.

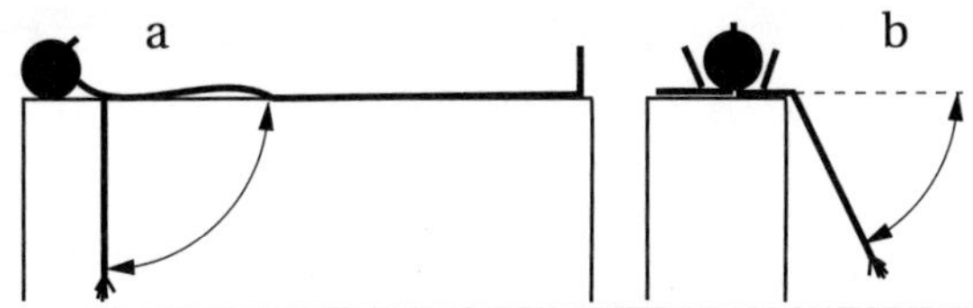

Figure 51. Shoulder vertical (backward) extension (a) and horizontal extension (b). The other shoulder must rest on the table.

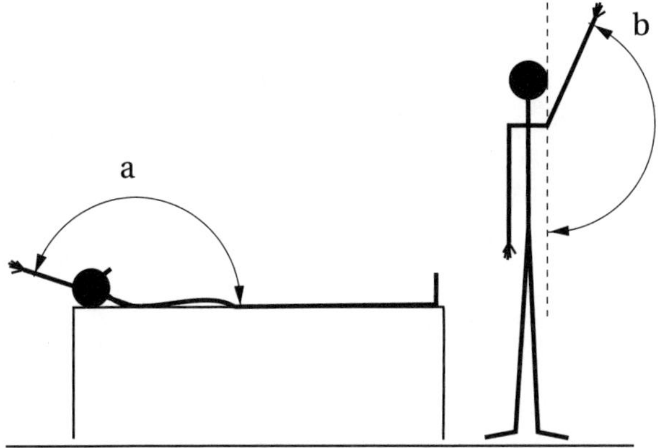

Figure 52. Shoulder forward flexion (a) and abduction (b). While measuring forward flexion the thoracic and lumbar spine must rest flat on the table. When measuring abduction the whole spine must be straight.

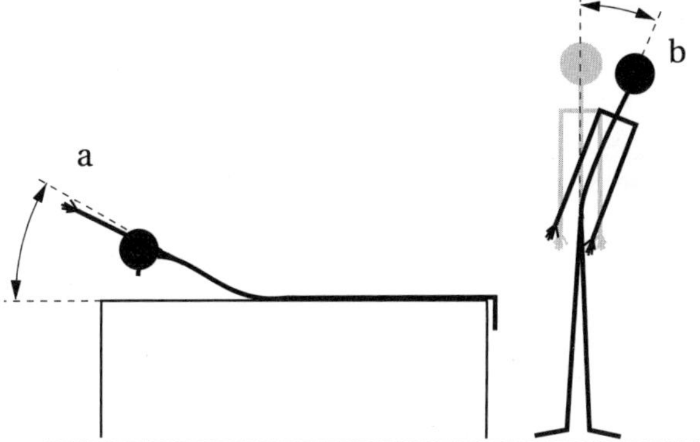

Figure 53. Lumbar and thoracic spine extension (a) and lateral flexion (b). When measuring extension pelvis rests on the table.

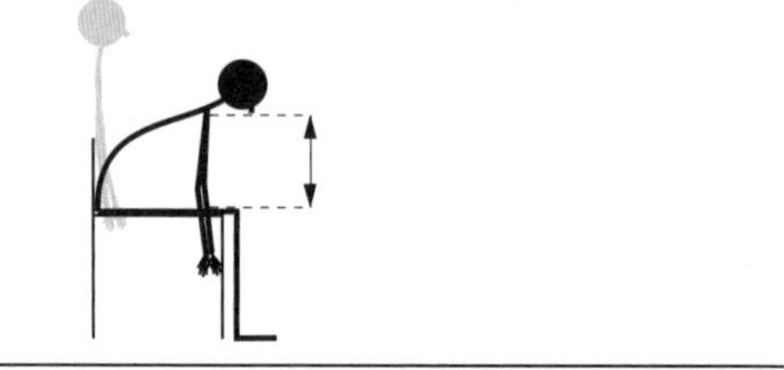

Figure 54. Lumbar spine forward flexion. The pelvis is kept straight (no movement in hip joints).

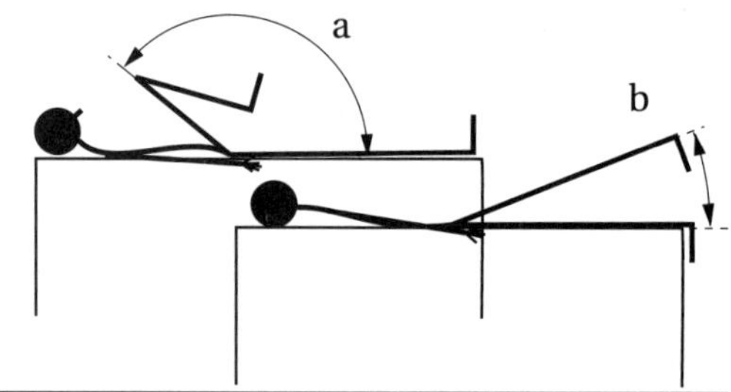

Figure 55. Hip flexion (a) and extension (b). When measuring flexion the other thigh rests flat on the table to keep pelvis straight. When measuring extension, the front of the other thigh rests on the table to keep pelvis straight.

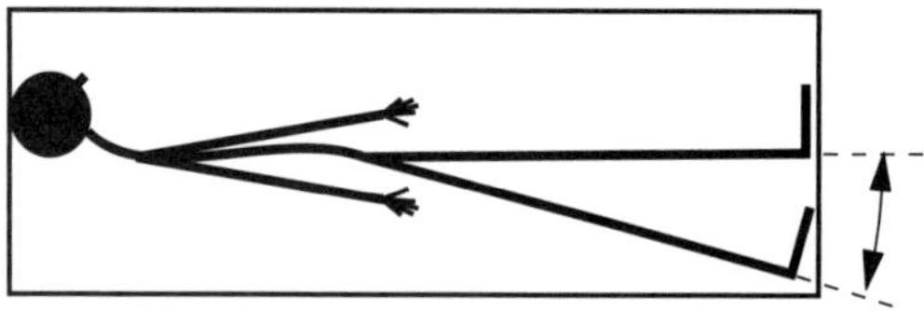

Figure 56. Hip abduction

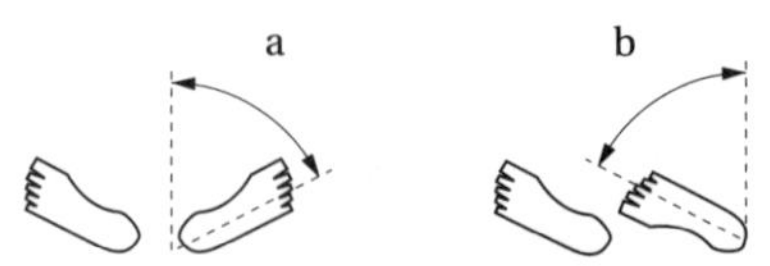

Figure 57. Hip rotation (a) external and (b) internal

11

TECHNIQUE

Technique refers to solving movement and tactical tasks effectively. The athlete calls upon the best in his or her physical potential—size, weight, joint mobility; the best in his or her motor potential—strength, speed, agility, coordination, and endurance; and the best in mental potential—intelligence, willpower, experience. All these potencies are orchestrated in ways suitable to the motor task and according to the rules of a given sport.

Rules of the sport determine the goals of technique.

In acrobatics, diving, gymnastics, and figure skating, making a good impression on the judges (who can otherwise deduct points) by performing difficult, sometimes dangerous movements or complex combinations of movements is what counts. In these sports, techniques are precisely described, performed in an unchanging environment without anyone's interference. The athlete must develop motor abilities as much as it takes for a flawless performance of preprogrammed movements. This is the first group of sports.

In track and field, swimming, and weightlifting, techniques facilitate reaching maximal and objectively measurable results. Here too rules prohibit interfering with an athlete's performance, but technique is judged not by its look or difficulty but by the result measured in time, distance, or weight. Good technique is whatever permits the athlete to fully use his or her motor abilities while adhering to the rules. This is the second group of sports.

In contact sports (boxing, fencing, wrestling), racquet sports (badminton, tennis), and team games (basketball, football, volleyball, hockey), technique helps in overcoming an opponent despite the opponent's resistance. In these sports technique is combined with tactics, reaction to constantly changing situations, and outpsyching the opponent. The best technique is whatever scores (within the rules) and it has to be adjustable to changing conditions. This is the third group of sports. In this group of sports motor abilities are subservient to technique. An athlete develops strength, speed, endurance, and flexibility the better to perform technique (punch, touch, pin, pass, shot)—just the opposite to the relation of technique to abilities in the second group of sports.

How quickly, exactly, and permanently an athlete learns technique and how well he or she applies it depends on his or her age, emotional state, motivation (its level and direction), talents, intelligence, temperament, knowledge, and skills. Also important are the coach's personality, use of teaching methods, knowledge of the technique and ability to analyze it, and the quality of the coach's verbal skills (important for describing the technique and for correcting mistakes), and the conditions in which learning takes place.

The optimal level, or amount, or quality of each of these factors is different for each athlete and it changes in the process of training. Too much, too little, or the wrong kind of motivation prevents proper learning, for example, as would learning with inadequate or too sophisticated equipment or sparring partners. And so does knowing too little or too much (when the athlete spends too much time on already mastered exercises and gets bored).

The essence of learning technique is learning and perfecting sensory-motor habits. A sensory-motor habit is a learned activity of sensory and motor processes intentionally practiced to the point of automatization. The physiological aspect of a sensory-motor habit is based on forming and making permanent the conditional reflex connections that cause the same set of motor reactions to respond to the same set of stimuli. Formation of a sensory-motor habit proceeds through several stages: first generalization of excitation in motor centers of the cortex (when beginners concentrate on general form of movement, its spatial relationships, are overly tensed and make unnecessary additional movements); next, to concentration of excitation in the proper motor centers (relaxed and economical movements, their spatial form approaches the required model, and attention is focused on particular details of technique, its rhythm and speed); and to ultimately to automatizing the whole action (no need for conscious control of the movement, which happens by itself in the right situation). The secondary signal system (reacting to verbal representation of sensory signals) that replaces the original sensory (auditory, visual, tactile, kinesthetic) signals plays a significant role in the process of forming sensory-motor habits.

Participation of the consciousness in forming sensory-motor habits permits their plasticity (adjustability in changing situations) and effectively learning new actions through mental training (visualization, ideomotor exercises). Sensory-motor habits can be open or closed. Open habits are adjustable to unexpectedly changing situation; closed habits are appropriate when the movement is performed in relatively unchanging situations and there is no need to adjust for the unexpected. In sports of the closed sensory-motor habits, athletes strive to precisely perform preprogrammed movements. They perfect these habits by drilling exactly in the prescribed forms of movements. While drilling they learn to notice (by muscle and joint sense) the most minute deviations from the proper form that, in the case of a gymnastic skill, ruins the routine or that underuses an athlete's power in a track and field throw. In the open habit sports, as soon as athletes know the basics of technique, the coach should constantly put them in situations that demand making choices and applying technique in various conditions. Perfection of the open habits means making them more plastic—more adjustable to various situations. Plasticity is necessary in sports with changing conditions, such as contact sports, games, skiing, or sailing.

Proper sports technique has a great deal to do with sensory-motor habits. Technique or technical skill is the capability of performing certain sensory-motor habits. The capability of reflexive, effective application of these habits in a contest is called technical-tactical skill.

Because of the influence of gymnastics and military drills, many coaches of sports requiring open sensory-motor habits wrongly concentrate athletes' attention only on the form of movement. In the open habit sports, however, technique should be evaluated in relation to the situation and not only by its spatial form or its speed. Teach techniques in conditions as close as possible to the actual application in competitions. Show technique in a typical situation, in the third group of sports against an opponent, and then have athletes practice it in this situation. Simplify the situation (attack or defense of the opponent) as much as it takes for the athlete to get the technique right. Then as the athlete progresses, in the course of several workouts, gradually remove restrictions from the opponent to make the situation realistic. Success in competition depends not so much on the number of techniques known to an athlete but on the ability to apply known techniques in tactical situations. Teach not only how to move in any technique but in what situations, when, and how to use this technique.

Give athletes your immediate verbal feedback on their effectiveness in addition to the nonverbal feedback they will get from the action itself.

To achieve great automatization of the technique and to make it applicable in competitions, an athlete must use other than strictly technical exercises in which his or her attention is focused only on how to move. In competition an athlete has to focus attention on tactics and on several changing actions of the opponent and referees. As soon as the athlete masters basic structure of the technique, he or she should practice in conditions resembling competition to learn applying the technique without thinking how to do it. The athlete's technique (sensory-motor habits) should be so mastered that in competition he or she can observe the opponent and focus on tactics and not on how to move. The technical-tactical skills that are required to apply technique in competition and that are developed by practicing in conditions resembling competition are: speed and adequacy of reaction; distancing; anticipation; concentration, mobility, and divisibility of attention; telling a feint from the real action; and the ability to change technique in mid-action.

Athletes of contact, racquet, and team sports have to learn how to perform the techniques and then have to learn what it takes to apply these techniques. Do not make the common mistake of teaching and polishing the technique while forgetting to teach how to apply it in competition. In these sports, as soon as the athlete gets the basic structure of the technique right, teach him or her the application of this technique in conditions increasingly resembling competition. The technical-tactical skills and psycho-motor reactions you thus teach in training will be those necessary in competition.

There are three stages in learning technique (whether single skills or a whole repertoire of sports skills):

1. Learning the technique. This may be difficult as the technique may resemble none of the normal, everyday movements and there may be many techniques to be learned. At this stage the decisive factor in learning is the coach. The coach controls conditions, can adjust the exercises and the pace of teaching to the needs of the athlete. As long as the athlete wants to learn a coach using the right methods can successfully teach.

2. Applying technique during a workout against an active opponent. Here the coach has less influence. It is harder to isolate the problem points and a lot depends on the athlete's talents and attitudes. The coach can help by devising the right tasks for a practice game or sparring.

3. Applying technique in competition. This is the most difficult stage and the measure of the athlete's talent and the coach's professionalism. The athlete faces unrestricted actions of the opponent. The coach has the least influence at this stage. Often during the contest there is no communication between the coach and athletes. Mistakes cannot be corrected until the next competition and the coach can comment and advise only before or after.

Here are the contradictions in the process of teaching technique and technical-tactical skills that the coach has to reconcile:

1. The need to stabilize and automatize sensory-motor habits has to be reconciled with the need to make these habits adjustable to varying conditions of the game or fight.

2. Initially sensory-motor habits (techniques) are taught in their standard, basic, or classical form, but later, when standards are automatized,

athletes are encouraged to individualize their techniques and develop their own style.

3. At the basic level of learning the technique, the athlete's attention is directed at the way he or she moves. The athlete is conscious of every detail of the technique. As the athlete progresses movements become automatic and the athlete can do technique paying little if any attention to its elements. The athlete's consciousness is on which techniques to use, not how to do them.

Attention and teaching technique

To learn and to apply technique athletes have to direct and focus their attention. The optimal direction and focus differ from sport to sport, and within the same sport change depending on the activity. While learning the athlete should direct the attention inward and focus it narrowly on his or her movements and associated sensations. In contact sports and team games where an athlete has to react to a changing situation, while still learning how to do the technique, he or she soon has to direct attention outward—to external clues such as actions of the training partner. When analyzing exercises, workouts, competitions, and planning training, the coach and the athlete direct their attention outward and focus it widely on their impressions, experiences, and options.

To be successful while playing or competing the athlete has to focus in the specific way required by the sport.

Wide external focus is required in team games where an athlete reacts to situations involving movements of many players, a ball or puck, and distances to goals and lines. Tennis also requires a wide external focus because of the size of the court.

Narrow external focus is required whenever there is contact between opponents (boxing, fencing, wrestling) or where distance is small (table tennis, one-on-one encounters in team games).

Narrow internal focus is required in the closed sensory-motor habit sports (gymnastics, weightlifting, track and field jumps and throws) where athletes use internal sensations for their clues and shut off nearly all external stimuli beyond some awareness of the equipment or apparatus.

Selectivity of attention refers to noticing what is important in a given situation while rejecting all that is not important.

Mobility of attention refers to shifting it at will or as needed (and not because of being easily distracted) from one object or action to another, such as changing from an attack to defense when noticing the beginning of a counterattack.

Divisibility of attention refers to focusing it on several objects or doing more than one thing at a time. For example, a soccer player has to follow the path of the ball, the movement of partners and opponents, and has to see the goal post.

Although sports specific attention can be developed as a by-product of plying the sport, you may want to devise exercises that facilitate this development. In individual contact sports when an athlete practices technique with a partner, tell him or her to pay attention to, for example, partner's feet during a few repetitions, to partner's hips during the next few repetitions, then to partner's shoulders, and finally to partner's face. This exercise, while teaching which body part can give what clues or early warnings of the opponent's actions, makes the athlete focus and maintain attention on chosen objects. The athlete will discover how much focus is beneficial and how much is detrimental to the quality of technique. Changing the features the athlete focuses on prevents boredom. This is especially important with children because of their short attention span. You do not want them to change the direction (from external to internal) or the width of their attention focus to any other than what is conducive to best performance in their sport.

In sports where distances are greater (tennis, team games) tell athletes to pay attention to the ball or puck only, then to the ball or puck and a certain player or players.

Types of technique

There are five types of technique:

1. elementary (simplified basic structure of the movement used for teaching beginners);

2. standard (generally accepted way of performing movements that works for majority of athletes, taught as soon as the elementary form is learned);

3. individual (adaptation of the standard technique to the individual athlete—his or her personality, temperament, body build);

4. innovative (introduction of a new, different movement to accomplish the task, as for example, the introduction of the Fosbury flop in high jump), which, when proven effective, becomes a new standard; and

5. model (based on a mathematical model derived from current and projected world class performances).

Technical training

In sports disciplines in which there is no contact with an opponent (e.g., gymnastics, swimming, track and field), technical training is relatively easier than in those sports disciplines where there is contact (ball games, individual contact sports). In both cases technical training has much in common with coordination training.

Technical training means acquiring movement skills and habits, which is accomplished in four phases.

1. Acquainting the athlete with the movement action

2. Teaching the athlete the movement action

3. Consolidating the athlete's learning of the movement action

4. Perfecting the athlete's movement action

Preconditions of technical training

The assumptions are that the athlete shows

- marked coordination;
- motor talent for a particular sport;
- imagination; and
- a level of development of motor abilities, especially of strength and speed.

Teach fundamental techniques of a given sport during the sensitive periods of those coordination abilities that are essential for given techniques. For example, teach techniques requiring considerable speed-strength, such as jumps and weightlifting snatch and pull and jerk (stressing technical perfection and not the amount of weight), at the ages of 11 to 14 because this is a period of rapid increase in speed-strength abilities. Coordination abilities are predispositions while technique is the skill of using these abilities. Coordination abilities are developed by learning new movements, and in turn they allow an athlete to learn more difficult skills. Coordination abilities, technique, and results are closely related.

Principles of technical training

1. Use correct teaching methods from the very beginning to teach effective skills. Knowing the speed and rhythm in the current model of a track and field throw, for example, try to gradually recreate these characteristics. This requires adjusting the conditions of the exercises (size and weight of equipment) to the present abilities of the athlete. Such an approach paid off in case of Soviet throwers (Petrov and Papanov in Legkaya Atletika number 8, 1980, quoted in Raczek 1991).

The above does not mean that you should copy the whole technique of a world class athlete and try to teach it to the children. This would violate other principles.

2. Progress from easy skills to difficult ones—not too easy because it bores, and not too difficult because it frustrates. Match exercise partners with a similar level of skill. In techniques that require accuracy and speed, develop accuracy first and speed later.

3. Progress from known skills to new skills. Determine what knowledge and skills are basic for a given sport. Teach these basics first and then gradually add advanced information and skills.

4. Teach technique parallel with tactics but refrain from too difficult, stressful, overly competitive situations with beginners. Conditions too real with too much stress lead to learning quickly but incorrectly. A child thrown in a pool may learn how to keep the head above the water but will not learn how to swim well. Similarly, a beginning fighter exposed to a series of quick attacks will get nervous, tensed, awkward, and frustrated rather than learn to anticipate attacks and defend against them. Teach basics in easy situations and quiet conditions. It takes longer but the learned skills are more accurate, adjustable, and permanent, and they facilitate learning more advanced techniques and tactics.

5. Match technical training to an individual's potential (physical, psychological, physiological, motor). Your athletes have different body build, fitness, health, interests, temperament, type of mental imagery (auditory, motor, verbal, visual, tactile, mixed), type of mental activity (descriptive, observational, interpretive, erudite, fantasy-prone, emotional), mobility of nervous processes, and physical mobility. Some are extroverts (open, sociable, bold, at ease in new situations), some introverts (closed, reflective, inhibited, sensitive). All these different persons have to be treated and taught differently. Match teaching methods to the athlete's strengths. To benefit extroverts do exercises at a fast pace, vary

exercises and change their character and speed often, do frequent short breaks, exercise in large groups stressing teamwork, make explanations lively and humorous, and use mainly synthetic methods (learning by doing the whole technique). In case of educational problems use strong stimuli such as reprimands. Before competitions create a friendly carefree group atmosphere, make them wait and warm-up with the group and in contact with coach. Introverts, on the other hand, benefit from a slower pace of exercises, done for long periods of time, accurately, with less variety and less frequent changes. Use a greater proportion of analytical methods with introverts, and see to it they do most exercises alone. Before competitions introverts like to concentrate alone, far from noisy people. Do not use sharp commands with them.

Teach an athlete who is well-coordinated but has slow reaction how to anticipate an opponent's actions. Also teach him or her a wide range of techniques. Teach how to instantly improvise if an athlete has a quick reaction time. Enlarge the arsenal of techniques and tactics of an athlete who prides him- or herself in fighting technically. Develop aggressiveness of an athlete who loves a hard struggle and does not care for fancy moves.

Motivate young, beginning athletes for doing the exercises right. As they mature motivate them for achieving long-term training goals. Remember that each athlete has a different level of motivation.

6. Use diverse exercises. The more exercises the athlete knows the easier he or she learns new techniques. Athletes with a large "thesaurus" of movements often skip the first phase of learning new sensory-motor habits, which is trying recreate general spatial form of movement while experiencing generalization of excitation in motor centers. They start with a good image of the technique and can easily recreate its spatial form. They proceed right away to the second phase—work on details, rhythm, and speed. This is called "transfer of sensory-motor skills."

7. Vary conditions of exercising.

8. Teach maintaining self-control.

9. Capitalize on the phenomenon of transfer from the nondominant side. Exercising the "worse" arm further improves the technique of the "better" arm. Symmetry in exercises lets athletes perform a high number of attempts without overloading one limb or side of the body. Doing exercises with the "worse" side forces one to get to know the movement better. This greater knowledge of technique helps the athlete in better performance.

In games and individual contact sports there is also a tactical advantage, of course, to being ambidextrous.

10. Give and get immediate feedback. Exchange information with your athletes. Let them know how they do so they can make corrections on the spot. Observe your athletes and listen to them so you can better teach them. The most important feedback is from the kinesthetic (muscle and joint) sense. To help sharpen perception of this sense, reinforce its signals with signals from additional sources of information that act on other senses. For example, a figure skater has difficulty jumping with several turns because of poor control of the arms. Let him or her hold bells in the hands while practicing these jumps. The bells will give additional feedback about the movement of the arms and thus will help the skater correct their movements. The skater will try to notice kinesthetic sensations that accompany correct movement and to recreate them without the bells' help.

11. Train the athlete's mind as well as his or her body. Explain to athletes or aid them in discovering why techniques work, why some athletes learn some techniques easier, why different exercises develop different elements of technique. Tie your explanations with subjects (e.g., biology, physics) that athletes learn at school.

Athletes who are aware of the rationale behind techniques and of the functions of the exercises in teaching, perfecting, and correcting these techniques learn faster and better.

12. Train the athlete in versatility. The future champion needs to be proficient with both sides of the body, with many techniques, in various situations. Use many various exercises while teaching the children. This will develop general fitness, and coordination, as well as keeping them from being bored. A good foundation of general fitness and well-developed coordination makes it easy to learn progressively more difficult skills.

13. Prepare the athlete with theory as well as practice. An athlete should know how to perform and when to apply each technique, and how changes in the rules affect techniques. They should know how their sport and its training methods are evolving.

14. In open habit sports, teach technique first without an opponent, then with a passive opponent, then with an active opponent performing known and previously announced actions, then in free struggle, and eventually in competition.

15. Make learning and practice systematic. Workouts must be sufficiently frequent to continue progress based on what was learned in previous workouts. Of course, subjects or tasks of subsequent workouts must also be related, again to allow for continuity of progress. Longer than necessary breaks in training cause forgetting of skills and undo recently automatized sensory-motor habits.

Stages of teaching and learning technique

1. Acquainting with technique: Give its name, a general description, explain its applicability in competition, and demonstrate it.

a. The whole technique at real speed

b. The technique broken down into elements

c. The whole technique in slow motion

d. And again the whole technique at real speed.

Your demonstration must be always flawless. If you cannot do something yourself then show a video, movie, or photographs of a model performance. Accompany your demonstration with explanations. Make your explanations of the technique and its applications brief and clear. The right use of words helps in learning sports techniques. You can point out what is not immediately obvious. Tell athletes what they should look at, what they should hear, what they should feel, what they should imagine, what to aim for, and what mistakes to avoid in subsequent phases of the technique. Use appropriate metaphor or comparison to make your explanations memorable. Do not try to pass along all your knowledge of a given technique during one workout or even one demonstration. Give only that information absolutely essential at a given stage of learning for understanding and correctly practicing the technique. As athletes master technique give more in-depth explanations and tips.

Demonstration is most important at the initial stages of teaching technique. For athletes of national and higher class, visual demonstration is not necessary. It is enough to tell them what the task is and they will exercise right.

Remember: the way you demonstrate and explain a technique influences an athlete's attitude toward it. Make sure the athletes you train appreciate the importance and are enthusiastic about this technique.

2. Teaching the technique.

- By the synthetic method, doing the whole technique at a pace typical for it if the technique is not complicated

Children's attention span is short so you have to incorporate this technique into a variety of exercises, games, and plays to keep children interested.

Synthetic methods are preferred by extroverts.

- Teaching the technique by the analytic method, one element at a time if the technique is complicated

Those elements are made into separate, preparatory exercises. Putting these exercises together eventually leads to learning the whole technique. You have to know the technique perfectly to divide it into elements and to devise preparatory exercises. You also have to know your athletes well to match the exercises to them. Not all athletes will benefit from the same preparatory exercises and not all athletes will put the exercises together in the same sequence. Do not require perfection in these partial or preparatory exercises. These are only fragments of the whole technique.

Analytic methods are preferred by introverts.

- Teaching the technique by the mixed method, consisting of:

a. Attempts at performing the whole technique

b. Practicing single difficult elements

c. Perfecting by the synthetic method with resort to the analytic method in case of difficulties with particular elements of the technique.

Breaking some techniques into elements can adversely affect proper movement coordination in these techniques. Do not use mixed and analytic methods for teaching such techniques. Use these methods only for teaching techniques the elements of which are not significantly altered when done separately.

- Teaching the technique by the "from whole action to single technique to whole action" method. This method goes further than synthetic method. Here whole actions, such as a simplified game or contest, are attempted. Explain the rules and present a few basic techniques without detailed descriptions, just enough to give a rough idea of what to do, and let the athletes play. The athlete has to grasp the general idea of the sport (in the case of beginners) or of the particular tactical solution taught in such a way. After the play point out separate skills or techniques that were used by athletes and teach these skills one by one; then apply them again in action. Stress the application of newly learned skills in realistic conditions, in a training game or fight.

Children like this method because it is more fun to play than to drill single techniques, the application of which they do not always understand. The play makes them aware of the role of particular techniques in the game and motivates them to do the drills when it is time to do it. Remember that children join a team because they want to play the sport, not to drill! This method is also liked by very individualistic athletes and those who want to win without regard for flashy techniques.

This method lets you find out quickly who has a talent for your sport and who does not before you and the youth invest a few months in drilling the basics (which often bores and turns off some talented players), only to learn that they do not have what it takes to play. In sports requiring great precision of movements (boxing, fencing, volleyball), you must allow enough time for practicing single techniques without stress, even with assistance—otherwise the athletes will not learn advanced skills.

- Teaching the technique by task method, where you present the situation and let the athletes figure out the technique to solve it. For example, in volleyball you can position the players on the court and pass the ball so it flies too low for even a "bump" (receiving with forearms). Give the task: keep the ball in play (bounce it high enough so your partners can play it). As the athletes try various movements tell them what is good about them and what the drawbacks are until someone attempts a slide and a bump. Praise that player and explain why this move is better than others and taught as a standard technique. From that point on proceed with the standard demonstration. Another example, more advanced: Give to athletes as their task, to invent and arrange in proper sequence exercises for teaching the slide and a bump.

One more example, this one from judo. The task: throw an opponent who resists your attack by pushing you away with stiff arms. After several tries judoka will discover that merely breaking the opponent's grip does not guarantee success. It may simply cause the opponent to quickly change the grip and continue to stiff-arm any attacks. Someone may eventually notice that if they cause the opponent to make several steps walking or running while they break the grip the throw is more likely to succeed. The attacker finds that the stiff-arming opponent cannot regrip when his or her balance is broken, which is more likely when the opponent is walking or running. After the athletes discover how to synchronize moving (walking or running) with the opponent while breaking his or her grip, they will not be stopped by a passive, stiff-arm defense.

The value of the task method is that athletes are made to think on their own, to use and expand their knowledge of the game.

- Teaching the technique by the problem method, similar to the task method, where after solving the original task athletes get new tasks. You present the situation, athletes find the solution, but then new problems arise and athletes must solve them. A sample problem: How to avoid being hit. Young boxers exercise in pairs. One throws a straight right to the face while the other tries to avoid it. Usually, the defenders will try moving back, to the sides, or diving down, for example. Eventually someone will try to hit or slap the attacking arm. If not, you can suggest it by telling them to use their arms. After some trying they will discover that the surest block is with the palm of the open glove hitting the opponent's glove or wrist. You can reinforce this conclusion by pushing with your little finger at the shoulder, elbow, forearm, and wrist of someone's outstretched tensed arm trying to move it sideways. This will show how easily one can redirect a limb by controlling its end. Once they have tried the block; ask them which hand should be used for blocking so they do not open themselves to the left straight. When they see that their left hand should block their opponent's right, ask at what distance from their face they should block so their head is covered by their guard and their arms and forearms do not stop protecting their trunk. If they uncover themselves their opponent should hit them in the exposed targets.

In this teaching method the athletes themselves discover principles of technique and essential skills. This increases their interest, motivation, self-sufficiency, and initiative. Knowledge acquired on one's own by creative trial and error is better assimilated and more permanent than if served ready-made. For the coach, the problem method and the task method are more demanding than standard methods. You have to know what problems to pose for what level of athlete at what stage of intellectual and biological development. You have to know your techniques inside out—doing them right is not enough, you have to be able to analyze their most minute details. If you are not meticulous in matching the problems to your athletes' level of skill and maturity, your athletes will keep missing effective solutions for a long time and workouts will fall apart.

As teaching devices, you can recommend practicing alone, with a partner, in front of a mirror, at the athlete's own pace, and then at a pace imposed by you.

3. Consolidating the technique. Have the athlete perform the technique:

- at various speeds in easy conditions;
- on signal;
- simultaneously with a whole group;
- at his or her own pace; or
- in more difficult but constant conditions.

4. Perfecting technique. Have the athlete perform the technique:

- in increasingly difficult conditions;
- in changing conditions announced and unannounced by the coach; and
- in contests.

In the three groups of sports, because of their different goals and the role technique plays in them, you should pay attention to different elements of technique. Teaching a gymnastic or skating evolution, for example, attend to forming an exact, precise image of the movement and all its elements. Teaching a soccer or basketball pass as soon as player has fair control of the ball, athletes must pay most attention to anticipating the moves of receiving partner and the opponents.

Introduce no more than one new technique or one new variation of technique in any one workout. This allows you to arrange exercises in such a way that athletes: a) warm up just right for this one technique; b) gradually arrive at the technique, one easy step at a time; and c) learn the connection between these partial exercises and the whole technique, so when they have a problem they know which exercises will fix it. Dedicate as many subsequent workouts to that technique as it takes to make it usable. Athletes must have time to digest the information and then practically apply the results of their deliberations in their next workout. Limiting instruction to one technique or variation at a time helps them retain the skill. Although it may seem to slow down the pace of learning, this measured rate of instruction actually facilitates progress because the skill is learned more reliably. Teaching one technique per workout keeps it from turning into a sermon. Each new technique requires description, explanation, and occasional corrections. Trying to teach several techniques breaks the flow of exercises and causes an unending flow of words instead. Use words sparingly, to the point. Find what descriptions help your athletes better grasp the technique. Praise good performance and point out mistakes—briefly. Say what was good or bad about a given attempt so an athlete knows what to keep in mind while practicing. Sensitive persons, those with weak temperaments (phlegmatic, melancholic) or introverts can be easily discouraged by criticism. They need more encouragement and praise. People with strong temperaments (sanguine, choleric) or extroverts can deal with critique better.

Technical mistakes, their causes and fixes

The formation of technical defects in the course of learning is inevitable. Spotting and removing technical mistakes is an important factor in teaching skills. Mistakes occur with first attempts at a technique, usually in the form of extra movements, excessive tension, wrong amplitude, wrong trajectory of movements, and improper rhythm. Even the best coaches cannot totally eliminate mistakes from the process of learning techniques. If learning without mistakes were possible every coach could make world champions in the course of a few workouts.

Sports mastery is achieved, not for lack of weak points or technical mistakes, but thanks to the perfection of an athlete's talents and strong points. The coach should look for and develop an athlete's strengths and eliminate major technical mistakes that clearly lower effectiveness in contests, rather than dwelling on minor mistakes. In the process of training you should balance choices among teaching new skills and habits, developing or perfecting strong points of the athlete, and removing technical mistakes. Your priority is teaching and perfecting habits that bring success in competition.

Technical mistakes are divided as follows (Czajkowski 1991b):

1. Typical and atypical

a. Typical mistakes occur very often and with all students, as for example, excessive tension, extra movements.

b. Atypical mistakes occur rarely, usually resulting from individual features of a particular athlete, from his or her build, or strength imbalances.

2. Local and chain

a. Local defects are when one link in the chain of movements is wrong but it does not influence the quality of other elements of the technique.

b. Chain defects are when one mistake causes others, for example, a wrong grip on the racquet adversely affects the moves of a tennis player. Correct the grip and the strokes will improve too. You cannot eliminate stroke defects without first correcting the grip. Another example: Lifting the head too fast during the low start for sprints may cause lifting the trunk too soon and thus ruin the start.

3. Unfixed and fixed

a. Unfixed defects are mistakes that are not habitual, not automatized yet, often occurring at early stages of learning. Correct mistakes as soon as they are formed to prevent them turning into fixed ones.

b. Fixed defects are mistakes that are turned into habits, automatized movements, which makes their removal difficult. Sometimes it is more efficient to learn a new technique than to correct fixed mistakes in the old one.

4. Competitive and noncompetitive

a. Competitive mistakes occur only during competitions. The athlete performs well during workout but, under the stress of competition and with opponents' interference, deviates from correct technique.

b. Noncompetitive mistakes occur during workouts. The athlete makes technical mistakes even under the easy conditions of the workout—such mistakes are sure to be repeated during competition.

5. Athlete-related and coach-related

a. Athlete-related mistakes are those faults committed in spite of proper teaching, as for example, because of a lack of talent, not paying attention to demonstrations and explanations, wrong focus and direction of attention when applying technique, too high or too low motivation, lack of confidence, or being overly excitable.

b. Coach-related mistakes are those faults due to wrong demonstration, lack of proper explanation, applying wrong teaching method, teaching when athletes are tired, bad organization of the workout, violating principles of didactics (exercises too difficult), or a low level of knowledge and skills.

The first attempt at a technique is very important. It will stay in an athlete's memory for a long time. Make sure that you do your best in choosing and arranging exercises so as to make the first try a success.

Typical causes of technical mistakes are:

a) insufficient general physical fitness or lack of optimal level of needed motor ability (Sharkey 1986);

b) not understanding the essence of the technique or exercise;

c) improper image of the technique;

d) difficulty in receiving and interpreting kinesthetic signals;

e) wrong emotional state while learning (too excited, bored, ashamed, scared); and

f) adverse conditions of learning (bad light, too cold, too hot, bad equipment).

To remove technical mistakes athletes should initially exercise in eased up conditions, without stress, paying attention only to the correct form of the movement. Correct one mistake at a time. Otherwise you will overwhelm a child's ability to focus attention. Only when one mistake is corrected can you start to work on the next one. Later on, you must use situations demanding divisibility of attention, making choices, dealing with surprising actions—in other words, situations similar to contests. In a contest an athlete must decide what to do rather than how to do it. The athlete's attention (in open habit sports) is concentrated on the actions of the opponent, distancing, and timing, and not on how to move. This is why a technical mistake cannot be removed by strictly technical exercises even if the mistake is not caused by insufficient strength, speed, endurance, flexibility, or coordination. In those cases when an athlete makes a technical mistake because of insufficient development of any motor ability, that ability must be improved first before applying technical exercises to correct the mistake.

Carefully choose exercises and other means of teaching and perfecting technique so as to limit the number and gravity of mistakes. Mistakes are inevitable while learning new skills, but right demonstration, description, and choice of exercises, and immediate feedback and accurate corrections may prevent solidification of mistakes into habits.

Evaluation of technical training

There are several ways to evaluate the process of training in technique.

1. Coach's observation and recording the technical behavior (use of and proficiency with techniques) of an athlete on special forms

2. Tests of techniques and of special fitness

3. Biomechanical analysis

4. Video record

5. Analysis of official documents (for example: score sheets)

The above methods of gathering information on an athlete's use of technique provide you with data that you can use for direct or indirect evaluation of the athlete's technical proficiency.

Table 52. Examples of data used for direct evaluation of technique (direct criteria) (Bober 1992)

Sports discipline	Indicator	Desired value
Basketball	% of accurate throws	maximum
Soccer	% of accurate shots from an assigned distance and at assigned part of the goal	maximum
Volleyball	number of good receptions and passes per time unit	maximum
Team handball	time of running and dribbling on an assigned distance	minimum
High jump (track and field)	a. position of general center of gravity in relation to the bar, b. lowering of the general center of gravity at the end of run-up in Fosbury flop	a) minimum (natural 6.0" scissors 2.6" flop -3.3") b) optimum (43-45% of body height)
Long jump (track and field)	% of foot length on which reaction force acts	optimum (38-68%)
Ski jump	ratio of distance to velocity upon leaving the chute	maximum
Butterfly (swimming)	deviation of speed at any instant from average speed	minimum
Backstroke (swimming)	frequency of movement cycle	optimum (0.77 Hz)
Low start (track and field sprints)	% of body weight supported by arms at the "set" command	optimum (73-82%)
Sprinting (track and field)	length of stride, angular velocity of bending the knee before support phase	optimum (stride length 1.14-1.26 of body length, angular velocity 3-6 rad/s)
Speed skating (1500 m to 3000 m)	angle between trunk and transverse plane	optimum (15°)
X-country skiing	ratio of the push-off phase to duration of the whole step (on flat surface)	optimum (60%)

Table 53. Examples of data used for indirect evaluation of technique (indirect criteria) (Bober 1992)

Sports discipline	Indicator	Desired value
Basketball	time difference between jump from the layout with and without ball	minimum
Team handball	time difference between agility run while dribbling the ball and without the ball	minimum
Running (track and field)	ratio of work to energy expenditure	1
Hurdles	time difference between running hurdles and sprint on the same distance	minimum
High jump	difference between height of the bar and the body height	maximum
Acrobatics (somersault on a trampoline)	time difference between simple jump and the somersault	minimum

12

TACTICS

The chapter on techniques inevitably had references to tactics interlaced. Making techniques second permits an athlete to focus on the interplay of techniques and tactics necessary in any sports engagement, an interplay embodied in the term **technical-tactical skills.** This chapter focuses on the tactical side of that equation.

Tactics refers to ways of conducting a sports contention that further achieving a set goal. In a sports contest effective tactics are those that give advantage at the time and place crucial for the outcome. Racing across the field or rink and putting the ball or puck in the goal when the clock is stopped, or making a wrestling takedown out of bounds, no matter how good it looks, counts for nothing while a less spectacular action done when it counts scores. Choice of tactics is determined by the athlete's and by his or her opponent's quantity and quality of techniques, their physical abilities, personality traits, and mental strength. The importance of tactics differs in various sports disciplines, being greater in ball games and individual contact sports than in gymnastics or in track and field. In track and field's running events, for example, tactics refers mainly to the evaluation of opponents and then distribution of energy; in jumps and throws it is also deciding which attempts to skip and which attempts to concentrate on. In gymnastics tactics will relate to planning the routines to accentuate the strong points of the gymnast.

Preconditions of teaching tactics

There are several preconditions to teaching tactics.

- Sufficient fitness
- Sufficient technical skills
- Sufficient mental fitness
- Sufficient knowledge and experience

Experience shows that tactical skills are not just an expression of an athlete's talent. Sudden changes of situation, quick switching from attack to defense and from defense to attack, the need to constantly apply new surprising combinations of techniques, tactical variants, and tactics—all this requires that tactical skills be learned from the very first days of training. An athlete's intuition alone will not suffice. It has to be augmented by solid knowledge and experience.

The purpose of teaching tactics is to develop skills and abilities to organize and effectively wage a winning sports campaign. Teaching tactics has three main goals.

- Instilling knowledge of tactics
- Developing tactical thinking
- Developing tactical skills

These three goals permit dividing the teaching of tactics into theoretical and practical preparation, an artificial division that eases the task of explanation. Instilling knowledge of tactics, for example, although it seems to be strictly theoretical is best done with reference to the practical experiences of the athletes. Developing tactical skills, seemingly a purely practical activity, is based on good knowledge of tactics (theory).

Teaching a theory of tactics starts with the main tactics of the athlete's sports discipline, then teaches the general principles of tactics of sports. Starting from the athlete's own discipline is necessary because children are concrete (not good with abstracts). Besides, you have to teach the tactics simultaneously with the techniques of their sports anyway. Teaching about other sports tactics will give the athlete better insight into his or her sport and let him or her creatively apply tactical concepts from other, related sports.

Teaching tactical theory involves developing the following elements.

- The ability to acquire, classify, and update theoretical knowledge
- Tactical thinking—necessary for using tactical knowledge and skills and for decision making in changing situations
- Anticipation (trying to foresee developments and having alternative actions ready)
- Divisibility of attention—important for acquiring *relevant* information during the action, classifying it, and assigning relative importance

- Willpower and emotional maturity—self-control, perseverance, decisiveness, and courage

Teaching the practical aspects of tactics involves learning the tactical skills and developing the habits of using them. It also develops the self-evaluation needed for determining one's limitations and choosing tactics that take those limitations into account.

Observe the following principles when teaching practical aspects of tactics.

- While teaching technique do not separate it from its tactical setup.
- Reinforce the image of tactical skills acquired during a (practical) workout with theoretical analysis.
- Teach and perfect tactical skills initially without an opponent, then against a passive opponent, then against an active opponent, and finally in competition.
- After athletes have mastered the main tactics, introduce variants of these tactics.
- After athletes vave mastered several variants of the main tactics, teach matching them to various situations for best solutions.
- Use every opportunity to teach the skill of observing and analyzing sports contests—particularly those of future opponents.
- Teach athletes to objectively evaluate their own tactical actions.

There are four stages of learning tactics.

1. Learning particular tactical actions and basic cooperation within a team

2. Learning several relatively adjustable tactical schemes, suitable for typical situations in contests

3. Learning to apply flexibly and precisely mastered tactics and combinations while taking into consideration one's potential.

4. Learning to plan tactics depending on the weaknesses and strength of the opponent and learning to change planned tactics or their variants if evaluation of the opponent turns out to be inaccurate.

Tactical thinking is used for and developed by initial planning of the tactics, carrying them out, and then evaluating their effectiveness. Planning requires gathering information about an opponent and then developing several tactical variants to deal with the opponent's tactics.

Carrying out the planned tactical plans involves first evaluating the correctness of the athlete's choice of tactics. This evaluating is done during at least the first seconds of an engagement and is most evident, for example, in the first round of a boxing match. Maturity of tactical thinking shows itself in creatively and instantly adjusting planned tactics to the current reality—while confronting the opponent. Tactical thinking during the struggle consists of:

- analyzing and accurately evaluating the current situation;
- choosing the most effective actions during particular moments of the struggle; and
- finding the means for most effectively caring out the plan of the match.

Tactical thinking is used in preparing the plan of encounter—the choice of tactics and techniques. Good tactical thinking in ball games contests, for example, is demonstrated in accurate reconnaissance of the opponent, preparing a general tactical plan, setting up attacks well, taking the initiative, imposing one's style of playing, anticipation of an opponent's actions, and showing the skill of changing tactics during the play.

All this depends on an athlete's imagination, correct perception, and interpretation of the actions, which in turn depends most on experience. Correct perception and interpretation of a situation is helped by knowledge of tactical situations. Tactical skills rely on purposeful and planned observation of the opponent, aimed at gathering specific data. The athlete must see and understand movements, actions, and the mental and physical state of the opponent to guess the opponent's tactics. This requires acute perceptiveness because an opponent wants to hide plans and deceive by providing false clues. It is not enough to see—one has to understand the meaning of what one sees. Knowing the names of the techniques one looks at helps with recognizing and classifying them. Imagine a spectator who does not know your sport. The spectator may enjoy the excitement of the struggle and aesthetic qualities of it without ever realizing who wins, who loses, and why. You, on the other hand, see elements of setups, deceptions, planning—that you can name and therefore understand the meaning of. Many coaches make the mistake of teaching techniques and tactics without giving them names and explaining their function in various situations. An athlete who cannot name an opponent's action cannot recognize it, cannot understand the opponent's tactic, and will be surprised by it.

Creative tactical thinking depends on the athlete's mastery of technique so techniques become second nature, and depends on the athlete's fitness so fatigue does not interfere with thinking or with carring out the planned actions.

In gymnastics or figure skating tactical thinking is concerned with exact performance of the routine, foreseeing problem spots, and planning ahead how to recognize and mask trouble. In track and field, swimming, rowing, and other sports where athletes compete against time or space, tactical thinking relates more to deciding how to distribute one's energy—for which attempt should one mobilize more or less of one's energy. In contact sports, racquet sports, and ball games athletes have to accurately perceive, analyze, and react to a situation all in an instant. Knowledge of techniques and tactics, keen senses, speed of thinking, proper focus, and direction of attention are all more important for tactical thinking in this group of sports than in the other two.

Evaluating the effectiveness of tactics refers to confronting the plans with actual performance—what was carried out how and to what effect. In evaluating tactics avoid generalizing too much. What works or does not work against one opponent may not work or may work against another, so neither the athlete nor the coach should discard any given tactic because it does not work in one match.

Principles of tactics

Certain principles of tactics are common for all open-habit sports where the athlete must adjust to changing conditions. These principles are:

1. Continuity of maintaining initiative. Continuity of maintaining initiative means that athletes ought to seize the initiative and keep it no matter if they attack or defend.

2. Active defense. Active defense means that athletes must be active all the time so that, even when defending, they create opportunities for counterattacking.

3. Counterattack. Skill at counterattacking helps keep the defense active, taking the initiative away from the opponent and putting him or her on the defensive.

4. Surprise. Surprise can be achieved by using any kind of tactics as long as the opponent cannot quickly adjust to it. The tactic itself can be known to the opponent—it just has to be applied unexpectedly.

5. Change of plans and variants. Skillful changes of tactical plans and of their variants can surprise opponents and are a must when facing changing situations. Research shows that athletes or teams that mastered 3-4 tactics (and their variants) win. Knowing a greater number of tactics (with their variants) but less well is not advantageous.

6. Observation of future opponents. Objective evaluation of one's own and of opponent's tactics is necessary for planning tactical training. Evaluation of an opponent's tactics is often easier than of one's own. To get objective information do not start with your opponent's tactics but first evaluate yourself and how you compare to your opponent.

Teaching tactics

1. Theoretical preparation (Ulatowski 1971)

In the preparatory period of macrocycle, the athlete concentrates on:

- improving knowledge of theory of the athlete's own sport;
- learning new contest rules; and
- studying new tactics and new tactical variants of known tactics.

In the main competitive period, the athlete:

- acquaints him- or herself with the opponent's tactics;
- learns the rules and regulations of competitions; and
- familiarizes him- or herself with the sites of future competitions (this is also needed for visualization, an essential element of mental preparation).

In the transitory period, after the main competitions, the athlete:

- analyzes causes of achievements and failures;
- analyzes tactics applied in the competitive period; and
- devises tactical concepts for the new macrocycle.

2. Practical preparation (Ulatowski 1971)

In the preparatory period, the athlete:

- practices new tactics and new tactical variants; and
- perfects physical fitness, techniques, and mental abilities as required by new tactics.

In the main competitive period, the athlete:

- perfects various tactics; and
- corrects errors.

Principles of teaching tactics (Weineck 1983)

1. Teach tactics early and together with techniques.

2. Intensify tactical training from ages 10 to 13. This is the sensitive period of motor development, especially of coordination, and thus the best time for learning techniques and tactics.

3. Develop the athlete's mind as well as his or her body. The athlete needs to know rules and regulations and have the ability to adjust tactics to changes in these rules. Developing the athlete's mental activity is also essential to the ability to distinguish the important from the unimportant. The athlete needs knowledge of tactics of other sports and ability to apply this knowledge to his or her sport. Athletes, from the very beginning of their training, should be able to plan tactical actions, carry them out, and evaluate them. Achieving this goal requires athletes' full participation in planning and preparation for competitions they are going to take part in and in evaluating their performance after competitions.

4. The athlete needs to learn tactics first without an opponent, then with a passive opponent, then with an active opponent who performs known and preannounced actions, then in free struggle and in competition.

5. Teach only one tactical variant per workout. Following this principle will keep athletes from confusing one maneuver or tactic with another. They will remember each tactic better.

6. Use demonstration to teach new tactics and variants of tactics. Even advanced athletes, who can learn and perfect new techniques often without having it demonstrated to them, benefit from seeing demonstra-

tions of tactics. Children need a good demonstration even more. Tactical situations involve more details than single techniques or simple combinations. There is more to pay attention to—position and movements of all players on the field, distance to the lines, safety areas, position of the referee, opponents' actions and intentions to name a few examples.

Methods of teaching tactics

There are two basic ways of teaching tactical skills.

1. Teaching and developing the ability to use specific, set tactical schemes

2. Developing the ability to make correct decisions in various situations

The goal is for the athlete to be able both to carry out preplanned tactics and recognize opponent's tactics as well as to improvise, taking full advantage of arising opportunities.

All teaching method discussed in previous chapters are used to teach tactics and in addition there are specific methods of teaching tactics. These specific methods form four groups (Raczek 1991).

1. Methods of teaching how to distribute efforts such as:

- exact realization of planned distribution of effort;
- increasing athlete's activity and intensity of actions;
- extending the distance to the finish, time of play, or fighting until a given score is reached;
- introducing rested opponents during the practice contest; and
- quick mobilization for effort—on a signal, for example.

2. Methods of teaching purposeful application of techniques. Athletes' effectiveness depends not so much on the number of techniques mastered as on the skill to use them in the right situations. Methods that teach this skill are:

- exercises requiring choosing the right techniques—for example, an exercise partner attacks in ways that open him or her up only for certain counters;

- introducing an opponent who acts with increasing intensity, while also increasing the variety of techniques he or she uses;

- mock competition against exercise partners who simulate tactics of the future opponent; and

- assigning development of a tactical plan.

3. Methods of teaching cooperation with partners (applicable in team sports):

- introducing reserve players during practice games; and

- teaching and practicing combinations and tactical variants that involve all players on the field and change the roles of all players.

4. Methods of teaching the skill of changing tactics during the contest:

- switching combinations and tactics on a signal;

- sudden situation changes requiring quick and creative adjustment of tactics; and

- competing against opponents that differ in their style and their tactics.

Recap

The athlete is not only the subject in a sports contest but also the object of constant attacks. He or she must be intellectually and emotionally prepared to take it, act intelligently and quickly, have good self-control, and must like to cooperate in a team. All these characteristics are best developed in conditions similar to a contest or in the contests themselves. In such conditions the tactically well-prepared athlete will learn understanding the tactical task, evaluating the situation, his or her place in it, self-control, being calm, dealing with obstacles, and trusting the coach. All this will prevent stress that may otherwise result from the difference between the athlete's expectations and reality.

Having developed such characteristics means intellectual and emotional readiness for sports competition.

Coaches and instructors, be warned: oversimplification and lowering standards in teaching tactics may prevent an athlete from learning self-reliance in analyzing situations and making decisions. Athletes who believe the fallacy that to attack they must have superiority, when they feel that they haven't got it, get discouraged and passive and lose the contest. Tactical choices can make the difference. It is possible to win against an opponent that is superior in certain respects as long as one chooses his or her tactics wisely—to fully use his or her strengths and take advantage of an opponent's weaknesses— and then carries these tactics out.

13

SAMPLE P. E. LESSONS

These examples show how you can teach skills while maintaining a high level of activity. These lessons or workouts are planned to minimize down time and have the children kids flow from one activity to the next.

P. E. Lesson for Children—Developing Endurance

Group size—15-20
Age—10-12
Location—school's field
Equipment—10 markers, on the field drawn huge figure of a moose
Duration—50 minutes
Goal—running endurance
Task—acquainting with new endurance exercises

Workout part	Exercises	Time or reps	Notes on organization and methodology
I. 15 min.	1. Assembly in file, greeting, count off to two, and announcement of today's task	2 min.	Giving the goal and the task has intellectual, educational, and motivational significance.
	2. Marching and singing or clapping out a rhythm		In line around the field
	3. Fast marching and singing or clapping out a faster rhythm		In line around the field
	4. Jog forward and circle one arm forward.	2 times across the field	In a file along the long axis of the field. Change arm after each crossing of the field.
	5. Jog backward and circle one arm backward.	2 times across the field	In a file along the long axis of the field. Change arm after each crossing of the field.

Workout part	Exercises	Time or reps	Notes on organization and methodology
I. (cont.) 15 min.	6. Imitation of picking up a ball, throwing it up, and catching while jumping	5 times	Scattered, facing the teacher.
	7. Running on all fours in all directions	0.5 min.	Only if grass surface.
	8. In pairs, grip each other's right hand and off balance each other.	0.5 min.	Instead of 7 if no grass.
	9. Leg raises to the front.	6 reps per leg.	
	10. Jumps in pairs, facing each other, hands on each other's shoulders	6-8 jumps	Each pair consists of "1" and "2." When "1" jumps "2" presses down on "1's" shoulders.
	11. Tag "stork." The stork stands on one leg, puts one arm under his or her raised thigh, and holds his or her nose with the hand of that arm.	1-2 min.	Two or three storks chase simultaneously. Limit the area for the action.
II. 25 min.	1. Jog-run-jog-run-jog-run	3-4 times	In line, jog along diagonal lines and run along two short sides of the field.
	2. Run along labyrinth (see figure 38 on page 112).	4-5 times	Use whole field. Teacher leads.
	3. Run in pairs holding each other by the hand.	0.5 min.	One partner resists. Change roles.
	4. Run along a thunderbolt (see figure 38 page 112).	2 times	
	5. Stand and spread legs maximally to the sides, arms spread sideways.	5-8 sec.	Scattered, facing the teacher.
	6. Run along shape of the moose (see figure 38 page 112).	3 times	Run very fast along the moose's legs and horns.
III. 10 min.	1. Jog around the school building, take deep breath while raising arms, exhale while lowering arms.	3 min.	Leader—one of students
	2. Go to a shower.		

Note: With younger children, stress the versatile development of the whole person, aerobic character of effort, variety of exercises, play forms of exercises, imagination, and divert attention away from fatigue, which is the point of the runs along the shape of the thunderbolt, labyrinth, and moose.

P. E. Lesson for Youth—Developing Endurance

Group size—15-20
Age—15-18
Location—woods, hills or local terrain
Equipment—trees and bushes, or what have you
Duration—60 minutes
Goal—running endurance
Task—maintaining the pace of running

Workout part	Exercises	Time or reps	Notes on organization and methodology
I. 20 min.	1. Assembly in file, greeting, and announcement of today's task	2 min.	
	2. March in extended file across terrain.	2-3 min.	
	3. Jog across terrain.	2-3 min.	In line, lead by coach/teacher
	4. Easy run, slalom among trees or landscape features.	5 min.	Lead by designated student
	5. March uphill, on signal on all fours.	5 min.	In file
	6. Running up the tree (or wall)	1 min.	Who will make more steps
	7. Try to uproot the tree (or goalpost).	5-8 reps	
	8. Support the leg on the tree and lean trunk in all directions.	5 reps per leg	Place leg as high as possible.
	9. Skip A uphill	1 min.	In file
	10. Running hurdles over bushes	1-2 min.	In line, change attacking leg
	11. Jog and every few steps jump and reach to a tree branch.	2 min.	In line, change the reaching arm
	12. Run downhill.	3-5 reps	Distance 50-80 meters
II. 30 min.	1. Accelerations in "pyramid run": jog 30 sec. and run 30 sec.; jog 30 sec. and run 45 sec.; jog 30 sec. and run 60 sec.; jog 30 sec. and run 75 sec.; jog 30 sec. and run 60 sec.; jog 30 sec. and run 45 sec.; jog 30 sec. and run 30 sec.; 30 sec. jog	10 min.	Jogging always 30 sec., pay attention to proper sprinter's arms' work
	2. Stretching (lunges, splits)	5 min.	Hold the stretch.

Workout part	Exercises	Time or reps	Notes on organization and methodology
II. (cont.) 30 min.	3. Run intervals of 500-600 meters at 80% of HR_{max}	15 min.	Maintain running pace, correct the technique, fill breaks by jogging 2-3 min.
III. 10 min.	1. Climb any tree and try to relax lying on a branch, or if there are no trees, lie supine on the ground and "write" words with limbs. If lying on the ground is not possible, students can stand in pairs facing each other, one student "writes" letters or words with a hand and the other student tries to read them.	5 min.	
	2. Continuous jogging back to place of assembly	5 min.	
	3. Go to a shower.		

Notes: With youth of this age (15-18), stress mixed anaerobic-aerobic efforts because of the increased activity of fructokinase—an enzyme facilitating anaerobic processes.

Use more task-oriented methods than play, and teach details of running technique.

P. E. Lesson for Children—Developing Strength

Group size—15-20
Age—10-12
Location—school's gym
Equipment—8-10 medicine balls (2 kg)
Duration—45 minutes
Goal—general strength training
Task—acquainting with strength exercises with medicine ball

Workout part	Exercises	Time or reps	Notes on organization and methodology
I. 12-15 min.	1. Assembly in double file, greeting, and announcement of today's task.	2 min.	
	2. Jog all over the floor among medicine balls.	2 min.	Balls scattered all over the floor before the workout
	3. Run on all fours among the balls.	1 min.	End up by collecting the balls.
	4. Game: "Catch the snake's tail"	4 min.	Make two snakes.
	5. Walk on all fours with back toward the floor.	0.5 min.	Walk in any direction.
	6. Run in pairs holding each other by the hand.	1 min.	Around the gym
	7. Run pushing the partner.	1 min.	Around the gym
	8. Jump alternatively on one and on both legs over supine partner.	1 min.	Partner lies on his or her back, change after 30 seconds.
	9. Synchronized crawling in pairs	1 min.	Both partners do the same movements.
	10. Cock fight in a half squat	0.5 min.	In pairs
	11. Jog around the gym, every other student picks up a medicine ball	1 min.	Initially in one line then form two lines, only one line holds the balls
II. 25 min.	1. Throw the ball for distance	5 min.	In pairs, facing each other
	2. Try to take the ball away	5 min.	In pairs, alternate the defender and the attacker
	3. Squat holding the ball	2 min.	Partner counts, after one min. switch

Workout part	Exercises	Time or reps	Notes on organization and methodology
II. (cont.) 25 min.	4. Throw the ball backward overhead.	1 min.	Partner tries to catch the ball.
	5. Jump forward and sideways over the ball.	10 reps	Each rep is one cycle (forward jump, quarter turn, sideways jump, quarter turn).
	6. Pushups with hands on the ball	max.	One works, other counts, then switch.
	7. Throw the ball forward from behind the head to the partner.	10 reps	After the throw, squat and touch the floor with hands.
	8. Kick the ball to the partner.	10 reps	Alternate the legs (five reps per leg).
	9. Lying on the floor, feet to feet, hand the ball to the partner.	5 min.	Start with the ball on the floor, held in outstretched arms behind the head.
	10. Basketball game "to five passes" (five passes=one point)	5-8 min.	10.Four teams, two teams play on each half of the floor
III. 5 min.	1. Balance the ball on the head.		Partner counts seconds.
	2. March holding the ball in both hands behind the back.		Push chest forward.
	3. Return the balls.		As directed by the teacher
	4. Go to a shower.		

Note: If children are bored with some exercises of part II, teacher can do 1 or 2 games and free exercises with the ball. The whole workout or lesson should not be dedicated strictly to strength exercises because at this age other exercises, such as speed or agility exercises, still develop strength.

P. E. Lesson for Youth—Developing Strength

Group size—15-20
Age—15-18
Location—school's gym
Equipment—10 medicine balls (2-4 kg), jump rope, weightlifting bar, chinning bar, gymnastic box
Duration—50 minutes
Goal—general strength training
Task—acquainting with circuit training

Workout part	Exercises	Time or reps	Notes on organization and methodology
I. 12-15 min.	1. Assembly in double file, greeting, and announcement of today's task	2 min.	
	2. Arm circles forward and backward	0.5-1 min.	Youth scattered around the gym
	3. Jog in place.	0.5 min.	Same as above
	4. Jog in place, clap hands under the knee.	1 min.	Clap on signal.
	5. Jog around the gym, make pairs.	0.5 min.	
	6. In pairs, grip each other's hand, pull partner off balance.	1-2 min.	Hold by the same hands, change hands.
	7. In pairs, both hands on each other's shoulders, push partner off balance.	1-2 min.	
	8. In pairs, one jumps up, other presses down on his or her shoulders.	2 min.	Change roles after one minute.
	9. In pairs, lying on the floor face to face, arm wrestle.	1-2 min.	Change arm after each match.
	10. In pairs, tag partner on the lower leg.	1 min.	This is a standing exercise
II. 30 min.	1. Form six teams.	1 min.	Coach appoints six captains, captains recruit 2-3 teammates.
	2. Circuit training	29 min.	Make three circuits.
	2a. First station—Throw medicine ball at the wall	7-10 rep	Throw at full power.
	2b. Second station—Jump rope, hop on both feet	max rep	Until next station is free

Workout part	Exercises	Time or reps	Notes on organization and methodology
II. (cont.) 30 min.	2c. Third station—Chin-ups on the bar	7-10 rep	Girls and weaker youth do bent arm hang.
	2d. Fourth station—Lie prone on the box, feet secured, raise trunk until level with floor, clap hands in front of the head.	max rep	Partner may hold the feet.
	2e. Fifth station—Push-ups	7-10 rep	Girls and weaker youth do half push-ups.
	2f. Sixth station—Curls with bar		In pairs, bar held in natural grip
III. 3-5 min.	1. Clean up the stations.		
	2. March in a line, swing arms back and forth in horizontal plane.		
	3. March, inhale raising arms above head, exhale lowering arms.		
	4. Lie on the back, eyes closed, raise one leg off the floor and "write" one's name with the foot.		Repeat with the other leg.
	5. Go to a shower.		

Note: Maintain a high pace of movements in part II of the workout, to develop endurance besides strength. In case youth are overly tired make the whole group do a few flexibility exercises.

P. E. Lesson for Children—Developing Speed

Group size—15-20
Age—10-12
Location—school's gym
Equipment—4 volleyballs, 14-16 bean bags
Duration—45 minutes
Goal—encouraging participation in exercises and games developing speed
Task—improving reaction time

Workout part	Exercises	Time or reps	Notes on organization and methodology
I. 20 min.	1. Assembly in a circle, greeting, and announcement of today's task	2 min.	Teacher in the center
	2. Easy run toward the center and back	5-6 rep	Hold hands running toward the center, raise arms in front of the teacher, then run backward lowering the arms.
	3. Scattered around the gym, on signal: a) do cross-legged squat, hands on knees b) lie on the abdomen, arms raised c) sit with legs apart, arms reach forward	2-3 min.	Demo during exercise #2 a) one clap b) two claps c) three claps Point out the last one to react.
	4. Game: "Puddle" (In a circle, face center, hold hands, run around and pull others inside to the puddle).	2-3 min.	Change direction of circling.
	5. Game: "Avalanche" (Scattered around, one chases rest like tag, the caught ones join chaser, and holding each other's hands catch others)	until all caught	
	6. Relay with dribbling and throwing the ball up: catch, dribble, catch, throw, catch, dribble, and so on until coming close to a wall, throw at the wall, catch, turn around, pass to next in line, go to the back of the line.	2 turns	Make four teams. Point out the winning team. Stay in teams for next exercise.
	7. Game: "Star" (The same four teams assemble in four lines every 90° around a circle, everybody facing the center. At a signal teams shift 90° along the circle. Fastest and most orderly team wins.)	4 rotations	Two full rotations clockwise, two counterclockwise. After each complete rotation change positions within teams, those that stood close to the center go to the end of their team's line.

Workout part	Exercises	Time or reps	Notes on organization and methodology
I. (cont.) 20 min.	8. In pairs, push each other off balance.	2-3 min.	
	9. "Pedaling" while lying on the back	1 min.	
II. 20 min.	1. Form 2 or 4 teams. One at a time run and jump over bean bags, return walking to the end of the team line.	3 reps	Bean bags every 1 meter (3 feet) in 2 (7 meter) or 4 (3.5 meter) lines.
	2. Jog around the gym, accelerate on signal.	4 circles	After two circles change direction.
	3. Race "There and back" along the length of the gym and touch the end wall, from high start, from sitting with legs straight, from lying on the back with head toward direction of the run. Return to the end of the team and assume the same starting position.	3-4 min.	In 2 or 4 teams
	4. Game: "Day and night" (Two files, one called 'day' the other 'night,' stand back to back along the center of the gym. Teacher shouts 'day' and the 'day' line chases 'night' and vice versa.	2-3 min.	
	5. Run with high knee raises, initially in place then in various directions as ordered by teacher	2 min.	Start scattered just as the 'day and night' had ended
III. 3-5 min.	1. Lie on the back, raise legs and touch floor behind the head with toes.	8 reps	Scattered as in the above
	2. Lie on the back, raise one leg off the floor and "draw" geometrical figures with the foot.		Do each figure with right and left leg
	3. Stand up without using hands.		
	4. Teacher praises the most active ones.		
	5. Go to a shower.		

Note: Conducting a workout with children, use games and plays that stress speed of reaction and maximal speed of movements.

In the speed workout the part I (the warm-up) is longer than in other workouts and it may be longer than the part II, the (main) part.

P. E. Lesson for Youth—Developing Speed

Group size—15-20
Age—14-16
Location—stadium
Equipment—8-10 gymnastic canes
Duration—45 minutes
Goal— improving speed
Task—perfection of the low start

Workout part	Exercises	Time or reps	Notes on organization and methodology
I. 15 min.	1. Assembly in a file, greeting, and announcement of today's task	2 min.	
	2. Jog around the track.	1 lap	
	3. Easy run with quick turns while maintaining the same direction of running	1-2 min.	One turn clockwise, second counterclockwise, etc.
	4. Skip A (knees high) while holding hands with arms crossed	1 min.	See illustration, p. 79. Start in a file, along the long side of the field.
	5. Chain tug (One file, every other student faces back, students hook up their elbows, the side that makes chain move in the direction they face wins.)	1-2 min.	
	6. Game of tag in pairs—tag by slapping the buttock	2-3 min.	
	7. High start after forward roll	3-5 reps	Scattered, on the grass, all face in the same direction
	8. March while circling arms forward and backward	1 min.	March toward designated side of the track.
II. 25 min.	1. Bound along the track. Leap into footsteps of the preceding student.	1-2 min.	In one line, on the track, knee of the leading leg firmly bent
	2. Lunge forward, hold low position, hands on the front knee.	1-2 min.	Scattered on the grass
	3. Attempt front split.	1-2 min.	Switch legs
	4. In pairs, chase partner that starts standing 2 meters ahead	2-3 min.	On the track, teacher gives signal.

Workout part	Exercises	Time or reps	Notes on organization and methodology
II. (cont.) 25 min.	5. Swing up leg bent at the knee, holding on to partner's shoulder.	5-6 reps	Face in opposing directions; and swing the knee on the opposite side from the shoulder being held.
	6. Low start and sprint to a cane held by partner 3-5 meters away.	5-6 reps each	On the track, change roles after each start.
	7. Jog with accelerations.	1/2 lap	In a line, on the track, accelerate on signal (whistle).
	8. Easy run with acceleration on the curve	1 lap	In line, on the track
	9. Jog in place on the grass, on signal assume low start position.	1-2 min	
III. 5 min.	1. Relax jogging on the grass		In groups, talking allowed
	2. Pointing out those exercising best		In a loose group
	3. Go to a shower.		

Notes: With this age group accentuate speed-strength exercises.

This workout is designed for track and field athletes.

P. E. Lesson for Children—Basketball

Group size—15-20
Age—10-12
Location—school's gym
Equipment—15-20 basketballs
Duration—45 minutes
Goal—learning techniques of basketball
Task—learning grip and high pass

Workout part	Exercises	Time or reps	Notes on organization and methodology
I. 15 min.	1. Assembly in one file, greeting. Introduction—individually—each student runs to the teachers and gives "high five"	2 min.	Balls prepared before the lesson form a slalom
	2. Explanation and demonstration of today's task	1 min.	
	3. Count to two in file, right turn (form a line)		
	4. Jogging "slalom" among balls while circling one arm forward at a time	Teacher decides	Teacher goes to the head of line and leads jogging
	5. Change direction of jogging and make arm circles backward.	Teacher decides	
	6. Jogging "slalom" among balls, touching the balls with one arm and then withdrawing it quickly	Teacher decides	
	7. Pick up the nearest ball and jog in place. Teacher demonstrates correct technique of the grip.	Teacher decides	Teacher takes such a position that everybody can see him or her
	8. Lean forward, touch the floor with the ball, count to three, straighten up and raise the ball as high as possible, count to three.	Teacher decides	
	9. Jog to another location on the court.		
	10. In pairs, jump up while partner resists by pressing on jumper's shoulders. "Ones" pair with "twos," ball on the floor by the "one's" foot, "two" faces "one," "one" puts one foot on the ball, hands on the "two's" shoulders and presses down. "Two" tries to jump up.	Teacher decides	After X repetitions change roles.

Workout part	Exercises	Time or reps	Notes on organization and methodology
II. 25 min.	1. Both partners grip the ball and struggle for it.	Teacher decides	
	2. Take the ball and come close to the wall, bounce the ball off the wall, and catch as demonstrated by teacher in warm-up, item 7.	Teacher decides	
	3. Play tag with ball held in proper grip. The chaser (without the ball) has to touch the escaping student's ball. There can be more than one chaser.	Teacher decides	
	4. Jog following the teacher, form pairs ("one's" with "two's") one ball per pair		
	5. Stop and face each other in pairs, practice passes	Teacher decides	
	6. Practice passes in pairs while walking forward and backward.	Teacher decides	
	7. Practice passes in pairs while moving to the sides.	Teacher decides	
	8. Practice passes while running up to the arriving ball.	Teacher decides	
	9. Form two circles (one "ones," one "twos") each with one student in center. Pass the ball between center student and others	Teacher decides	
	10. Play "to five passes" (five passes=one point)	Teacher decides	Each circle is now a team. Extra balls taken away by the teacher
III. 5 min.	1. Jog to the ball, balance it on head	Teacher decides	
	2. Sit down on the floor, place ball between feet, touch the ball and count to three or put hands on the ball and slowly roll it forward as far as possible.	Teacher decides	
	3. Sit on the ball—who will make best Rodin's "Thinker"	Teacher decides	
	4. Stand up, walk to the exit, and give your ball to the teacher.		
	5. Go to a shower.		

P. E. Lesson for Children—Soccer

Group size—15-20
Age—9-11
Location—soccer field
Equipment—15-20 light soccer balls, 10-14 cones
Duration—45 minutes
Goal—learning techniques of soccer
Task—learning technique of controlling the ball, perfection of pass, shot with upper and inner surface of the foot, high pass

Workout part	Exercises	Time or reps	Notes on organization and methodology
I. 15 min.	1. Assembly in one file, greeting, count off to four, distribution of balls	2 min.	Along longer side of the field. Appointed student takes bag with balls to one end of the file and moving down the file gives a ball to each student.
	2. Run leading the ball across the field.	Teacher decides	Spread in the file but do not switch place. Keep ball close to the foot.
	3. "Ones" and "threes"on one side of the field, "twos" and "fours" on the other. On command "Change" students run to the opposite side of the field, first without balls, and next leading the ball.	Teacher decides	
	4. Balls lined up on one side of the field, students divided into four teams on the other. On signal run to one's ball, and then lead it back to their spot on the starting line. Team that does it first wins.	Teacher decides	
	5. Students scatter. Kick up the ball dropped from hands and when it falls down, catch it after one bounce.	Teacher decides	
	6. Kick up the ball dropped from hands and when it falls down, jump up and catch it before it lands.	Teacher decides	
	7. Kick up the ball dropped from hands and when it falls down, turn around and catch it before it lands.	Teacher decides	
	8. Kick up the ball dropped from hands, make a forward roll and catch the ball when it falls down.	Teacher decides	

Workout part	Exercises	Time or reps	Notes on organization and methodology
I. (cont.) 15 min.	9. Two teams lined up along the center of the field, each faces its own goalpost (no goalkeeper). On signal students lead the ball and 16 meters from the goalpost shoot. Team that gets more goals wins.	Teacher decides	
II. 25-30 min.	1. Penalty shots with inner and upper surface of the foot.	Teacher decides	
	2. Game 1:1 with one goalpost (no goalie).	Teacher decides	
	3. Two teams play, two goalposts (1-2 meter wide, no goalies.	Teacher decides	
	4. Game: "Goalie and sniper" (Students in pairs take turns shooting and goalkeeping.)	Teacher decides	Each pair places cones to mark two goalposts 3 meter wide facing each other and 10 meters apart.
III. 5 min.	1. Lie supine on the ball , roll body forward and backward.	Teacher decides	
	2. Lie supine, ball on the abdomen, deep breathing.	Teacher decides	
	3. Return ball to the teacher.		
	4. Go to a shower.		

P. E. Lesson for Children—Volleyball

Group size—15-20
Age—9-11
Location—school's gym
Equipment—15-20 volleyballs
Duration—45 minutes
Goal—learning techniques of volleyball
Task—learning technique of the bump

Workout part	Exercises	Time or reps	Notes on organization and methodology
I. 15 min.	1. Assembly	2 min.	
	2. Tag in pairs	1 min.	
	3. Tag in pairs, hold each other's right then left hands. Tag on the calf.	2 min.	Switch hands after 1 min. This game forces moving in low position (strongly bent legs).
	4. Jog and pass the ball from hand to hand around the waist.	Teacher decides	
	5. Jog, throw the ball up with both hands and catch it with both hands.	Teacher decides	Elbows straight at the moment of release, catch above the head with elbows slightly bent. Optionally hands can be positioned as in upper reception.
	6. Jog, hold the ball behind the back and throw it up and catch it in front.	Teacher decides	
	7. March, throw and catch the ball with the same hand. Change hands.	Teacher decides	
	8. March, throw ball with one hand, catch with the other. Ball flies above the head.	Teacher decides	
	9. March and roll the ball down over the shoulder and upper back from one hand to another.	Teacher decides	Keep switching the hands.
	10. March. Raise knees high and carry the ball under the raised knee.	Teacher decides	
	11. Place ball on the floor and jump over it forward, backward, and side to side.	Teacher decides	

Workout part	Exercises	Time or reps	Notes on organization and methodology
I. (cont.) 15 min.	12. March around one side of the court and along the net. Marching along the net throw the ball over it and catch it by squatting and reaching for it under the net.	Teacher decides	
II. 25-30 min.	1. In pairs face each other standing 6-8 meters apart. Throw ball underhand with both hands, keep the elbows straight. Start the throw from low position and straighten the knees during the throw. Catch the ball with both hands, elbows straight.	Teacher decides	Use one ball, the other one on the floor nearby. Pay attention to bending and straightening the knees during throwing.
	2. Throwing partner turns his or her back toward the catcher and throws the ball with both arms backward over the head. The catcher positions his or her arms as if in upper reception.	Teacher decides	Both partners must bend and straighten their knees as they throw and receive the ball. If the throw is inaccurate catcher moves to it using slide step.
	3. Roll the ball to the partner. Keep arms straight when rolling and when receiving it.	Teacher decides	Low posture, one leg forward.
	4. The same as above but roll the ball once to the left, once to the right to force partner to make 2-3 sliding steps to it.	Teacher decides	To increase intensity use two balls.
	5. Demonstrate the bump.		
	6. In pairs, one sits with legs straight, hands on the floor behind the back. Partner facing him or her stands near his/her feet and holds the ball in outstretched hands at the head level. Without warning release the ball. The sitting partner must position arms so the ball bounces off his or her forearms.	Teacher decides	Change after every 3 reps.
	7. The same as above, instead of sitting partner is lying on the floor.	Teacher decides	The standing partner has to throw the ball up to give more time for falling. Change after every 3 reps.
	8. In pairs, stand 6-7 meters apart and face each other. One throws the ball up and forward the other must move forward and bump it back.	Teacher decides	Tell the class that arms have to be held lower when bumping forward then when bumping up. Pay attention to bent knees and sliding steps. Change after every 3 reps.

Workout part	Exercises	Time or reps	Notes on organization and methodology
II. (cont.) 25-30 min.	9. The same as above but throw ball slightly to the side so the receiver moves to the sides.	Teacher decides	To increase intensity use two balls.
	10. In pairs, keep passing the ball using the bump.	Teacher decides	
	11. The same as above but with additional tasks after bumping the ball: a) squat and touch the floor, b) sit down, c) jump up, d) move back and return, e) move to the side and return.	Teacher decides	
	12. The same as exercise 10 but change trajectory of the ball—once low, once high.	Teacher decides	
	13. In pairs, bump over the net. Partner moves close to the net, to attack line, to the end line.	Teacher decides	
	14. Everybody takes a ball and bumps it at 2-3 meters above the head. Try to use as little space as possible.	Teacher decides	
	15. The same as above but alternate high and low bumps.	Teacher decides	
	16. The same as above but moving in all directions.	Teacher decides	
	17. Throw the ball far forward, run after it, and bump it up immediately after its first bounce off the floor.	Teacher decides	
	18. Race of the lines. Run to the marker while bumping the ball. Return running to the end of the line.	Teacher decides	3-4 teams. Do each race only once.
	19. The same as exercise 18 but keep bumping the ball during return.	Teacher decides	
III. 5 min.	1. March around the gym. On command, walk high on the toes and raise ball high above the head.	Teacher decides	
	2. March (normal).	Teacher decides	

Workout part	Exercises	Time or reps	Notes on organization and methodology
III. (cont.) 5 min.	3. Stand with legs wide apart. Ball held in straight arms above the head. Trunk circles.	Teacher decides	
	4. Stand with legs wide apart. Roll the ball along figure eight between the feet. Shift bodyweight after the rolling ball to feel stretch in alternate legs.	Teacher decides	
	5. Sit with knees bent, soles on the floor, hands on the floor behind the back. Shake the muscles of the thighs and lower legs.	Teacher decides	Place the ball on the floor.
	6. Lie on the back, arms along the body. Inhale deep and raise the arms forward and up. Exhale and slide the arms sideways back to initial position.	Teacher decides	
	7. Stand up, pick up the ball, march toward the exit and give the ball to the teacher.		
	8. Go to a shower.		

P. E. Lesson for Children—Judo

Group size—15-20
Age—10-12
Location—school's gym, mat
Equipment—15-20 judo jackets and belts
Duration—45 minutes
Goal—learning techniques of judo
Task—learning technique of Supporting Foot Lift-Pull Throw (Sasae Tsurikomi Ashi)—how to pull with arms and when to block the foot

Workout part	Exercises	Time or reps	Notes on organization and methodology
I. 14 min.	1. Assembly, kneeling in one file	1 min.	
	2. Sit and cross legs. Rotate joints starting with the neck and hands, ending with feet.	2 min.	
	3. March on all fours around the mat, initially forward, then sideways, and backward.	2 min.	
	4. March on all fours forward. On command do a rolling front breakfall (Mae-mawari Ukemi).	2 min.	
	5. In pairs, one remains on all fours, facing center of the mat. The other grabs the collar of kneeling partner and does breakfalls over the partner while holding the collar.	2 min.	Form pairs while marching, at the end of exercise 4. Do one breakfall on each side and then change roles.
	6. Stand up, hold partner's right hand in your right hand and do breakfall jumping over his or her forearm.	2 min.	Initially supporting partner bends his or her knees to lower the height of falling. Do one breakfall on each side and then change roles.
	7. Tug. In pairs, stand facing each other, grab partner's one sleeve (right hand left sleeve, while partner grabs the right sleeve with his or her left hand). Try to make him or her step forward.	1 min.	Change hands after each win. Change partners each 15 seconds.
	8. Cock fight. In pairs, stand on right leg, hold left leg with the left hand. Force opponent to step off the mat section or to put left foot on the mat.	2 min.	Place judo belts of each pair on the mat to mark their game area if mat is not divided into sections. Change legs after each win. Change partners each 20 seconds.

Workout part	Exercises	Time or reps	Notes on organization and methodology
II. 26 min.	1. Demonstration of Supporting Foot Lift-Pull Throw (Sasae Tsurikomi Ashi).	1-2 min.	Explain the need for helping the thrower by exaggerating the step of the foot to be blocked, by following his or her pull, and by falling when pull and block are roughly right.
	2. In pairs, practice Supporting Foot Lift-Pull Throw (fit in only, no throw) with one step forward and back.	5 min.	Change sides after each three tries, then (after six tries) change roles. Coach or teacher moves from pair to pair and lets everybody fit in and fits in with everybody so students get the feel of the good technique from both points of view.
	3. In pairs, practice complete Supporting Foot Lift-Pull Throw (fit in and throw) with one step forward and back.	10 min.	Partner falls if pull and block are roughly right. Coach or teacher does the same as in exercise 2, plus throws and lets him- or herself be thrown.
	4. In pairs, standard judo grip, step on opponent's foot and do not let him or her step on yours.	2 min.	
	5. The same as exercise 4 but it is OK to throw if opponent lost balance. The thrown opponent cannot resist.	2 min.	
	6. In pairs, practice complete Supporting Foot Lift-Pull Throw with one step forward and back. As soon as partner falls enter groundwork by applying Broken Upper Four-Corner Hold (Kuzure Kami Shiho Gatame).	2 min.	The ground fighting technique of Upper Four-Corner Hold has to be known from previous workouts.
	7. Demonstration of defense (turning to the side and rolling the opponent over the body) against the Upper Four-Corner Hold.	1 min.	
	8. Individual practice of the defense.	1 min.	
	9. In pairs, one applies Broken Upper Four-Corner Hold, the other tries to get free by turning to the side and rolling the opponent over.	2 min.	

Workout part	Exercises	Time or reps	Notes on organization and methodology
III. 5 min.	1. Sit-ups	1 min.	
	2. Support trunk on straight arms and toes (like push-up). Bring the right leg under the left until right hip touches the mat. Return to initial position and do the opposite side.	1 min.	New exercise so it will be done slowly making it a good cool-down.
	3. Crawling on the back.	0.5-1 min.	Corrective exercise.
	4. Assembly in one file. Bow.	0.5 min.	
	5. Go to a shower.		

APPENDIX A

Balancing Volume and Intensity of Work

Variations of the pulse rate measured in the morning, in comparison to the previous morning and evening values, are used to determine what types of efforts ought to be used in that day's workout.

Long-lasting studies of athletes have revealed that each workout causes changes that are related to an increased tension of either the sympathetic nervous system or the parasympathetic nervous system. Increased tension of the sympathetic system results from using mostly intensive efforts in a workout. Increased tension of the parasympathetic system results from extensive training methods and the employment of a high volume of work in a workout. To gauge the effect of the workout on these two systems, the index of efficiency of recovery (I_{ER}) may be used in conjunction with the evening and morning heart rate comparisons.

$$I_{ER} = \frac{(HR2-HR3)}{(HR2-HR1)} \cdot 100 \qquad \text{Example: } I_{ER} = \frac{(183-121)}{(183-64)} \cdot 100 = 52\%$$

HR1—heart rate before the workout
*HR2—heart rate immediately after the main part of the workout.
HR3—heart rate five minutes after the end of the main part of the workout (in the sixth minute of a cool-down).

*The heart rate stays at the level it was during an exercise for only the first ten seconds after finishing the exercise. For measurements to be accurate start to count the heartbeats no later than two to four seconds after the exercise. Count the beats during six seconds and multiply the number by ten to get the heart rate per minute.

Knowledge of the degree of recovery after the main workout permits corrections in the intensity and volume of workouts of individual athletes:

1) I_{ER} between 50-60%, evening heart rate and morning heart rate up 5-7 beats per minute—means the loads are optimal, not leading to overworking.

2) I_{ER} between 50-60%, evening and morning heart rate down 3-5 beats per minute—means the total load is optimal, but there is an incorrect

proportion between the time of effort and its intensity (the time is too long).

3) I_{ER} between 50-60%, evening and morning heart rate up 10-15 beats per minute—means the total load is optimal but intensity is too high.

4) I_{ER} above 60%, evening and morning heart rate without changes—means the ability to adapt to the load was not fully used and load needs to be increased.

5) I_{ER} above 60%, resting heart rate with a tendency to go down—means it is possible to increase intensity by using more intensive loads.

6) I_{ER} above 60%, resting heart rate up 5-10 beats per minute—means it is possible to increase the time of work, using longer-lasting efforts.

7) I_{ER} less than 50%, resting heart rate without changes—means the total load exceeded the ability to compensate. These symptoms are always accompanied by a loss of weight and a longer reaction time.

8) I_{ER} less than 50%, resting heart rate up—means overworking, caused by loads that are too intensive.

9) I_{ER} less than 50%, resting heart rate down—means overworking, caused by efforts that last too long.

Evening heart rate is taken around 2200 hours (10 P.M.), 10 minutes after going to bed. Morning heart rate is taken 4-5 minutes after waking up, while still in bed. (References to changes in the evening and morning heart rate mean "changes the evening and morning following the main workout relative to the usual approximate average.")

The above recommendations are to be applied to the main workouts of the microcycle, but the measurements and calculations have to be done every day, after every workout, to spot any irregularities of recovery.

This is an adaptation from *Science of Sports Training: How to Plan and Control Training for Peak Performance* by Thomas Kurz (Island Pond, VT: Stadion Publishing Company, Inc.) 1991.

APPENDIX B

Selection

Here are tables with information related to selection for specific sports.

Table A1. Structure of somatic and fitness requirements in selected sports according to Wojciechowski after Raczek (1989)

Sports	Leading features	Essential features	Assisting features
Basketball Volleyball	Body height, agility (softness and precision of movements)	Speed, endurance, jumping ability	Flexibility, strength of the arms and the back
Boxing	Speed, agility	Strength of arms and back, endurance, BMI over 100	Flexibility, strength of legs
Diving Figure skating	Agility, BMI over 100	Strength, flexibility	Endurance, speed
Rowing	Body height, long limbs	Strength of the back, arms, and legs	Speed, flexibility
Speed skating Cross-country skiing Middle- and long-distance runs	Endurance, strength of legs, BMI over 100	Agility, strength of the back, speed	Flexibility, strength of arms
Swimming	Endurance, flexibility of shoulders and ankles, coordination, sense of water	Body height, speed, strength, BMI over 100	Speed
Wrestling	Agility (softness and precision of movements)	Strength of arms, back, legs, endurance, BMI over 100, speed	Flexibility
Shooting	Precise coordination of movements	Endurance	Strength, flexibility, speed
Fencing	Agility in fast movements	Body height, strength of legs, endurance, BMI over 100	Flexibility

Table A2. Tests and norms for track and field sprinters at subsequent stages of training according to Tabachnik after Raczek (1989)

	Initial sports preparation	Basic sports preparation	Sports specialization	Sports perfection	Sports mastery
Test/Age	10-12	13-15	16-17	18-19	20 and older
60 m	9.00-8.60 s	7.60-7.40 s	7.20-7.00 s	6.90-6.80 s	6.65-6.55 s
100 m		11.80-11.60 s	11.3-11.0 s	10.7-10.5 s	10.35-10.25 s
200 m		24.0-23.7 s	22.8-22.5 s	21.5-21.0 s	20.7-20.4 s
30 m low start	5.00 s	4.60-4.40 s	4.30-4.20 s	4.15-4.05 s	3.95-3.85 s
30 m flying start	4.00 s	3.30-3.10 s	3.10-3.00 s	2.85-2.80 s	2.75-2.70 s
150 m		18.2-18.0 s	17.1-16.7 s	16.0-15.8 s	15.2-15.0 s
300 m		40.2-39.2 s	37.2-36.2 s	35.8-35.2 s	33.4-32.6 s
broad jump no pre-run	230-240 cm	250-260 cm	280-285 cm	290-300 cm	300-315 cm
triple jump no pre-run	6.50-6.80 m	7.40-7.80 m	8.00-8.20 m	8.50-9.00 m	9.5-10.0 m
deca jump no pre-run		26-28m	31-32 m	34-35 m	35-36 m

Table A3. Stage goals for female swimmers from 10 to 20 years old according to Svoboda after Raczek (1989)

Age Event	10	11	12	13	14	15	16	17	18	19	20
100m backstroke	1:35.0	1:27.2	1:19.7	1:16.7	1:14.1	1:11.8	1:09.9	1:08.4	1:07.3	1:06.3	1:05.6
200m backstroke	3:23.0	3:06.2	2:50.3	2:43.9	2:38.3	2:35.5	2:19.5	2:26.2	2:23.8	2:21.8	2:20.2
100 m breaststroke	1:48.7	1:39.7	1:30.7	1:27.3	1:24.3	1:21.7	1:19.6	1:17.8	1:16.6	1:15.5	1:14.7
200 m breaststroke	3:50.9	3:34.3	3:14.4	3:07.0	3:00.7	2:55.1	2:50.6	2:46.8	2:44.0	2:41.8	2:40.0
100 m butterfly	1:31.8	1:24.2	1:16.6	1:13.8	1:11.2	1:09.1	1:07.3	1:05.8	1:04.7	1:03.8	1:03.1
200 m butterfly	3:19.3	3:02.8	2:46.1	2:39.9	2:34.4	2:29.7	2:25.8	2:22.6	2:20.2	2:18.3	2:16.8
100 m crawl	1:24.7	1:17.7	1:11.2	1:08.5	1:06.2	1:04.2	1:02.5	1:01.1	1:00.1	0:59.3	0:58.6
200 m crawl	3:01.8	2:46.7	2:32.5	2:26.7	2:21.7	2:17.4	2:13.8	2:10.8	2:08.7	2:06.9	2:05.5
400 m crawl	6:20.3	5:48.8	5:16.4	5:04.4	4:54.1	4:44.1	4:37.7	4:31.6	4:27.0	4:23.3	4:20.5
800 m crawl	13:02.8	11:58.0	10:50.0	10:25.5	10:04.3	9:45.7	9:30.5	9:17.9	9:08.6	9:01.0	8:55.2
200 m medley	3:28.4	3:11.1	2:53.3	2:46.7	2:41.1	2:36.1	2.32.1	2:28.7	2:26.2	2:24.2	2:22.7
400 m medley	7:15.7	6:39.6	6:03.6	5:49.8	5:38.0	5:27.6	5:19.1	5:12.0	5:06.9	5:02.6	4:59.3

Table A4. Fitness tests used for initial selection of children 10-12 years old for cross-country skiing according to Kuzniecowa after Raczek (1989)

Tests		Grades		
		very good	good	sufficient
30 m sprint (flying start) (s)	boys	3.8-4.2	4.3-4.8	4.9-5.2
	girls	4.8-5.1	5.2-6.0	6.1-6.5
60 m sprint (high start) (s)	boys	9.0-9.2	9.3-9.6	9.7-10.0
	girls	9.5-10.0	10.1-10.7	10.8-11.5
Long jump (no pre-run) (cm)	boys	over 180	170-180	160-169
	girls	over 170	160-170	150-159
Triple jump on both legs (no pre-run) (m)	boys	over 6	5-6	4-6
	girls	over 6	5-6	4-6
Vertical jump (cm)	boys	over 55	50-55	40-49
	girls	over 50	45-50	35-44
Push-ups (number)	boys	over 8	5-7	3-4
	girls	over 5	3-4	1-2
Chin-ups (number)	boys	5-8	3-5	1-3
	girls	5-8	3-5	1-3
300 m run (s)	boys	up to 54	55-60	61-70
	girls	up to 58	59-64	65-75
Continuous run at 60% of maximal speed (m)	boys	over 3000	2000-3000	1000-1999
	girls	over 2000	800-2000	500-799

Table A5. Norms of physical fitness test (Raczek 1989)

Test	Age / Sex	7	8	9	10	11	12	13	14	15
Sprints 20 m (s)	boys	4.3	4.1	3.9						
	girls	4.5	4.2	4.0						
40 m (s)	boys	7.6	7.3	6.9						
	girls	8.0	7.6	7.2						
60 m (s)	boys				10.3	10.1	9.7	9.3	8.9	8.7
	girls				10.7	10.5	10.1	9.9	9.8	9.7
Endurance run following a leader (min)	boys and girls	5	6	7						
600 m (min)	girls				2:43	2:42	2:35	2:34	2:33	2:32
1000 m (min)	boys				4:23	4:17	4:08	3:59	3:51	3:45
3 kg medicine ball throw (cm) *—1 kg ball **—2 kg ball	boys	530*	720*	530**	430	480	560	670	820	910
	girls	460*	610*	460**	360	420	490	560	620	640

Table A6. Norms for recruiting children into sports based on indicators of motor abilities development according to Guzalowski (1977) after Raczek (1989)

Motor ability	Age / Sex	8	9	10	11	12	13
Strength —of back muscles (kg) as measured by a dynamometer attached to the floor	boys	65	75	80	100	110	120
	girls	45	60	70	80	90	95
Speed —six repetitions of the cycle: standing on attention, squat, hands on the ground, extend legs back, back to squat, return to standing on attention (s)	boys	8.7	8.6	8.5	8.5	8.3	8.2
	girls	9.0	8.9	8.8	8.7	8.6	8.5
Speed-strength —long jump without pre-run (cm)	boys	170	175	180	185	190	195
	girls	150	155	160	165	170	175
—vertical jump (cm)	boys	40	40	50	55	55	60
	girls	40	40	50	55	55	60
Strength-endurance —static—90° flexed arm hang (s)	boys	30	35	40	45	50	55
	girls	20	25	30	30	35	40
—dynamic—lying on the back, hands behind the head, raise trunk and legs to touch elbows to knees (number)	boys	55	60	65	70	75	80
	girls	30	35	40	45	55	60
General endurance —500 m run (min)	boys	1:45.0	1:42.5	1:40.0	1:37.5	1:35.0	1:32.5
	girls	1:50.0	1:47.5	1:45.0	1:42.0	1:40.0	1:37.5
Flexibility —sit and reach (cm)	boys	+8	+9	+11	+11	+11	+13
	girls	+10	+11	+12	+13	+14	+15
Agility —difference between results of a 60 m sprint and of pendulum run 4 x 15 m (s)	boys	5.5	5.4	5.3	5.2	5.1	5.0
	girls	5.8	5.7	5.6	5.5	5.4	5.3

APPENDIX C

Endurance Development

Here are figures and tables with more information on endurance development.

The curve of endurance development points to significant predispositions and the great potential of children at an early school age. These early predispositions are based on the high efficiency and harmonious functioning of the systems responsible for adaptation to effort and of a child's movement apparatus.

In comparing endurance achievements of boys and girls of various ages, the data shown in figures A1, A2, A3, and A4 seem to be specially interesting.

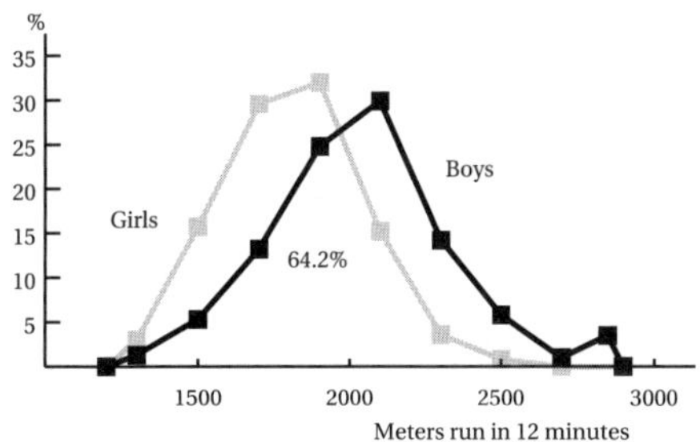

Figure A1. Distribution of frequency of occurrence of 12-minute run results in 8-year-old boys and girls (Drabik 1989)

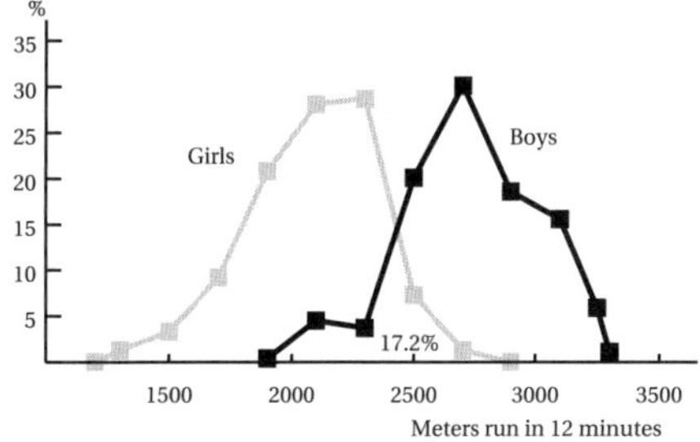

Figure A2. Distribution of frequency of occurrence of 12-minute run results in 19-year-old boys and girls (Drabik 1989)

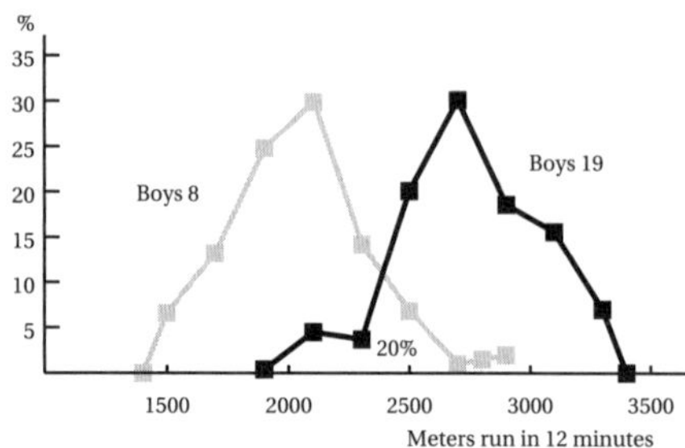

Figure A3. Distribution of frequency of occurrence of 12-minute run results in 8- and 19-year-old boys (Drabik 1989)

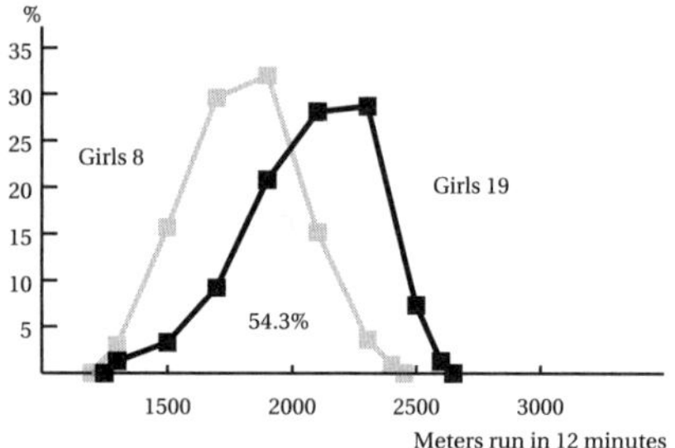

Figure A4. Distribution of frequency of occurrence of 12-minute run results in 8- and 19-year-old girls (Drabik 1989)

The conclusion can be drawn from the above data that among boys of the same age group similar results are less common than among girls, and that among eight-year-old boys and girls more have similar results than among nineteen-year-old youth of both sexes.

Figures A5 through A9 show the course of development of endurance of girls from various populations and in various group size for the researched age groups. Only in Canadian (figure A5) and Norwegian (figure A6) studies did best results appear for 17- and 18-year-old girls—the period of nearly maximal biological potential for young women. This curious result throws into question the results of measurement of the dynamics of endurance development from other studies. The data in Figure A8, as an example, show the difference in findings. The lower endurance of biologically mature girls as compared to girls 12 years old (which is what Figures A5 and A6 suggest) is counterintuitive and, Rachek (1987a) says, difficult to consider normal. This phenomenon results not only from morphological and functional differences between girls and boys but also from lowered physical activity and unwillingness to undertake strenuous efforts on the part of the maturing girls. One can try to change the level of endurance of those girls. An effort perhaps worth undertaking in the name of improving their biological potential.

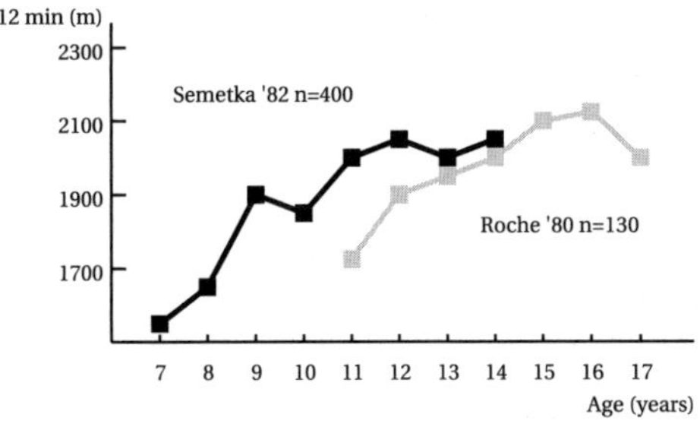

Figure A5. Development of girls' endurance (Canadian and Czechoslovakian research)

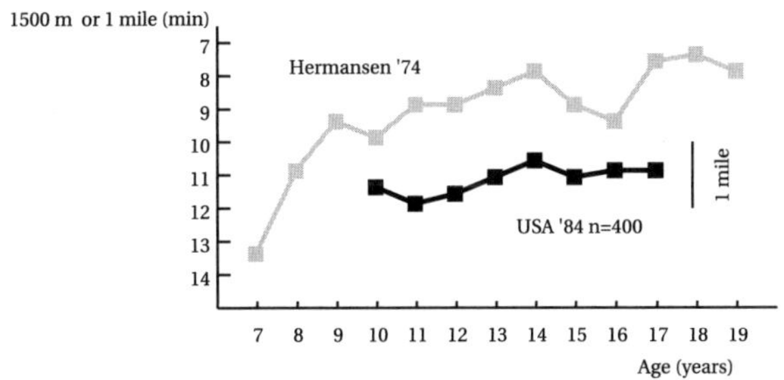

Figure A6. Development of girls' endurance (Norwegian research)

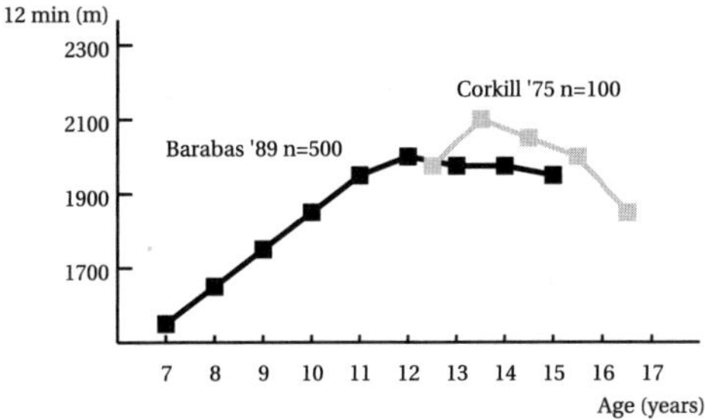

Figure A7. Development of girls' endurance (Hungarian and New Zealand research)

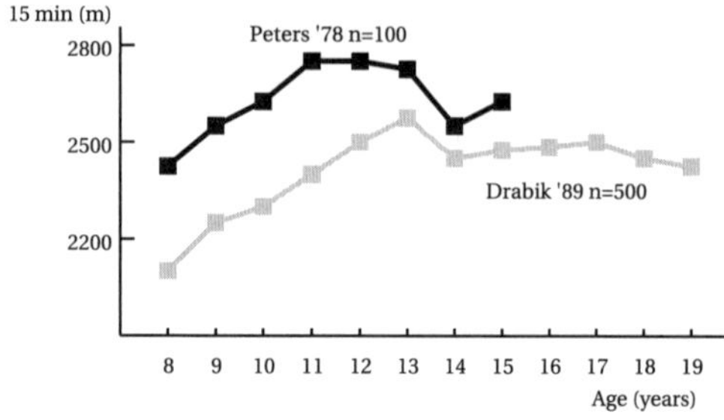

Figure A8. Development of girls' endurance (Polish and German research)

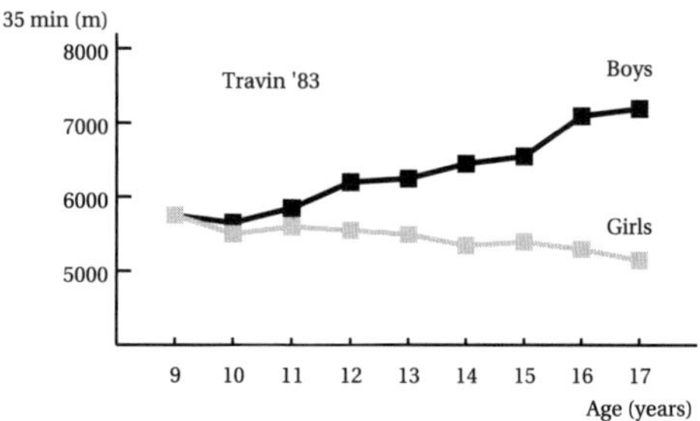

Figure A9. Development of girls' and boys' endurance (Russian research)

Tables A7 and A8, on pages 217-218 following, present information on the likelihood of fast (F), average (A), or slow (S) development of endurance during school age. These periods of development occur at various ages depending on height, mass, and BMI and at yet different ages if somatic features are not considered but only results (I).

The coach or p. e. teacher looking at these tables can assume, for example, that for a very tall boy (+90 in row II) who is 12 or 13 years old, the period of fast development of endurance is long past. This boy is in a period of biological development not favorable to developing endurance. Another boy, of age 10 or 11, for example, with high BMI (+90 in row IV) is in a period of fast development of endurance. If his type of biological development does not change, he will have another period of fast development of endurance from 17 to 18. The important issue is that the sensitive periods in development of motor abilities depend not only on the age but on the stage of physical development. Stocky children will have these sensitive periods at different ages than slim ones, tall children at different ages than small children. Through applying endurance exercises during sensitive periods (especially during those marked F), the teacher or coach further stimulates the natural, fast development of endurance that occurs during those periods.

Table A7. For boys: Sensitive periods in physical development and in endurance as measured by 12-minute run depending on the level of results(I), body height (II), body mass (III), and BMI (IV) (Drabik 1989)

I
+90—individuals with results of the run over 90th percentile
-10—individuals with results of the run under 10th percentile
80%—remaining individuals
II
+90—individuals with body height over 90th percentile
-10—individuals with body height under 10th percentile
80%—remaining individuals
III
+90—individuals with body mass over 90th percentile
-10—individuals with body mass under 10th percentile
80%—remaining individuals
IV
+90—individuals with BMI (body mass index) over 90th percentile
-10—individuals with BMI (body mass index) under 10th percentile
80%—remaining individuals

Pace of development: F-fast, A-average, S-slow

Age		8-9	9-10	10-11	11-12	12-13	13-14	14-15	15-16	16-17	17-18	18-19
Body height			F	S	S	A	F	A	S			
Body mass			S		S	S	F	A	A			
BMI		A	S		A		F	S	F			
Whole population		F			S							
I run results	+90			S		F	S		F		S	
	-10	F							A		A	
	80%	F			S							A
II body height	+90	F					S					
	-10	F			S			S				
	80%	F										
III body mass	+90	A		A			F					
	-10		F		F							
	80%	F			S	S						S
IV BMI	+90	S		F		S					F	
	-10	F	F		A		S					
	80%	F			S							

Table A8. For girls: Sensitive periods in physical development and in endurance as measured by 12-minute run depending on the level of results(I), body height (II), body mass (III), and BMI (IV) (Drabik 1989)

Pace of development: F-fast, A-average, S-slow

Age		8-9	9-10	10-11	11-12	12-13	13-14	14-15	15-16	16-17	17-18	18-19
Body height		F	F	F	F	F	A					
Body mass		S	S	S	F	F	F	A				
BMI		F			A		F	A				
Whole population		F		A	A							
I run results	+90	F			S							
	-10			F								
	80%	F		S	A							
II body height	+90	F										
	-10	A	F		F							
	80%	F		F	A							
III body mass	+90	F	F		F							
	-10	F			S							
	80%	S		F								
IV BMI	+90	F										
	-10	F										
	80%	F	S	F								

Table A9, on page 219 following, lists Polish (Drabik) norms in the 12-minute run for children and youth from various countries. Polish norms were based on data for the whole age group, for less and for more physically active, slim and overweight, of higher and of lower aerobic fitness, and so on. (The same is probably true for norms for other countries.) It is to be expected that for each of these groups norms would differ somewhat. The norms for the physically active should be the model for everybody, because physical activity is an important factor influencing the functional state of persons. Therefore, the ranges of values given here have value as information rather than as actual models to be followed.

Table A9. Results (in meters) of 12-minute run qualifying as good (B grade) according to various authors. B—boys, G—girls

Age	Auerbach 1978		Bovend'eerd t1980		Corkill 1975		Roche 1980		Semetka 1982		Spring 1980		Drabik 1989	
	B	G	B	G	B	G	B	G	B	G	B	G	B	G
8									2112-2445	1830-2132	2000	1800	2037-2441	1760-2055
9									2295-2653	2060-2397	2200	2000	2185-2629	1911-2280
10	2200	2050							2331-2669	1986-2220	2200	2000	2244-2682	1938-2319
11	2400	2200					2037-2577	1731-2188	2460-2846	2135-2449	2400	2200	2280-2704	2041-2373
12	2550	2250	2450-2550	2125-2225	2760-2799	2200-2319	2262-2634	1921-2266	2552-2883	2223-2573	2400	2200	2406-2788	2147-2489
13	2750	2350	2475-2600	2075-2200	2800-2879	2320-2399	2398-2744	1911-2464	2604-2949	2158-2479	2600	2400	2473-2863	2152-2490
14	2900	2350	2525-2650	2050-2225	2880-2999	2000-2439	2644-2938	2051-2390	2739-3109	2218-2548	2600	2400	2563-2926	2056-2435
15	3000	2350	2575-2725	2025-2150	2960-3159	2200-2359	2606-2975	2036-2488			2900	2600	2606-2937	2076-2405
16			2600-2775	2025-2175	3120-3199	2080-2239	2676-3037	2054-2592			2900	2600	2652-3041	2095-2390
17			2700-2825	2025-2125			2725-3124	2047-2425			3100	2800	2685-3077	2079-2407
18			2625-2750	2000-2625							3100	2800	2701-3086	2044-2393
19											3100	2800	2743-3162	2072-2219

Table A10. Percentile values of results (in meters) of the 12-minute run for boys (Drabik 1989)

Percentile	Age											
	8	9	10	11	12	13	14	15	16	17	18	19
95	2587	2731	2790	2822	2892	2933	3029	3040	3127	3101	3150	3269
90	2441	2629	2682	2704	2788	2863	2926	2937	3041	3017	3086	3162
75	2208	2430	2474	2510	2612	2688	2775	2801	2877	2857	2910	2975
50	2036	2184	2243	2279	2405	2472	2562	2605	2651	2654	2700	2742
25	1842	1963	2032	2061	2154	2247	2361	2394	2444	2440	2480	2563
10	1652	1807	1822	1866	1968	2029	2114	2167	2205	2239	2331	2414
5	1540	1673	1684	1771	1833	1896	1970	1995	2080	2130	2199	2209

Table A11. Percentile values of results (in meters) of the 12-minute run for girls (Drabik 1989)

Percentile	Age											
	8	9	10	11	12	13	14	15	16	17	18	19
95	2142	2348	2420	2465	2558	2571	2522	2487	2462	2463	2485	2414
90	2055	2280	2319	2373	2489	2490	2435	2405	2390	2407	2393	2219
75	1910	2117	2135	2207	2348	2360	2264	2267	2263	2245	2222	2171
50	1759	1910	1937	2040	2146	2151	2055	2075	2094	2079	2043	2071
25	1613	1710	1732	1873	1968	1982	1892	1905	1958	1922	1873	1888
10	1480	1531	1567	1733	1781	1818	1749	1789	1765	1778	1682	1688
5	1410	1427	1441	1636	1703	1725	1671	1700	1636	1620	1541	1563

Table A12. Percentile values of results (in meters) of the 15-minute run for boys (Drabik 1989)

Percentile	Age											
	8	9	10	11	12	13	14	15	16	17	18	19
95	2950	3194	3157	3343	3356	3497	3573	3548	3632	3625	3702	3720
90	2800	3064	3022	3207	3229	3377	3444	3422	3583	3583	3641	3687
75	2591	2830	2832	2962	3034	3153	3237	3242	3396	3378	3440	3499
50	2385	2559	2568	2683	2810	2933	3016	3046	3156	3189	3194	3258
25	2179	2272	2323	2419	2545	2694	2734	2838	2929	2945	2938	3071
10	1981	2109	2110	2248	2318	2451	2470	2553	2671	2720	2742	2918
5	1879	1943	1997	2113	2178	2281	2327	2390	2535	2554	2628	2758

Table A13. Percentile values of results (in meters) of the 15-minute run for girls (Drabik 1989)

Percentile	Age											
	8	9	10	11	12	13	14	15	16	17	18	19
95	2525	2732	2832	2933	2999	3052	2936	2970	2931	2970	2975	2869
90	2438	2640	2725	2811	2880	2957	2836	2868	2835	2902	2878	2761
75	2284	2453	2522	2610	2719	2784	2653	2668	2676	2716	2648	2620
50	2089	2235	2308	2394	2511	2554	2438	2482	2483	2501	2473	2464
25	1899	2011	2090	2199	2285	2333	2245	2266	2308	2318	2260	2279
10	1761	1839	1862	2049	2094	2128	2041	2101	2105	2149	2070	2052
5	1645	1719	1706	1942	1999	2001	1965	2004	2000	1991	1962	1929

GLOSSARY

Here are explanations of terms that are not found in most dictionaries and that were not explained in the text right where they appeared.

AAHPERD test—fitness test available from American Alliance for Health, Physical Education, Recreation and Dance, 1900 Association Drive, Reston, VA 22091.

Acyclic exercises—each movement is followed by a different movement, subsequent movements are rarely exactly the same, for example, techniques of gymnastics, wrestling, or ball games.

Anaerobic threshold—the point at which muscles use more oxygen than can be supplied to them. At that time lactic acid starts to accumulate in the blood.

Cardiorespiratory system—heart, blood vessels, and lungs.

Circuit training—where exercises are performed at stations, each exercise at a separate station.

Competitive period—that part of the training year during which an athlete competes most.

Concentric contractions—those involving shortening of the contracted muscles, such as when raising a load.

Continuous exercise methods—involving constant long work at low to medium intensity.

Cyclic exercises—each movement is repeated rhythmically, for example, walking, running, swimming, cycling, and rowing.

Cyclic sports—those where the event consists of rhythmically repeating certain movements, such as running or cycling.

Deadlift—stand straight, bend forward at the hips, grasp the barbell with both hands and lift it by straightening the body.

Dynamic contractions—those involving a change of length of contracting muscles (can be either concentric or eccentric).

Dynamic exercises—those involving movement.

Dynamic strength—used in fast movements (a form of speed-strength).

Eccentric contractions—those involving lengthening of the contracted muscles, such as when lowering a load.

EUROFIT test—fitness test available from Council of Europe, Committee for the Development of Sport, EUROFIT, Rome.

Explosive strength—the ability to apply maximum force in minimum time.

Extensive training methods—relying on a high volume of work.

Fartlek—exercise consisting of alternating fast and slow running over natural terrain.

"Good morning"—with a barbell on your shoulders behind your neck, lean forward at the hips and then straighten up.

HR_{max}—maximal number heartbeats per minute. HR stands for Heart Rate.

Intensity of exercises—amount of work (tonnage, mileage, repetitions) per time.

Intensive training methods—relying on high intensity of work.

Interval exercise method—a strictly regulated duration of exercises and the rest between them; a number of repetitions of each exercise and its rest period. The rest period does not allow for full recovery so the athlete begins each new exercise still feeling the fatigue from the previous one.

Interval run—see Interval exercise method.

Interval training—see Interval exercise method

Macrocycle—many microcycles, usually divided into mesocycles of a few microcycles each, assembled into training cycles lasting several months.

Mesocycle—a set of a few related microcycles lasting approximately one month.

Microcycle—a set of workouts that can last from two days to a week, and that can be repeated.

MOPER test—fitness test as described by Kemper (1983)

Motor ability—movement ability such as speed, strength, endurance, agility, or dexterity.

Neuromuscular system—in this work, specifically referring to the skeletal muscles and those parts of the nervous system that control them.

Preparatory period—period of preparation for the competitive period.

Psychomotor—related to psychological aspects of movement, for example, reaction time and movement coordination.

Repetition maximum (RM)—the maximum load that can be lifted before failure. For example, 1 RM (repetition maximum) load is a load that can be lifted only once.

Repetitive exercise methods—involving repeating certain exercises during the workout. Intensity is constant. Rest periods allow full recovery. Each repetition of the exercise means repeated adaptation to work.

Spatial form—trajectory and position in space. Together with the temporal form (duration and timing), this term describes movement or sports technique.

Speed-strength—strength used in fast movements (dynamic strength) and to amortize fast-moving loads (amortizing strength). An example: Jumping from a height, one's legs amortize, or spread over time, the shock.

Speed-strength sports—those where mainly speed and strength determine results. Such sports include track and field's sprints, jumps, throws, as well as weightlifting.

Squat—stand straight, bend hips and knees until hamstrings make contact with the calves (full squat), or until the thighs are parallel to the floor (partial squat), then rise by straightening the legs.

Squat creep—in full squat on balls of feet, with the trunk kept nearly vertical, shift weight to one leg and make strides by stepping forward with the unweighted leg while externally rotating the weighted leg at the hip and pivoting on the ball of the weighted foot.

Static contractions—those in which the length of the contracting muscles does not change, such as exerting force against immovable objects.

Static strength—used to hold something or resist a continuously applied force as well as to move slowly against resistance.

Steady state—state at which functions of the body can continue without discomfort as long as there are adequate energy stores; when oxygen supply equals oxygen demand and the removal of carbon dioxide equals its production.

Strength-endurance—ability to exert medium force over many repetitions without fatigue.

Technical sports—those where precisely described techniques are performed without anyone's interference. Such sports include gymnastics and figure skating.

Transitory period—period when athletes reduce the amount of their training after a string of major competitions and before the next preparatory period.

Variable exercise methods—the time of performing each exercise varies. The intensity of exercises varies too and is lowered when partial recovery is needed.

Vegetative system—that of internal organs and blood vessels and the autonomous part of the nervous system that controls them.

Volume of exercises—number of repetitions, tonnage moved, mileage covered (See also, Intensity of exercises).

LITERATURE CITED

Aaken, E. 1979. *Die ausdauer der kinder.* Hilden: Edition Spiridon.

Adams, C. 1991. Swimmer with touch of gold. *The Burlington (Vermont) Free Press* 27 January, 1991, sec. C, p. 7.

American Academy of Pediatrics. 1990. Policy statement: Strength training, weight and power lifting, and body building by children and adolescents. *Pediatrics* 86, no. 5 (November 1990): 801-802.

Arnot, R., and C. Gaines. 1984. *Sportselection.* New York: Viking Press.

Astrand, P. O. 1970. *Textbook of work physiology.* New York: McGraw Book Company.

Auerbach, K. 1978. Vorschlage zur Bewertung der Laufausdauer im Sportunterricht der Klassen 5 bis 10. *Körpererziehung* no. 5: 212-217.

Barabas, A. 1989. Motor performance of Hungarian schoolchildren in *Children and exercise.* Champaign, Illinois: Human Kinetics Publishers.

Bellotti, P., G. Benzi, A. Dal Monte, A. Donati, E. Matteucci, and C. Vittorio. 1978. Classificazione degli sport a determinazione dei mezzi di allenamento. *Atleticastudi* no. 3-4: 49-54.

Black, E. J., K. R. Isaacs, B. J. Anderson, A. A. Alcantara, and W. T. Greenough. 1990. Learning causes synaptogenesis, whereas motor activity causes angiogenesis, in cerebellar cortex of adult rats. *Proceedings of the National Academy of Sciences USA* vol. 87 (July 1990): 5568-5572.

Bober, T. 1992. Technika sportowa. *Trening* vol. 2.

Bogdanowicz, J. 1968. *Fizjologia rozwojowa dziecka.* Warszawa: PZWL.

Bompa, T. O. 1985. *Theory and methodology of training.* Dubuque, Iowa: Kendall/Hunt Publishing Company.

Bovend'eerdt, J., H. Kemper, R. Verschuur. 1980. *De MOPER Fitness Test.* Haarlem: BV Uitgeverij De Vrieseborch.

Caine, D. J., and J. Broekhoff. 1987. Maturity assessment: A viable preventive measure against physical and psychological insult to the young athlete? *The Physician and Sportsmedicine* vol. 15 (March): 70.

Clarke, H. H. 1959. *Application of measurement to health and physical education.* New York.

Committee for the Development of Sport. 1988. *EUROFIT.* Rome: Council of Europe.

Cooper, K. H. 1981. *The aerobic way.* New York: Bantam Books.

Corkill, J., L. R. T. Williams, and K. Roberts. 1975. Twelve-minute run standards for New Zealand secondary schools. *New Zealand Journal of Health, Physical Education, and Recreation* vol. 8, no. 2: 67-71.

Cronk, C. E., and A. F. Roche. 1982. Race- and sex-specific reference data for triceps and subscapular skinfolds and weight/stature^2. *American Journal of Clinical Nutrition* 35, no. 2: 347-354.

Cureton, K. J., P. B. Sparling, B. W. Evans, S. M. Johnson, U. D. Kong, and J. W. Purvis. 1978. Effect on experimental alterations in excess weight on aerobic capacity and distance running performance. *Medicine and Science in Sports and Exercise* no. 10: 194-199.

Czajkowski, Z. 1991a. *Nauczanie techniki sportowej.* Warsaw: Resortowe Centrum Metodyczno-Szkoleniowe Kultury Fizycznej i Sportu.

Czajkowski, Z. 1991b. O bledach w nauczaniu techniki sportowej. *Sport Wyczynowy* no. 1-2/313-314: 102-105.

Denisiuk, L., and H. Milicerowa. 1969. *Rozwój sprawnosci motorycznej dzieci i mlodziezy w wieku szkolnym.* Warsaw: PZWS.

Dick, F. W. 1977. *Training and the growing child.* A lecture given at the Midlands Coaching Conference.

Drabik, J. 1983. Wybrane zdolnosci koordynacyjne osob w roznym wieku z uwzglednieniem symetrii i asymetrii ruchu. *Zeszyty Naukowe AWF Gdansk* no. 7: 255-259.

Drabik, J. 1989. *Wytrzymalosc i jej uwarunkowania somatyczne u dzieci i mlodziezy w wieku 8-19 lat.* Gdansk: AWF.

Drabik, J. 1991. *Kajakarstwo—teoria i praktyka (sport, turystyka, rekreacja).* Gdansk: AWF.

Drabik, J., and J. Kuszewski. 1989. Variability of body build of 13 year old boys as evaluated by weight/height indices. *Biology of Sport* no. 4: 269-277.

Drozdowski, Z. 1986. Biologiczne wartosci kultury fizycznej. *Materialy II Kongresu Naukowego Kultury Fizycznej.* Gdansk.

Duda, M. 1986. Prepubescent strength training gains support. *The Physician and Sportsmedicine* (February) vol. 14, no. 2: 157-161.

Eriksson, B. O. 1972. Physical training, oxygen supply and muscle metabolism in 11-13 year old boys. *Acta Physiologica Scandinavica Supplement* no. 384.

EUROFIT. *See* Committee for the Development of Sport.

Farfiel, W. S. 1960. *Fizyologya sporta.* Moscow: Fizkultura i Sport.

Filin, W. P. 1987. *Teorya i metodika yunosheskovo sporta.* Moscow: Fizkultura i Sport.

Filipowicz, W. I., and I. M. Turowski. 1977. O sportowej orientacji dzieci i mlodziezy oraz zmiennosci struktury ich motoryki. *Sport Wyczynowy* no. 11-12: 61-67.

Fixx, J. 1979. *Das komplete buch vom laufen.* Frankfurt am Main: W. Krüger Verlag.

Fomin, L., and W. Filin. 1975. *Altersspezifiche grundlagen der körperlichen erziehung.* Schorndorf: Hofmann Verlag.

Frolov, V. G., G. P. Yurko, and P. I. Kabachkova. 1974. Eksperimentalnoe issledovanye metodiki vospitanya obshchey vynoslivosti u doskolnikov. *Teorya i Praktika Fizicheskoy Kultury* no. 11: 36-38.

Geblewiczowa, M. 1973. *Badania nad szybkoscia ruchow czlowieka.* Warsaw: AWF.

Gilbert, G. G., J. H. Montes, and J. G. Ross. 1984. Summary of findings from national children and youth fitness study. *HHS News.* Washington, DC: Department of Health and Human Services, Office of Disease Prevention and Health Promotion, U.S. Public Health Service.

Grosser, M., S. Starlschka, and E. Zimmerman. 1983. *Konditionstraining.* Munchen: BVL Sportwissen.

Gundlach, H. 1970. *O systemie zaleznosci pomiedzy zdolnosciami i umiejetnosciami fizycznymi.* Materialy Sympozjum teorii i techniki sportowej. Warsaw: Sport i Turystyka.

Guzalowski, A. A. 1977. Okresy krytyczne w rozwoju motoryki dziecka. *Sport Wyczynowy* no. 11-12: 57-60.

Harre, D. 1985. *Trainingslehre.* Berlin: Sportverlag.

Harre, D., and M. Hauptmann. 1988. Szybkosc i trening szybkosci. *Szkolna Kutura Fizyczna i Sport* Warsaw: Resortowe Centrum Metodyczno-Szkoleniowe Kultury Fizycznej i Sportu.

Havel, Z., and V. Horkel. 1985. Vztah nekterych ukazatelu pohybove vykonnosti na telesne vysce deti. *Trener* no. 12: 535-539.

Hebbelinck, M. 1984. The concept of health related to physical fitness. *International Journal of Physical Education* no. 1: 9-18.

Hermansen, L. 1974. "Individual differences." In *Fitness, Health and Work Capacity,* edited by L. A. Larson, 395-419. New York: MacMillan Publishing Company, Inc.

Hettinger, T. 1964. *Isometriches muskeltraining.* Stutgard: Georg Thieme-Verlag.

Hirtz, P. 1976. Untersuchungen zur entwicklung koordinativer leistungsvoraussetzungen bei schulkindern. *Theorie und Praxis der Körper Kultur* no. 4: 283-289.

Hirtz, P., ed. 1985. *Koordinative fähigkeiten im schulsport.* Berlin: Volk und Wissen Volkseigener Verlag.

Hollmann, W., H. Heck, H. Liesen, R. Rost, C. Bouchard, and K. Kawahats. 1978. Zur gesundheitlichen bodeutung des schulsports. *Sportwissenschaft* no. 2: 2-5.

Hollman, W., and T. Hettinger. 1980. *Sportmedizin-arbeit-und trainingsgrundlagen.* Stuttgart and New York: F. K. Schattauer Verlag.

Huberti, H. H., and W. C. Hayes. 1984. Patellofemoral contact pressures: The influence of q-angle and tendofemoral contact. *Journal of Bone and Joint Surgery* 66-A: 715-724.

Jeannotat, Y. 1980. Du test de Cooper e la VO_2max. *La Jeunesse et Sport* no.5: 106-109.

Karvonen, M. J., E. Kentala, and O. Mustafa. 1957. The effects of training on heart rate: A longitudinal study. *Annales Medicinae Experimentalis Et Biologiae Fenniae* no 35:305-315.

Kemper, H. 1983. The Moper Fitness Test: A practical approach to standard measurement of motor performances in the field of physical education in the Netherlands. In *Evaluation of Motor Fitness,* ed. J. Simons and R. Rensoned, 101-115. Leuven: I.L.O.K.U.

Kovar, R. 1980. *Human variation in motor abilities and its genetic analysis.* Prague: Charles University.

Kurz, T. 1991. *Stretching scientifically: A guide to flexibility training.* Island Pond, VT: Stadion Publishing Company.

Larson, L. A. 1966. An international research program for the standardization of physical fitness tests. *The Journal of Sports Medicine and Physical Fitness* no. 4: 259-261.

Leeds Education Department and Carnegie School of Physical Education. 1981. *A joint study of physical fitness in relation to schoolchildren (1978-1981).* Leeds: Leeds Education Authority.

MacDougall, J. D., P. D. Roche, O. Bar-Or, and J. R. Moroz. 1983. Maximal aerobic capacity of canadian schoolchildren: Prediction based on age-related oxygen cost of running. *International Journal of Sports Medicine* no. 4: 194-198.

MacDougall, J. D., H. A. Wenger, and H. J. Green. 1982. *Physiological testing of the elite athlete.* The Canadian Association of Sport Sciences. Ithaca, NY: Mouvement Publications.

Marciniak, J. 1990. *Zbiór cwiczen koordynacyjnych i gibkosciowych.* Warsaw: Biblioteka Trenera, Resortowe Centrum Metodyczno-Szkoleniowe Kultury Fizycznej i Sportu.

Martin, D. 1985. Auch die anzahl der jahre machts. *Condition* no. 6: 27-29.

Matvieyev, L. P. 1977. *Osnovy sportivnoy trienirovki.* Moscow: Fizkultura i Sport.

Mazur, B., M. Serapata, A, Scibich, and E. Pyda. 1975. Ocena wydolnosci fizycznej dzieci szkolnych z miasta Katowic na podstawie harwardzkiej proby stopnia. *Pediatria Polska* no. 50: 887-892.

Meinel, K. 1976. *Bewegungslehre.* Berlin: Volk und Wissen Volkseigener Verlag.

Micheli, L. J. 1990. *Sportswise: An essential guide for young athletes, parents, and coaches.* Boston: Houghton Mifflin Company.

Mikulik, S. 1990. Do they show no promise? *Sport: USSR and World Arena* no. 5 (326): 42-43.

Milicerowa, H. 1973. Budowa somatyczna jako kryterium selekcji sportowej. *Studia i Monografie* Warsaw: AWF.

Morrow, J. R., A. S. Jackson, and J. A. Bell. 1978. The function of age, sex, and body mass on distance running. *Research Quarterly for Exercise and Sports* 49, no. 4: 491-497.

Nabatnikowa, M. Y., ed. 1982. *Osnovy upravlienya podgotovki yunykh sportsmenov.* Moscow: Fizkultura i Sport.

Nadori, L. 1979. Analyse der ausdauer bei 4 bis 12 jährigen kindern. *Theorie und Praxis der Körperkultur* no. 1: 61-63.

Novikov, A. A., and Y. I. Chuiko. 1984. Na shto delat upor v podgotovkie olimpiycev? *Sportivnaya Borba* no. 1: 69-70.

Palgi, Y. 1980. *Physiological and anthropometric factors underlying endurance performance in boys and girls.* Dissertation for degree of Doctor, New York: Columbia University.

Peters, H., U. Pahlke. 1978. Niektóre zagadnienia dotyczace rozwoju wytrzymalosci w wieku szkolnym. *Wychowanie Fizyczne i Higiena Szkolna* no. 2: 41-43.

Peters, H., H. Philipp. 1985. Zur Messung der Ausdauerleistungsfahigkeit mittels sportmotorischer Tests. *Wissenschaftliche Zeitschrift der Deutche Hochschule für Körperkultur* no. 3: 494-500.

Protasova M. 1984. Train for balance. *Soviet Sports Review* vol. 25, no. 4: 157-158 (December 1990) translated from *Fizkultura i Sport* no. 6: 36-37.

Przeweda R. 1985. *Uwarunkowania poziomu sprawnosci fizycznej polskiej mlodziezy szkolnej.* Warsaw: AWF.

Puni, A. C. 1976. Wybrane zagadnienia teorii wolicjonalnego przygotowania w sporcie. in *Psychologia a wspólczesny sport.* Warsaw: Sport i Turystyka.

Raczek, J. 1978. Stan biologiczny wspólczesnej populacji szkolnej w swietle badan wydolnosci fizycznej. *Wychowanie Fizyczne i Sport* no. 1.

Raczek, J. 1986. Motorycznosc czlowieka. *Wychowanie Fizyczne i Higiena Szkolna* no. 6: 199-202.

Raczek, J. 1987a. *Doskonalenie wytrzymalosci w procesie treningu sportowego.* Warsaw: Instytut Sportu.

Raczek, J. 1987b. *Uwarunkowania rozwojowe szkolenia sportowego dzieci i mlodziezy.* Katowice: AWF.

Raczek, J. 1989. *Szkolenie mlodziezy w systemie sportu wyczynowego.* Katowice: AWF.

Raczek, J. 1991. *Podstawy szkolenia sportowego dzieci i mlodziezy.* Warsaw: Resortowe Centrum Metodyczno-Szkoleniowe Kultury Fizycznej i Sportu.

Roche, D. P. 1980. The Development of norms for run-walk tests for children aged 7 to 17. *CAHPER Journal* no. 7/8: 6-13.

Roshchupkin, G. V., and A. V. Gogin. 1989. Pryzhki v IV-X klassakh. *Fizicheskaya kultura v shkole* no. 3: 22-24.

Schilch, M., P. Löffler, and H. Hendel. 1975. Zur entwicklung der ausdauerfähigkeit im leichtathletischen grundlagentraining. *Der Leichtathletik* no. 34: 35- 37.

Semetka, M. 1982. Telesny vyvoj a pohybova vykonnost 7-14 rocnej populacje na Slovensku. *Trener* no. 1: 1-16.

Sergeev, K. 1990. Strong for their age. *Sport: USSR and World Arena* no. 9/90(330): 12 (September).

Sewall, L., and L. J. Micheli. 1986. Strength training for children. *Journal of Pediatric Orthopedics* no. 6:143-146.

Sharkey, B. J. 1984. *Physiology of fitness* Champaign, Illinois: Human Kinetics Publishers.

Sharkey, B. J. 1986. *Coaches guide to sport physiology.* Champaign, Illinois: Human Kinetics Publishers.

Sledziewski, D. 1989. Uczenie ruchu. *Trening* no. 3: 29-42.

Sozanski, H. 1972. Wybrane zagadnienia ksztaltowania szybkosci w procesie szkolenia sportowego. in *Podstawowe elementy wspolczesnego treningu cech motorycznych.* Warsaw: PKOL.

Sozanski, H. 1975. Sprawnosc fizyczna w teorii i praktyce sportu. *Sport Wyczynowy* no. 12: 9-17.

Sozanski, H. 1984. Wybrane zagadnienia treningu sportowego dzieci i mlodziezy. *Sport Wyczynowy* no. 4: 24-34.

Sozanski, H., and T. Witczak. 1981. *Trening szybkosci.* Warsaw: Sport i Turystyka.

Spring, P. 1980. Lieber länger laufen lernen. *Sporterziehung in der Schule* no. 7/8: 6-13.

Starosta, W., and A. Handelsman. 1990. *Biospoleczne uwarunkowania treningu sportowego dzieci i mlodziezy.* Warsaw: Resortowe Centrum Metodyczno-Szkoleniowe Kultury Fizycznej i Sportu.

Szczepanik, M. 1987. Cwiczenia ksztaltujace zdolnosci koordynacyjne u dzieci i mlodziezy. *Sport Wyczynowy* no. 12: 21-27.

Szewczyk, B. 1984. *Szkolenie mlodziezy uzdolnionej sportowo.* Warsaw: Materialy Glównego Komitetu Kultury Fizycznej i Turystyki.

Szopa, J. 1989a. Nowa koncepcja klasyfikacji i struktury motorycznosci czlowieka. *Antropomotoryka* no. 2: 3-7.

Szopa, J. 1989b. Zmiennosc ontogenetyczna oraz genetyczne i srodowiskowe uwarunkowania maksymalnej pracy anaerobowej—wyniki badan rodzinnych. *Antropomotoryka* no. 1: 37-49.

Szopa, J. 1993. Raz jeszcze o strukturze motorycznosci—próba syntezy. *Antropomotoryka* no. 10: 217-227.

Travin, J. G., and W. W. Diakonov. 1983. *Legkaya Atletika.* Moscow: Institut Fizicheskoy Kultury.

Tschiene, P. 1977. Einige neue aspekte zur periodisierung des hochleistungstraining. *Leistungssport* no. 5: 379-382.

Ulatowski, T., ed. 1971. *Teoria i metodyka sportu.* Warsaw: Sport i Turystyka.

Ulatowski, T., ed. 1981. *Teoria i metodyka sportu.* Warsaw: Sport i Turystyka.

Ulatowski, T. 1992. *Taktyka walki i wspólzawodzictwo sportowe* Warsaw: Wydawnictwa Urzedu Kultury Fizycznej i Turystyki.

Wazny, Z. 1975. *Sprawnosc specjalna w lekkiej atletyce.* Warsaw: Sport i Turystyka.

Wazny, Z. 1977. *Trening sily miesniowej* Warsaw: Sport i Turystyka.

Wazny, Z. 1989. *Modelowe wskazniki cech mistrzostwa sportowego.* Warsaw: Resortowe Centrum Metodyczno-Szkoleniowe Kultury Fizycznej i Sportu.

Weineck, J. 1983. *Optimales training.* Erlangen: Perimed Fachbuch-Verlagsgesellschaft.

Wilmore, J. H. 1982. *Training for sport and activity: The Physiological basis of the conditioning process.* Boston: Allyn and Bacon.

Wolanski, N. 1979. *Rozwoj biologiczny czlowieka.* Warsaw: PWN.

Wolanski, N., and J. Parizkowa. 1976. *Sprawnosc fizyczna a rozwój czlowieka.* Warsaw: Sport i Turystyka.

Wozniak, K. 1974. *Kanusport* Berlin: Sportverlag.

Zaciorski, W. M. 1970. *Ksztaltowanie cech motorycznych sportowca.* Warsaw: Sport i Turystyka.

INDEX

R

S